Linus Pauling

Scientist and Peacemaker

⇜⇜⇜

Photograph by Phil Stern

LINUS PAULING

SCIENTIST AND PEACEMAKER

←←←

edited by

Clifford Mead

Thomas Hager

Oregon State University Press
Corvallis

The paper in this book meets the guidelines for permanence and durability of the Committee on Production Guidelines for Book Longevity of the Council on Library Resources and the minimum requirements of the American National Standard for Permanence of Paper for Printed Library Materials Z39.48-1984.

Library of Congress Cataloging-in-Publication Data
Pauling, Linus, 1901-
  Linus Pauling : scientist and peacemaker / edited by Cliff Mead, Thomas Hager.-- 1st ed.
      p. cm.
Includes bibliographical references and index.
  ISBN 0-87071-489-9 (alk. paper)
  1. Pauling, Linus, 1901- 2. Science—History. 3. Scientists—United States—Biography. I. Mead, Clifford. II. Hager, Thomas. III. Title.
  Q143.P25 A3 2001
  540'.92--dc21
  00-011894

Oregon State University Press
101 Waldo Hall
Corvallis OR 97331-6407
541-737-3166 • fax 541-737-3170
http://osu.orst.edu/dept/press

OREGON STATE
UNIVERSITY

PREFACE

⇜⇜⇜

The concept of a centenary volume commemorating the hundredth birthday of Linus Pauling originated with coeditor Cliff Mead. In his position as Head of Special Collections at Oregon State University's Valley Library, Mead oversees the Linus Pauling Collection, the complete personal papers of this outstanding American scientist, humanist, and activist , a trove of hundreds of thousands of letters, articles, photographs, memoranda, and molecular models comprising his entire life's work. This vast and important collection is the source of many of the pieces in this book, a number of which have never before seen publication.

After enlisting the aid of Pauling biographer Tom Hager as coeditor, Mead decided that the best approach to a valuable and readable centenary volume would be that of a mosaic, modeled on similar works noting the centenaries of Albert Einstein and Niels Bohr published by Harvard University Press. These works were compilations of first-person accounts, historical reminiscences, illustrations, and short anecdotes that together cast a variety of lights on their subjects. This, it was decided, would work better than a narrative biography—which in any case would have been redundant in Pauling's case, because several biographies already exist.

This approach also offered the chance to make good use of written materials and photographs in OSU's Ava Helen and Linus Pauling Papers, making public some of the holdings that might otherwise be seen only by a relatively small number of researchers. In addition, Hager provided tapes of a number of interviews he held with Pauling's colleagues and contemporaries, which appear here in the form of marginalia.

Pieces included in the book were chosen for quality and comprehensiveness. It is impossible in any one volume to do complete justice to Linus Pauling's enormous life's work, but the editors hope that the selection here will give first-time readers about Pauling an intriguing taste of his interests and accomplishments, while providing more knowledgeable scholars with new and perhaps valuable source materials.

The result is an almost cubistic view, from many angles—personal and critical, contemporary and historical, first-person and third-person—of one of the central scientists in twentieth-century history. It is our hope that readers use these primary and secondary materials to form their own picture of a fascinating man.

Cliff Mead
Tom Hager
August 2000

ACKNOWLEDGEMENTS

We should like to take this opportunity to thank the many individuals who helped us with this project. In particular, we should like to acknowledge our indebtedness to Anna Coss, Faye Harkins, Chris Petersen, and Tracy Wells of the Special Collections staff; this book would not have been possible without their many hours of assistance and support. We should also like to thank the many student assistants in OSU Special Collections, including (but not limited to) Sadie Brundage, Jenessa Burmester, Jason Carver, Mike DeLoy, Kori Haddix, Fabio Hirata, Kimberly Ivancovich, Shannon Lowers, Marisa Meltbeke, Staci Otto, Emily Syphers, Nick Warner, and Ryan Wick. Karyle Butcher and Catherine Murray-Rust encouraged this project from the beginning. Lauren Kessler and Mary Steckel offered many helpful comments and advice.

The editors and publishers are grateful to the following contributors:

- Tom Hager for "The Roots of Genuis" and "The Triple Helix"
- Dr. Robert Paradowski for "A Pauling Chronology"
- Ava Helen and Linus Pauling Papers at Oregon State University for "My Best Friend," "Diary Excerpts," "Summer Employment," "Children of the Dawn," "The Incident on the Cliff," "Early Years of Physical Chemistry at Caltech," "The Original Manuscript for *The Nature of the Chemical Bond*," "Modern Structural Chemistry," "How I Developed an Interest in the Question of the Nature of Life', "Orthomolecular Medicine Defined," "An Episode That Changed My Life," "The Ultimate Decision," "Science and Peace," "Man—An Irrational Animal"; Neil A. Campbell interview "There Will Always be Something Interesting"; and "A World in Which Every Human Being can Live A Good Life"
- W.H. Freeman and Company for "The Discovery of the Alpha Helix"
- The American Academy for Achievement (www.achievement.org) for "Interview with Linus Pauling"
- Clara Shoemaker (for David Shoemaker) for "Linus Pauling, The Teacher"
- Jack Dunitz for "The Scientific Contributions of Linus Pauling," an edited version of an appreciation that appeared in *Biographical Memoirs of Fellows of the Royal Society*
- *Scientific American* for "Pauling and Beadle"
- Bruno Strasser for "Sickle-Cell Anemia"
- Gregory Morgan for "The Genesis of the Molecular Clock"
- National Broadcasting Corporation Inc. Meet The Press, copyright 1958 for "Meet the Press"

We would also like to thank the many friends, family members, colleagues and associates of Linus Pauling, whose comments, preserved in the Ava Helen and Linus Pauling Papers have informed the creation of this volume, and which appear as marginalia.

The editors would like to thank the following for photographs and illustrations:

- Phil Stern: pp. ii, 77, 90
- Terry Morrison: pp. 1, 226
- Ava Helen and Linus Pauling Papers, Oregon State University Special Collections: pp. 4, 5, 7, 8, 9, 10, 11, 13, 17, 20, 22, 26, 30, 32, 37, 40, 42, 47, 57, 61, 64, 69, 74, 80, 81, 82, 90, 92, 100, 101, 102, 103, 108, 114, 122, 128, 137, 140, 143, 144, 146, 153, 156, 162, 170, 178, 181, 186, 193, 200, 209, 211, 212, 216, 218, 226, 229, 230, 231, 232, 234, 235, 237, 238, 239, 240, 241, 243, 244, 245, 246, 247, 248, 250, 253, 254, 256
- Official Photograph, The White House, Washington: p. 18
- News and Communications Services, Oregon State University: pp. 191, 232
- National Broadcasting Company News: pp. 204
- Linus Pauling Institute of Science and Medicine, *Cancer and Vitamin C*: p. 47
- Cover Photo: Oregon State University News and Communications Services

TABLE OF CONTENTS

⇜⇜⇜

I

LINUS PAULING

Photograph by Terry Morrison

THE MAN

←←←

THE ROOTS OF GENIUS

Tom Hager

↢↢↢

Tom Hager spent five years researching the life of Linus Pauling while preparing two biographies, Force of Nature: The Life of Linus Pauling (Simon & Schuster 1995) and Linus Pauling and the Chemistry of Life (Oxford University Press 1997). Hager interviewed Pauling numerous times; talked to friends, colleagues, and family members; scoured archives; visited Pauling's childhood haunts; and pored over Pauling's personal papers in the Special Collections section of the Oregon State University Library, at Pauling's home, and in the files of the Pauling Institute, looking for the keys that would unlock and explain his subject's unique personality. The following essay distills from those efforts a few of the central influences that helped shape Pauling's sometimes contradictory genius.

I met Linus Pauling first in 1984. The occasion was a meeting of the American Chemical Society. I was covering the meeting as a correspondent for the *Journal of the American Medical Association*, and Pauling was slated to give a short talk on the medical benefits of vitamin C. I was the only journalist in the press room who expressed much interest. It had been thirteen years since Pauling had achieved international notoriety for his advocacy of very large doses of ascorbic acid to combat everything from the common cold to cancer. Most journalists felt the story had been done to death.

But I showed up in the scheduled lecture room, a bit early, interested more in the man than the vitamin. I knew that Pauling was the only individual to ever win two unshared Nobel Prizes. I knew that we shared some common background—both raised in the state of Oregon, both trained in science, both interested in medical research. I wanted to hear the greatest person my home state had ever produced, a man variously described as the world's greatest chemist, the greatest living American scientist, and a crackpot.

Pauling strode in, 83 years old, tall, erect, his white hair a wispy corona under a black beret. We were both a bit early; I was the only person in the room. He walked directly to me, introduced himself, and to my amazement began talking to me about the binding properties of tin. I understood very little of it, but I was spellbound. Metallic bonding, he said, had always interested him, and many questions were still unanswered. Pauling seemed to be thinking aloud, working through puzzles, solving theoretical problems as he spoke. He listened politely as I asked a few simple questions. He sketched as he spoke—I still have the page—and stopped only when he realized that the room was filling with an audience unlike any other I had seen at the meeting, a miscellany of buttoned-down scientists, sandaled health-food advocates, and long-haired students. It was time for his formal talk.

I listened, aglow, flattered that the Nobel Laureate had spent five minutes talking with me, a novice journalist. I was charmed by his friendly, enthusiastic manner. He had spoken to me like an equal. He had turned me into a fan.

My experience was not unique. Pauling treated almost everyone like an equal, at least until they demonstrated that they were closed minded, or cruel, stupid, or humorless. Everyone, whether student or teacher, world leader or lab assistant, was accorded the same even-handed, friendly, enthusiastic attention. He had many fans.

Our meeting spurred me to devote several years of my life to finding out more about Linus Pauling. Now, three books later—two of them biographies of Pauling—I remain impressed. I know a great deal more about him than I did on that day in 1984, a great deal more about his family and friends, colleagues and enemies, public successes and private defeats.

But important questions about Pauling remain unanswered. Like most biographers, I found that putting into reasonably good order the facts of his life—a long, diverse and productive life—was easy, while understanding Pauling at deeper levels—levels of emotion, personality, and motivation—was hard.

Pauling's larger-than-life personality was marked by what appear to be contradictions: a lifelong desire to put the world in order contrasted with an enthusiastic eagerness to shake things up; a deep desire for acceptance and normalcy counterpoised by a strong streak of maverick independence; a hankering for hermit-like isolation and solitary thought existing side-by-side with a love of the stage, of publicity and celebrity. Some observers found Pauling arrogant; many others loved him for his humor, humanity, and warmth. Various observers likened him to the Pope, to a fascist, a wizard, a king, a pillar of Ghandhism, an example of Hitlerism. He was a write-in candidate for senator. He was a target of the FBI. He was called brilliant. He was called a nut.

He was a complex individual.

What forces created Linus Pauling? Even after all this time and study, I cannot say. But I can provide some clues.

The first come from his early years. I think it significant that Pauling was born and raised in the Western U.S., in a place and at a time when the

I'll tell you something I remember about Linus. As you know, he spent several vacations with us, two at Wilhoit and one at the coast, Seaside, and would usually come to the house and stay for a day or two before we went on our vacation, and sometimes he would come out on his bicycle and stay Saturday night. Well, whenever he came, he was a dead loss to me as far as being a playmate, because he'd sit himself down with the *Encyclopedia Britanicaa* [sic] and starting with A and ending with Z, I'm sure that over a period of one or two years, he read every word in those thirty-two volumes.

Mary Conger, childhood friend

pioneer virtues of bravery, perseverance, and hard work were extolled; where people were valued for the work they did, not the name they carried; and where egalitarianism and openness were valued.

Most of his first nine years were spent in the farm town of Condon, in Eastern Oregon, where his father ran a pharmacy. His father's family was of sober and hard-working German immigrant stock; his mother's was somewhat more eccentric. On his mother's side, the Darling family, he had a grandfather who practiced law without a degree; a great uncle who communed with an Indian spirit; an aunt who toured the state as a safe-cracker (legally; she practiced her skills for a safe company); and a mother whose chronic anemia kept her bedridden for long stretches.

A bright boy, Pauling grew up with erratic adult supervision—especially after his father died when he was nine years old—a subsequent ability to act and think on his own, an expectation of success only after hard work, and romantic memories of cowboys, Indians, and a pharmacy filled with mysterious bottles, Latin labels, potions, and tinctures.

After his father's death, when his mother was relegated to running a boardinghouse on the edge of a much larger city, Portland, and was herself becoming ill, Pauling began exhibiting the counterbalanced traits of independence and duty that would characterize much of his life. As a teenaged "man of the house" he grudgingly took a series of part-time jobs to help his family make ends meet. Communication with his mother was strained, but he did his best to be supportive. At the same time, he developed a deep love of reading and learning, spending hours in the city's fine, large county library, impressing his elementary and high school teachers with his ability to memorize information, then use it creatively in solving problems. A childhood friend's demonstration of a toy chemistry set when Pauling was 14 got him interested in the field; he soon hammered together a small, rude laboratory in the basement of the boardinghouse and stocked it with begged, borrowed, and stolen labware and chemicals. Much of it he obtained on the sly from an abandoned smelter, smuggling home acids and equipment on the town's electric train, in canoes, and on wheelbarrows.

Using his father's old pharmacy books as a starting point, Pauling began learning that chemistry was built on a difficult but ordered system of knowledge. He spent much of his free time in high school down in the basement, learning by doing, creating low-grade explosives to scare girls and impress boys, reading, absorbing a wealth of knowledge about chemistry.

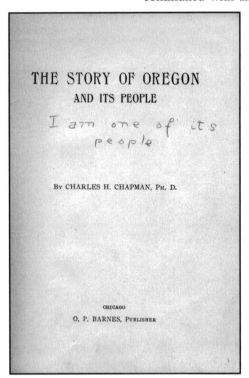

Pauling's fourth grade textbook with his penciled annotation

Ordered knowledge and the sense of control he got in the laboratory were important, too. There, he was the master; outside the laboratory, he was at the mercy of his mother, whose illness led to constant demands for help and whose marginally successful boardinghouse led to constant demands for more income.

The effort of keeping these disparate elements in balance led to twin crises in Pauling's senior year of high school. The first came at home. He wanted very much to attend Oregon Agricultural College (OAC, now Oregon State University), where his tuition would be free, and earn a degree in chemical engineering. His mother adamantly insisted that he take a permanent job at a local machine shop after graduating high school. Pauling decided to defy his mother and go to college.

Ava Helen Miller, at right, in costume for a play at OAC, 1922

The second crisis came from high school. OAC accepted Pauling early in his senior year. He realized that if he could get his high school diploma early, he could get an early start on college. State law, however, decreed that each high school student must take a full year of American history at the senior level. Pauling figured he could circumvent the rule by taking two terms of the required class simultaneously, but the principal saw things differently. He refused the request. Pauling responded by doing what he thought was right. He dropped out of high school.

Having demonstrated his independent streak, Pauling thoroughly enjoyed his time at OAC. He soon showed that he often knew more than his teachers, when it came to chemistry. By his junior year, he was teaching classes at the request of the chemistry department, and was becoming known as one of the smartest students on campus. His self-confidence grew accordingly. He bantered with his professors. He took oratory classes and developed a love of lecturing. He became optimistically convinced of the power of science to solve societal ills. Not even losing an attempt at a much-desired Rhodes Scholarship could dampen his enthusiasm for long.

In 1922 lightning struck, in the form of an 18-year-old girl. On his first day lecturing to a class of home economics students, on January 6, 1922, Pauling decided to start by measuring the class's basic knowledge. "Will you please tell me all you know about ammonium hydroxide, Miss . . ." He ran his finger down the registration sheet, looking for a name he could not possibly mispronounce. "Miss Miller?" He looked up and into the eyes of Ava Helen Miller, a small, strikingly pretty young woman with long, dark hair. She was smiling. And she knew a great deal about ammonium hydroxide.

Three years later—a period of courtship, separation when Pauling started graduate school at Caltech, and scores of sometimes steamy love letters—they were married.

Ava Helen was Pauling's lifelong love. She provided him the emotional sustenance he needed; she impressed him as being one of the smartest people he ever knew; she bore his four children.

Just as important, she redirected his energies from science to social issues. Ava Helen was raised in a politically active, left-wing family, where women were accustomed to speaking their minds and were expected to back their opinions with facts. Her own politics were activist and left-wing (merging into socialist).

The Pauling dinner table became a forum for talking about the issues of the day, from the candidacy of Upton Sinclair to the virtues of Roosevelt's White House. Pauling listened to his wife's views sympathetically, learned, and in the 1930s changed his political affiliation from Republican to Democrat. That was just the beginning. Ava Helen's outrage over the internment of Japanese-Americans during World War II became Pauling's, especially after their home was vandalized when they hired a Japanese-American gardener at the close of the war. Ava Helen's charitable attitude toward the Soviet Union became Pauling's. Ava Helen's interests in pacifism and world government became Pauling's.

In 1946, Ava Helen supported Pauling's concerns about the development of atomic weapons, and groomed him as a public speaker on the issue, providing tips on effective speech-making and pushing the content of his talks away from the science of the Bomb to its political repercussions. Under her careful eye, Pauling became one of the world's leading anti-Bomb activists. He was quite serious when, upon winning the Nobel Peace Prize, he noted that Ava Helen deserved a share. He later told reporters, very honestly, that if it had been up to him, he would have concentrated on chemistry. But he kept hammering away at activism, risking his career, in order to retain the respect of his wife.

Add to these influences—growing up in the West, the death of a father at an early age, a weak and demanding mother, a strong and activist wife— what appears to be a natural ebullience and optimism; a good brain coupled with an incredible memory; self-confidence born of early and applauded scientific success; a strong basic desire, common to so many scientists, to understand the world; and a true dedication to decreasing the sum of human suffering, and a picture of Pauling begins to emerge.

Readers of this book are invited to flesh out this sketch by reading the words of Pauling himself, and those of many of his colleagues, students, friends, and enemies in the following selections. Taken together, they form a mosaic portrait of a phenomenal man.

Corvallis — Saturday 16 Jan. 1982

The old Chem. Bldg was unlocked. I sat and stood for half an hour in the room on the second floor where I first saw my sweet love, 60 years ago, less two days. I stood at the front of the room and repeated my first words: "Will you tell me what you know about ammonium hydroxide, Miss..." (I then looked at my class book and selected one of the 25 names at random)"... Miller?" Ava Helen Miller made a good answer. This chance meeting has determined the nature of my life.

Linus Pauling

A PAULING CHRONOLOGY

Robert J. Paradowski

❧❧❧

*Linus Pauling felt deeply that he had been shaped by the values of the
Western frontier: self-sufficiency, restless energy, love of nature, inquisitiveness,
and hard work. One can see these traits in his scientific career, as his insatiable
curiosity drove him from one field to another. He liked to work on the
frontiers of knowledge, not in safe, crowded fields, and many of his greatest
discoveries were made in the interstices between disciplines—between
chemistry and physics, chemistry and biology, chemistry and medicine. Francis
Crick once called him "the greatest chemist in the world." When Pauling was
born, chemistry was a discipline dominated by Germans, but when he died, it
was dominated by Americans, and Linus Pauling did much to bring about
this transformation.*

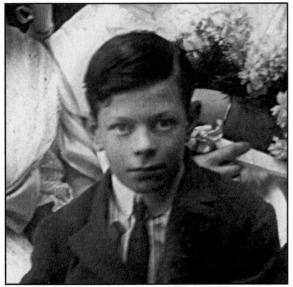

Linus Pauling in 1913, elementary school graduation

1901

Linus Carl Pauling is born in Portland on
February 28 to Herman and Lucy Isabelle
(Darling) Pauling, nicknamed "Belle." He is
named Linus after Belle's father and Carl
after Herman's.

1905

The Paulings move to the farming hamlet
of Condon, Oregon, where Herman opens
a drug store. William P. Murphy, who will
win the Nobel Prize for Medicine in 1934,
also lives in Condon at this time.

1909

After a fire destroys his drugstore, Herman
moves his family back to Portland.

1910

On May 12, Herman Pauling writes a letter
to the Portland *Oregonian* about his nine-
year-old son who is "a great reader" and

Linus Pauling with his mother and two sisters, Tillamook, Oregon, 1918

deeply interested in ancient history and the natural sciences. He asks readers of the newspaper to advise him about the proper works to procure for his child, who has "prematurely developed inclinations."

On June 11, Herman Pauling suddenly dies of a perforated stomach ulcer with attendant peritonitis.

1914
After witnessing a dramatic chemical reaction in the bedroom laboratory of his high-school classmate Lloyd Alexander Jeffress, Pauling decides to become a chemist.

1916
In the spring term at Washington High School Pauling takes his first semester of chemistry.

1917
At the start of the spring term, Pauling signs up for two semesters of American history, which are required to graduate, but the principal refuses to allow him to take the courses simultaneously, and he therefore does not receive a high school diploma. On October 6, Pauling begins school at Oregon Agricultural College (now Oregon State University) in Corvallis, Oregon.

Linus Pauling in chaps

1919

After Pauling leaves college to help support his mother and sisters, Oregon Agricultural College chemistry department offers Pauling, a sophomore, a full-time position as assistant instructor in quantitative analysis.

1920

Pauling writes to Arthur Amos Noyes about his interest in coming to the California Institute of Technology (Caltech).

1921

Pauling does his first research, on the effect of magnetism on the orientation of iron crystals when they are electrodeposited from an iron salt solution.

1922

Ava Helen Miller is a student in a class Linus is teaching, "Chemistry for Home Economics Majors," and Pauling meets her for the first time.

On June 22, Pauling graduates from Oregon Agricultural College and, at the end of the summer, leaves for Caltech in Pasadena.

1923

Pauling's first published work, written with Roscoe Dickinson, on the structure of molybdenite, appears in the *Journal of the American Chemical Society*.

At the end of his first year of graduate studies, despite family opposition, Linus and Ava Helen marry June 17, in Salem, Oregon.

Linus and Ava Helen Pauling wedding day, June 17, 1923

1925

Linus Carl Pauling, Jr. is born on March 10.

In June, Pauling receives his Ph.D. in chemistry, minoring in physics and mathematics, with his dissertation entitled "The Determination with X-rays of the Structure of Crystals."

1926

In January, the Guggenheim Fellowships are announced and Pauling is chosen as a fellow; he and Ava Helen go to Europe, leaving Linus Jr. with Ava Helen's mother.

1927

One of Pauling's greatest papers is published, "The Theoretical Prediction of the Physical Properties of Many-Electron Atoms and Ions, Mole Refraction, Diamagnetic Susceptibility, and Extension in Space."

> Linus's development was quite different from mine. I was completely lacking self-confidence by the time I was sixteen. And Linus, I gather, never lacked it.
>
> *Richard Morgan, Pauling's cousin*

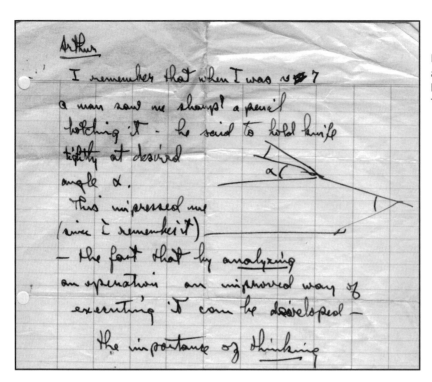

Linus Pauling
autobiographical note to
himself

Pauling returns to Caltech and is named Assistant Professor of
Theoretical Chemistry.

1930

In July, Pauling works on quantum mechanics in Germany at Arnold
Sommerfeld's Institute for Theoretical Physics. While visiting
Ludwigshafen, Pauling gets Hermann Mark's permission to use his
electron-diffraction techniques at Caltech.

In December, Pauling develops a new theory of the quantum mechanics
of the chemical bond.

1931

Peter Jeffress Pauling, the Paulings' second son, is born on February 10.

Pauling is appointed full professor at Caltech and, in September, receives
the first A. C. Langmuir Prize at a meeting of the American Chemical
Society in Buffalo, New York.

1932

Linda Helen Pauling is born on May 31.

Pauling meets and talks with Albert Einstein, who is at Caltech for the
winter. Einstein attends a seminar on the quantum mechanics of the
chemical bond by Pauling and tells reporters that he did not understand
the lecture.

1933

Pauling is elected the youngest member of the National Academy of
Sciences.

In June, he receives his first honorary degree, Doctor of Science, from Oregon State College.

1934

Pauling applies for and later receives a three-year grant from the Rockefeller Foundation to support research on the structure of hemoglobin and other biologically important substances.

1935

Pauling and E. Bright Wilson, Jr. publish *Introduction to Quantum Mechanics, with Applications to Chemistry*, a popular textbook for introducing chemists and physicists to the new field of quantum mechanics.

1937

Pauling is appointed Director of the Gates Laboratory at Caltech and Chairman of the Division of Chemistry and Chemical Engineering. Before accepting the position, he insisted on the title of director as well as chairman, as he realized he was not being given sufficient power to run the division the way he would like.

The Paulings' third son and last child, Edward Crellin Pauling, is born on June 4.

1939

The Nature of the Chemical Bond, and the Structure of Molecules and Crystals is published. This book, Pauling's greatest, becomes, by the end of the century, "the most cited book in the scientific literature."

1940

In hopes of defeating the Axis Powers—Germany, Italy, and Japan—who he believes are attempting to conquer the world, Pauling becomes involved in various types of war work in explosives, rocket propellants, and medical research.

In three days, Pauling develops the basic idea for a simple and effective instrument that can measure the partial pressure of oxygen in a gas. He and his collaborators at Caltech develop an oxygen meter, hundreds of which are later built for use in submarines and airplanes.

1941

Pauling receives the William H. Nichols Medal from the New York Section of the American Chemical Society for his fundamental contributions to the nature of the chemical bond.

Diagnosed with glomerulonephritis, a commonly fatal renal disease, Pauling is advised to cancel his memorial address at the Mayo Clinic and return home. A radical new treatment program developed by Dr. Thomas Addis, which stresses consuming a modicum of protein and drinking large amounts of water, is undertaken and followed by Pauling for the next fifteen years. He also takes various vitamins and liver extracts. This treatment is likely to have saved Pauling's life.

1942

Pauling and his wife speak out against the internment of Japanese-Americans.

Pauling, Dan Campbell, and David Pressman announce successful formation of artificial antibodies. Other researchers are unable to reproduce these exciting results.

In the fall, J. Robert Oppenheimer offers Pauling a job as Director of the Chemistry and Metallurgy Division for the Manhattan Project, working with the atomic bomb. Because of his nephritis and involvement with other war projects, Pauling declines.

1945

After three years of work, Pauling and Campbell announce successful development of a substitute for blood plasma called oxypolygelatin.

Pauling serves on a committee to help in the preparation of the Bush Report (about science in the U.S. after World War II), in which he argues that it is the responsibility of the Research Board for National Security to conduct research on how to avoid war.

After hearing about sickle-cell anemia from Dr. William Castle, Pauling gets the idea that cell sickling might be explained by abnormal hemoglobin in the sickled cells.

In August, Pauling becomes concerned upon learning of the atomic bombing of Hiroshima and Nagasaki. He begins giving talks about atomic bombs for local groups, restricting his remarks to the science and technology of the weapon.

At the urging of Ava Helen, he decides to devote a large portion of his time to learning about subjects relating to abolishing war from the world.

1946

He receives the 35th Willard Gibbs Medal of the Chicago section of the American Chemical Society.

At the request of Albert Einstein, Pauling joins in the formation of the Emergency Committee of Atomic Scientists, whose aim is to publicize the enormous consequences of the discovery of nuclear weapons.

1947

Pauling receives the Theodore William Richards Medal of the Northeast Section of the American Chemical Society.

Pauling, Richards Medal, 1947

He publishes a textbook, *General Chemistry*, which is an immediate success and revolutionizes the teaching of college chemistry.

The Royal Society of London awards him the Davy Medal.

In late December, Pauling writes a pledge on the back of a cardboard placard: "In every lecture that I give from now on, every public lecture, I pledge to make some mention of the need for world peace."

1948

In February, he is awarded the Presidential Medal for Merit for exceptionally meritorious conduct in the performance of outstanding services to the U. S. during and after World War II.

Pauling attacks again the problem of the structure of proteins and this time finds that he can formulate a structurally satisfactory helical configuration. As his model appears to contradict data from X-ray crystallography, he tells only Ava Helen about his structure.

1949

Pauling becomes president of the American Chemical Society. In his presidential address he urges American industrial corporations to support a scientific research foundation that will insure them a steady supply of new products. He also makes clear that he is not sympathetic with the aims of the American Medical Association. Liberals and conservatives in and outside of the scientific community criticize his address.

In April, Pauling and Harvey Itano, with Singer and Wells, present their results on sickle-cell anemia as a molecular disease at a meeting of the National Academy of Sciences.

1950

Pauling publishes *College Chemistry*, a more popular treatment of basic chemistry than his book *General Chemistry*. It is also a great success.

On November 13, testifying before the California Senate Investigating Committee on Education, Pauling explains for over two hours why he objects to loyalty oaths involving inquiry into a person's political beliefs.

1951

On February 28, his fiftieth birthday, Pauling communicates "The Structure of Proteins: Two Hydrogen-Bonded Helical Configurations of the Polypeptide Chain," to *Proceedings of the National Academy of Sciences (PNAS)*. Written with Corey and H. R. Branson, this paper appears in April.

The USSR Academy of Sciences attacks Pauling's resonance theory of chemical bonding as hostile to Marxism.

1952

Pauling plans to visit England to take part in a meeting on the structure of proteins. However, his request for a passport is denied: "the [State] Department is of the opinion that your proposed travel would not be in the best interests of the United States." He eventually receives a limited passport, but misses the conference, where Rosalind Franklin's crystallographic photos of DNA are displayed for the first time.

1953

Pauling and Corey publish "Stable Configurations of Polypeptide Chains," an extensive summary of their work on protein structure, in the *Proceedings of the Royal Society*. It becomes one of his most heavily cited publications.

1954

In October Pauling learns that he has been awarded the Nobel Prize in Chemistry for "his research into the nature of the chemical bond and its application to the elucidation of the structure of complex substances."

Pauling and his family travel to Stockholm where, on December 10, he receives the Nobel Prize from King Gustav Adolph VI.

1955

On July 15, Pauling and over fifty other Nobel laureates issue the Mainau Declaration, which calls for an end to all war, especially nuclear war.

In November, Pauling appears before the Senate Subcommittee on Constitutional Rights. He testifies that he is not and has never been a communist, open or concealed.

1956

Pauling receives the Amadeo Avogadro Medal in Rome. He gives a speech on Avogadro in Italian, as translated for him by an Italian chemist in Illinois.

Pauling and Caltech receive a Ford Foundation grant and form a team of scientists exploring the molecular chemistry of mental disease. Pauling believes many cases of mental disease are most likely the result of gene-controlled mental abnormalities.

1957

On May 15, Pauling speaks to students at Washington University, where he states that no human should be sacrificed to any nation's program of perfecting nuclear weapons. Because of the enthusiastic response to his speech, he composes an appeal to end atomic-bomb tests, which is promptly signed by over one hundred members of the Washington University science department. The famous United Nations bomb test appeal is conceived and widely circulated.

1958

On January 15, Linus and Ava Helen Pauling present the petition to halt bomb tests, plus a list of over nine thousand signers, to Dag Hammarskjöld at the United Nations.

In February Pauling debates, on television, issues of fallout and disarmament with Edward Teller.

In April, Pauling and seventeen others file a lawsuit against the United States Defense Department and the Atomic Energy Commission to stop nuclear tests.

No More War!, a passionate analysis of the implications of nuclear war for humanity, is published.

Pauling is elected to the Soviet Academy of Sciences.

He publishes a paper on the genetic and somatic effects of carbon-14. In this influential paper, he estimates the effect of one year of bomb tests on the next generation.

1959

In April, he formulates the hydrate microcrystal theory of anesthesia.

The Paulings attend the Fifth World Conference against Atomic and Hydrogen Bombs in Hiroshima, Japan. Pauling is the guiding member of a drafting committee that writes the "Hiroshima Appeal," the principal document issued by the conference. He and his wife deliver lectures at various institutions.

Pauling talked about what he was interested in and what he was interested in was everything ... almost.

Verner Schomaker, long-time colleague

1960

From Sunday, January 31, until Monday morning, February 1, Pauling is trapped on the ledge of a steep cliff near his ranch. His disappearance creates great concern, and his rescue makes news in many publications.

On June 21, Pauling testifies before the Senate Subcommittee to Investigate the Administration of the Internal Security Act in Washington, D.C. He is asked to furnish the letters of the individuals who helped him gather the signatures for his U. N. petition, but expresses concern that they may be subjected to harassment as he has been. He is ordered to reappear.

On October 11, Pauling again appears before the Subcommittee and, under threat of being held in contempt, refuses to reveal the names of those who helped circulate his petition. He is eventually excused without punishment.

1961

On January 2, *Time* magazine chooses the scientists of the United States as its "Men of the Year." Pauling is one of the scientists on the cover.

On January 16, Linus and Ava Helen Pauling issue "An Appeal to Stop the Spread of Nuclear Weapons" following a nuclear test carried out by France.

1962

On April 24, President Kennedy orders the resumption of atmospheric nuclear tests. On April 28 and 29, Linus and Ava Helen Pauling, with several hundred other demonstrators, march before the White House in protest. On the evening of April 29, Linus and Ava Helen Pauling enter the White House as guests of President and Mrs. Kennedy, who have invited many American Nobel Prize winners to a dinner party.

Pauling receives an honorary high school diploma from Washington High School, in Portland, Oregon.

In the November elections, Pauling receives 2,694 write-in votes for United States Senator from California.

1963

Pauling files a libel lawsuit against William F. Buckley's *National Review*, claiming that they recklessly and maliciously intended to destroy his good reputation.

On October 10, the day that a partial nuclear test ban treaty goes into effect, the Nobel Peace Prize Committee of the Norwegian Parliament announces the awarding of the 1962 Nobel Peace Prize to Linus Pauling.

Reaction by the U.S. media is largely negative—*Life* magazine declares the announcement "A Weird Insult from Norway." Caltech also does nothing to honor his achievement.

At the end of October, Pauling announces that he has accepted an appointment, effective November 1, as a research professor at the Center for the Study of Democratic Institutions in Santa Barbara, California. There he hopes to continue his work in science, medicine, and world affairs. He leaves Caltech after a forty-two-year association.

On December 10 in Norway, Pauling receives the Nobel Peace Prize for 1962. Because of his dissatisfaction with the attitude of the Society toward him, the bomb-test suits, and his Nobel Peace Prize, he resigns from the American Chemical Society.

1965

On August 12, eight Nobel Peace Prize winners issue an urgent appeal to world leaders for an immediate cease-fire and political settlement of the Vietnam War. Pauling, Albert Schweitzer, and Martin Luther King, Jr. are among the signers.

At a meeting of the National Academy of Science, Pauling announces a new theory of the structure of the atomic nucleus. The basic idea of his theory is that protons and neutrons are combined into spherons. He publishes "The Close-Packed-Spheron Theory and Nuclear Fission" in *Science*.

1967

Pauling takes a one-year leave of absence from the Center for the Study of Democratic Institutions to accept a position as professor of chemistry at the University of California in San Diego. He misses contact with other scientists and wishes to return to supervising experimental work.

Albert Schweitzer (left) and Pauling in Lambarene, West Gabon, near the mission hospital founded by Dr. Schweitzer, 1959

In December, Ava Helen is hospitalized after suffering a small stroke. She recovers completely.

1969

Pauling accepts an appointment at Stanford University as Professor of Chemistry.

1970

Pauling publishes "Evolution and the Need for Ascorbic Acid" in *PNAS*.

He is awarded the International Lenin Peace Prize for 1968-1969.

His best-selling book, *Vitamin C and the Common Cold*, is published. The book will win the Phi Beta Kappa Book Award in 1971 as one of the most distinguished and important works published in 1970.

1971

Dr. Ewan Cameron notifies Pauling of his work in Scotland, administering vitamin C to cancer patients. Pauling replies, stating that he feels strongly that ascorbic acid may be of great value in the prevention and treatment of cancer. This correspondence marks the start of a fruitful collaboration.

1972

Cameron and Pauling submit a paper, "Ascorbic Acid and the Glycosaminoglycans: An Orthomolecular Approach to the Treatment of Cancer and Other Diseases," to *PNAS*. In a controversial decision, *PNAS* decides not to publish the work. The paper is eventually published in *Oncology*.

1973

Pauling is named Director of the Laboratory of Orthomolecular Medicine, a forerunner of the Linus Pauling Institute.

Pauling and David Hawkins edit *Orthomolecular Psychiatry: Treatment of Schizophrenia.*

Linus and Ava Helen travel to the People's Republic of China. They are among the first Americans to do so in the era of détente.

1974

The Institute of Orthomolecular Medicine changes its name to the Linus Pauling Institute of Science and Medicine.

Pauling retires from Stanford University.

1975

Linus and Peter Pauling publish *Chemistry.*

President Gerald Ford presents Pauling with the National Medal of Science. The previous Nixon Administration had twice postponed the award.

Ava Helen Pauling, Linus Pauling, and President Gerald Ford at the awarding of the National Medal for Merit to Linus Pauling, 1975 (official White House photo)

1976

Pauling delivers the Centennial Address, entitled "What Can We Expect for Chemistry in the Next 100 Years?" to the American Chemical Society in New York.

During the summer, Ava Helen experiences troubles with her digestion, and a physician discovers that she has a large tumor in her stomach. She has a three-quarter gastrectomy and recovers well from the surgery.

Pauling publishes *Vitamin C, the Common Cold, and the Flu*, an updated version of his earlier book.

1977

Governor Bob Straub of Oregon declares June 1 "Linus Pauling Day" in Oregon.

1978

Pauling receives the Lomonosov Gold Medal, the highest award of the Soviet Academy of Science.

1979

Pauling is the first recipient of the United States National Academy of Sciences Medal in the Chemical Sciences.

Cameron and Pauling publish *Cancer and Vitamin C,* about the nature and causes of cancer, prevention and treatment, and the role of vitamin C in treating the disease.

1981

Pauling delivers the inaugural Ava Helen Pauling Lecture for World Peace at Oregon State University.

On November 1, Ava HelenPauling is awarded the 5th Ralph Atkinson Award, in celebration of her efforts on behalf of civil liberties and peace. It is her last public appearance.

After several hemorrhages, she dies of stomach cancer on December 7, following an illness that lasted 5 years and 3 months.

1982

In June, Pauling takes a sentimental trip to Oregon and Washington. He revisits several places where he and Ava Helen spent time together. He sees, for the first time, the grave of his grandfather Linus Wilson Darling, in the Condon Cemetery.

1983

Pauling publishes the 25th Anniversary Edition of *No More War!*

Pauling announces the discovery of a new type of chemical bond that can mimic, for small molecules, the kind of bonding believed to exist in bulk metals.

1984

Pauling receives the American Chemical Society's most prestigious award, the Priestley Medal, for his contributions to chemistry and to the Society.

1986

How to Live Longer and Feel Better, a popular account of Pauling's ideas on nutrition and health, is published. The book makes the *New York Times* best-seller list.

In April, Pauling announces plans to give all of his papers, as well as those of his wife, to his alma mater, Oregon State University. In December, the first 125,000 (of an eventual 500,000) items arrive on the OSU campus.

I am writing to ask if you would be interested in being my agent in connection with a book on which I have begun to work. The book has a tentative title *The Nature of Life—Including My Life*. I enclose a first draft of what might be the first chapter of the book. Recently I have been thinking about the last chapter, which I think would be on the mind-body question: Is there one basic reality, the mind, or perhaps the body, or are there two such realities?

Linus Pauling to John Brockman, March 24, 1992

Linus Pauling receiving Vannevar Bush Award, 1989

1987

Pauling and Cameron begin to advocate the use of vitamin C in the treatment of AIDS.

Pauling delivers a special series of the George Fisher Baker Non-resident Lectures in Chemistry commemorating the 1937 Lecture Series; entitled "The Nature of the Chemical Bond."

1989

Pauling receives the Vannevar Bush Award of the National Science Foundation.

He participates in the discussions about "cold fusion" and offers a chemical explanation for what some have interpreted as a nuclear phenomenon.

1991

Pauling publishes an appeal to stop the rush to war in the Persian Gulf, asking that leaders concentrate on negotiations and economic sanctions instead.

Matthias Rath and Pauling theorize that ascorbate deficiencies are a primary cause of heart disease.

In December, Pauling is diagnosed as having rectal and prostate cancer. Pauling undergoes two surgeries to treat the cancer, but otherwise chooses vitamin C megadoses as his primary form of therapy.

1994

On August 19, Linus Pauling dies at Deer Flat Ranch, Big Sur, California.

MY BEST FRIEND

Linus Pauling

❧❧❧

*Scientific careers are made of more than a strong interest in the natural world.
As Pauling points out in this appreciation of his friend, Lloyd Jeffress,
personal interactions often play a vital role in guiding and motivating the
development of scientific talent. Jeffress's friendship was critical twice in
Pauling's life: first, when he introduced the adolescent Pauling to chemical
experimentation, igniting an interest that would last a lifetime; and second,
when Jeffress and his family encouraged Pauling to stick with his plans for
college despite the opposition of Pauling's mother. Pauling rarely saw Jeffress
after graduating from college. Despite that, he considered him his best friend
for the rest of his life.*

Lloyd Jeffress and I were about the same age. Since I first met him,
when, I think, I was twelve years old and had begun my high-
school studies in Washington High, Portland, Oregon, I have
considered him my best friend, even though I saw him only rarely after
1925. My respect for his insight began to develop when we were fifteen
years old. He came with me when I traveled seven miles, from Portland to
Oswego, to visit my grandparents. Standing in front of her little house, my
grandmother said to me, "Liney, what are you going to be when you grow
up?" and I immediately answered, "I am going to be a chemical engineer."
Lloyd then spoke up saying, "No, he is going to be a university professor."

There are two actions taken by Lloyd that greatly influenced my life.
When we were thirteen years old he and I were walking from the high
school towards his home, which was on the route toward my home, farther
away, when he asked me if I would like to see some chemical experiments.
I answered that I would, and we went to his bedroom on the second floor
of his parents' house. There he carried out two or three experiments, one
of which I remember very clearly. I was intensely interested, and when I
reached home I found my father's chemistry book and began reading it,
and also carried out a manipulation consisting, I think, only of boiling
some water over an alcohol lamp. I immediately began collecting chemicals
and apparatus, mainly given to me by family friends, one a druggist who

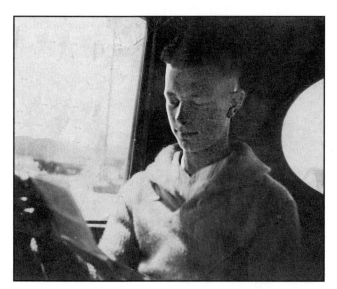

Teenaged Linus Pauling studies while on the train

had known my father during his life and the other the stockroom keeper in North Pacific Dental College. I was started on my career by Lloyd Jeffress.

The other influential action came three years later, when I was sixteen. I had applied for admission to the course in chemical engineering at Oregon Agricultural College, and had been accepted. During the summer I had a job in a machine shop. My employers were very pleased with me, as a responsible young person who could learn fast. They increased my salary with every paycheck, and wanted me to stay in the machine-shop business. My mother, as a young widow with three children (I have two sisters younger than I), was eager for me to continue in the machine-shop business and to bring in a not insignificant income. I was torn between my desire to do what my mother wanted me to do and my strong desire to learn more by going to college. By this time Lloyd's father and mother had died and he was living with his aunt and uncle, Mr. and Mrs. Brayman. Lloyd and his aunt and uncle argued with me strongly, urging me not to give up my plan of going to college. My mother accepted this decision, even though the next few years were difficult ones financially for her as well as for me. In a sort of compromise, I agreed two years later not to return for my junior year at the college but to continue working at my job as a paving engineer. Later in the fall I was given an appointment as a full-time instructor in quantitative analysis in Oregon Agricultural College, and was then able to return for my junior and senior years, with the loss of only one year.

I was with Lloyd during our freshman year in Oregon Agricultural College, and for some time was his roommate. He had signed up as working for a degree in electrical engineering, but he neglected his studies to some extent in order to carry out experiments in physics in his room in Corvallis, with apparatus borrowed from the physics department. I think that he decided then to shift to Berkeley to major in physics, although I am not sure about my memory on this point. At any rate, he became interested in medicine, and studied anatomy and other pre-medical subjects. I believe that he took one year out to study German and some other subjects independently. As a premed student he became interested in psychology, and got his bachelor's degree and then his Ph.D. degree in psychology at the University of California in Berkeley.

In 1923 my wife and I were married in Salem, Oregon, the 17th of June. Lloyd served as my best man at the wedding, which was held in the home of one of my wife's sisters, with the wedding attended by a good group of relatives and friends, perhaps about forty. A few months later my wife and I were living in a small apartment in Pasadena when Lloyd and a young woman, a student in Berkeley, turned up, saying that they wanted to get married. I went to a church nearby, which I had not attended at any time, found the minister, and asked if he could come to our apartment and carry out the marriage ceremony. Accordingly Lloyd and Sylvia were married in our small apartment, with my wife as Sylvia's attendant and me as Lloyd's best man. No one else was present except the minister. Sylvia's parents lived in Los Angeles, but they were very strongly opposed to her marriage to Lloyd. I do not know whether the rift between Sylvia and her family was ever healed—at any rate I never heard about any solution to the problem.

Every few months we were able to see Lloyd and Sylvia when we visited Berkeley in order for me to talk to people in the college of chemistry of that University. One evening we attended the psychology party. I think that there were about seventy-five people present. Lloyd had, before the party, asked if I would participate in an exhibition of mind reading. We were all in a quite large room in the psychology building, perhaps 35 feet by 60 feet. There were chairs all around the perimeter, and a long table in the middle. Over and over again Lloyd would go out of the room, Edward Tolman or some other professor would gather up a dozen objects from people in the room and put them on the table, one of these objects would then be selected by someone, and everyone would be asked to look at the object at which this person was pointing and to remember which one it was. Lloyd was then asked to come back into the room. As he entered he would walk a few steps toward the table, then stop and stand still for a few seconds, then walk toward the table and around it looking at the objects, and finally would pick up the correct one, as his first choice. He repeated this action with a new selection of a dozen objects, perhaps half a dozen times, before giving up. The people at the party were, I think, getting more and more suspicious of me, but I do not think that they saw what was happening. Lloyd's scheme was a simple one. When he entered the room and stopped, standing still for a few seconds, he then began to walk, counting the steps as a, b, c,.... I was also counting the steps a, b, c,..., and when he took the step corresponding to the initial letter of the selected object I, who had been sitting quietly before, would raise my hand to scratch my ear or would cross my legs or would move my body, as a sign to Lloyd that the proper initial letter had been reached.

Lloyd's experimental work for his doctorate was on the psychogalvanic effect. The field of electronics had not been very well developed at that time. Lloyd used a d'Arsonval string galvonometer, which he himself constructed. His background in physics enabled him to carry out a study that very few graduate students in psychology would have attempted.

When my first freshman textbook, *General Chemistry*, came out in 1947, Lloyd suggested to me that he and I cooperate in writing a similar introductory textbook in physics. Nothing came of this proposal, probably because I was so engrossed in my research activities as not to be willing to take any time for that job.

Around 1946 a gift was made to the California Institute of Technology to support work on the functioning of the brain. I was a member of the committee to decide about the use of this money, the Hixon Fund committee. One of the other members was a psychologist who had married Richard Chace Tolman, my respected professor of physical chemistry and mathematical physics, with whom I had written a paper in 1925. Mrs. Tolman (Dr. Ruth Tolman) suggested that the committee set up a symposium on the scientific basis of psychoanalysis. After some months of effort on the part of the committee, this plan was given up, because we were not able to find anyone who could give a significant paper on the scientific basis of psychoanalysis. We then decided to hold a symposium on cerebral mechanisms. It was clear that the job of preparing for this symposium and running it would be a difficult one, and that we needed some knowledgeable person. At my suggestion, the job, a one-year appointment, was offered to Lloyd, and he came to Pasadena, living for that year in our house, while my wife and I and our children were in Oxford. When we came back the symposium was held. It was an outstandingly successful one. Lloyd worked for another year editing the papers, which were even then published in a book. The Hixon Fund committee then decided that the money should be used to support a professor, and we chose Roger W. Sperry. This was a good selection—Sperry later was awarded the Nobel Prize.

My wife and I saw Lloyd in Austin about five years before his death. He seemed not to be in very good health. Later he wrote that it had been difficult for him to accept Sylvia's death. I do not think that Lloyd had any belief in an afterlife. When he and I were about fourteen years old we went several months to Sunday school every Sunday, in a Christian Science Church. Lloyd's father and mother had been Christian Scientists, and I think his uncle and aunt also. Lloyd probably attended these Sunday school classes to please his father and mother, who were still alive then, and I went along in order to be with Lloyd.

Lloyd and I wrote to each other rather rarely. The last time that I talked with him was by telephone, when he was in the hospital in Austin, two weeks before his death. He had strong voice and spoke cheerfully, but he suggested that he did not have long to live, and mentioned his emphysema.

I have many friends, but I continue to think of Lloyd Alexander Jeffress as my best friend.

Diary Excerpts

Linus Pauling

✦✦✦

During the summer following his senior year of high school, when he was only sixteen years old, Pauling began to keep a diary. His scientific interests and objectivity were already present, as evidenced by one of the first entries. On August 30, 1917, he wrote, "I regret to say that I have this minute laid my fingers on the top of the little stove in which I was burning some waste paper, and in this manner have caused the formation of blisters fully 1/3 cm. in diameter on each of the four fingers of my dextrum. They are already visible, although formed only a minute ago. They do not interfere with my writing, but pain me considerably."

AUGUST 29, 1917

Today I am beginning to write the history of my life. The idea which has resulted in this originated a year or more ago, when I thought of the enjoyment that I would have could I read of the events of my former and younger life. My children and grandchildren will without doubt hear of the events in my life with the same relish with which I read the scattered fragments written by my granddad, Linus Wilson Darling. This "history" is not intended to be written in diary form or as a continued narrative—rather, it is to be a series of essays on subjects most important in my mind. It will serve to remind me of resolutions made, of promises, and also of good times had, and of important occurrences in my passage through this "vale of tears." It is to be my Father Confessor—at times—and my companion at other times. Often, I hope, I shall glance over what I have written before, and ponder and meditate on the mistakes that I have made—on the good luck that I have had—on the carefree joyety [sic] of my younger days; and, pondering, I shall resolve to remedy these mistakes, to bring back my good luck, and to regain my happiness.

AUGUST 30, 1917

On Tuesday, June 26, 1917, I began working at Aple's Meat Market, having worked earlier in the summer at the People's Market, but, owing to shortage of work, having been required to quit. On that same day Mrs. Grumbling, the girls' music teacher, called me up about finding a boy for

Linus Pauling, age
seventeen

some work. That evening I called up Mr. William Schweizerkopf, who, in partnership with Chas. Day, owns the Pacific Scale and Supply Co., the Howe Scale Co., the Brown Portable Conveying Machinery Co., etc, etc, etc, and made an appointment with him for the morrow. The next day I, having been getting $8.00 per week at Aple's, contracted with him for $35 per month. Having worked two days, I relinquished my position in the meat retailing line to _____, much to the disgust of Aple, whom I had told that I would work all summer.

On the following Monday, July 2nd, I began work in the machine shop of the Brown Portable Conveying Machinery Co. Two weeks later Mr. Schweizerkopf told me I would probably get $40 a month. A week afterwards I was raised to $45, which sum I received for my first month's labor. For the next month (which will end tomorrow), I am to receive $50, which will be increased about $5 because of my night work. I got $53.75.

At 6:15 Mamma wakes me up. I dress, eat breakfast, and leave for work at 6:55. At 7:30 my work begins, I sweep out the office, then go upstairs and encase myself in greasy overalls and shirt. At 12 P.M., after much anxious waiting for the hour, I eat my lunch and inhale a pint of milk through a glass straw, while avidly devouring a story in *All-Story*, or some other magazine. At 12:30 I begin the afternoon, quitting at 5. Last week and the week before I have worked from 6 to 9 P.M. on Monday—Wed—Friday, four bits being furnished by the company for dinner.

SEPTEMBER 5, 1917

I have been reading a library book which I got yesterday. Its name is "Modern Chemistry and Its Wonders," by Dr. Geoffrey Martin, an Englishman. It was written in 1915, and so contains references to the war and to "Kaiser William the Bad." The author makes the mistake, which I must avoid, of often saying such "as I have pointed out in my former book 'Triumphs and Wonders of Modern Chemistry' 2nd Ed., p. 60." etc. etc. This mistake is very obnoxious; that is, the mistake of so often referring to your own "former volumes." Otherwise the book is rather interesting; containing, as it does, numerous anecdotes relating to chemistry.

Lloyd (Simon), while working at the Portland Rubber Mills, made the acquaintance of Dave Beutler, who is a very good photographer; i.e., from the developing side. We three are going to install in our lab. (a 14' x 14' structure in Lloyd's basement) a complete developing, printing, enlarging, tinting, etc., establishment, enlarging a specialty. The company will probably purchase a second hand motorcycle for use in delivering and collecting work, and Lloyd will use it before and after school. If I get $5 to $10 a week throughout the year my college course will present few pecuniary difficulties. I might even take a year of graduate work and get the degree of Ch.E. I will specialize in the chemistry of photography as far as possible.

I have never seen Dave as yet, and Lloyd said that he was opposed to taking me into partnership until he discovered that I had a half interest in the laboratory, when he readily consented. Lloyd is a good friend.

I enjoy day-dreaming, and building castles in Spain. But I hope that these are not dreams or castles.

Yesterday and today the feeling has often come to me that never more will I go to school. I think of all the other students beginning their studies, I imagine how I am [sic] member of the graduating class, would appear at Washington, I remember the enjoyment I got out of my studies and school life in general, and I sometimes poignantly regret that I have decided to go to college without graduating from high school. I covet every term of education that I have, and would gladly have more. College still seems so dim and far away that I often forget all about it. In a month and a day from now I will be in Corvallis. I try not to think of College, because of the way it affects me. Why should I rush through my education in the way I am?

Paul Harvey is going to O.A.C. to study chemistry—big, manly Paul Harvey, beside whom I pale into insignificance. Why should I enjoy the same benefits he has, when I am so unprepared, so unused to the ways of man? I will not be able, on account of my youth and inexperience, to do justice to the courses and the teaching placed before me. But it is too late to change now, even if I wanted to—so I will only do my best. But perhaps every young college student feels as I do. I do not know. At any rate I will do my best. Perhaps it would be better to allow a year or two to elapse between my graduation and year of graduate work.

THURSDAY, SEPTEMBER 6, 1917

My ignorance about matters photographical is overwhelming. I must learn all I can before I go to O.A.C., so I will be prepared to take pictures there. Today I told Mr. Zeigler about Lloyd's $56 camera, but, as I had never seen it, I did not know whether it used plates or films.

The more look at myself in the mirror the more peculiar my physiognomy appears to me. I do not look at all attractive, but I am a prejudiced judge. I already have faint horizontal wrinkles in my forehead, and my upper lip projects to an unnecessarily great extent. I must remember to restrain it.

TUESDAY, SEPTEMBER 11, 1917

I got 4 rolls of film at Mason's today and two from Oscar (Carlson), a 25 yr. old Swedish scale expert at the shop. Some of these have two prints made, thus raising the price. Lloyd took the films over to Dave, on a motorcycle, I

He was always experimenting in the basement and the most awful odors would come up and go all through the house…We weren't supposed to go in that little room he closed off down in the basement.

Pauline Pauling Emmett, sister

think, and said that he would bring some things over to the laboratory, as a first step in moving.

I just today finished reading a quite interesting book, Cooper's "Two Admirals."

I believe I have found a good method of learning more Latin, especially as regards vocabulary. It is this; to memorize rhyming Latin poems and their translations. As a start, I am learning Moore's "To a Beautiful Milkmaid" and Father Prout's translation, "In Pulchram Lactiferam."

SUNDAY, SEPTEMBER 16, 1917

Tentative Resolutions.

I will make better than 95 (Mervyn's record) in Analysis (Math). (I made $99^6/_{11}\%$ in Analytic Geom.)

I will take all the math possible.

I will make use of my slide rule.

I will make the acquaintance of Troy Bogart.

I must go out for track, and <u>succeed</u>.

Early last fall, as I was crossing a field on the way to school with a bunch of boys, I found a slide rule. The other boys had stepped over the box in which it was, but I picked it up. I watched the advertisements in the daily papers for many days, but it was not advertised for. It is a polyphase duplex slide rule, made by Keuffel and Esser Co., and costing about $7.50. Its number is <4088-3>. It is 12 inches long and contains 12 scales.

Mr. Benedict, of the Pacific Scale and Supply Co., after a trip to a place where he was to set a scale, said that at some town he had seen a young man, with whiskers, dirt, and ragged clothes, whom he thought to be a tramp, but who was an O.A.C. student working in the harvest fields. He told him about me, and the young man said for Mr. Benedict to tell me to look him up at Corvallis. Bennie could not remember my name, never having known what it was. The young man, whose card is in an envelope marked "High School Reminiscences," although not belonging there, was named Troy Bogart, of Woodburn, Oregon, and is a Senior in Farm Crops at O.A.C.

On a blank page toward the front of this manuscript is a photo of Mrs. Linus Vere Windnagle, and an account of her marriage to Linus. This from today's *Oregonian*. I will save all reference to any Linuses or Paulings.

SATURDAY, SEPTEMBER 29, 1917

Mr. Schweizerkopf, after I had worked for him a month, said that I would be a success in anything I should take up. Mr. Day later said the same thing. Today Mr. Schweizerkopf said that if I were not going to college that they would find some work for me to do all the time, and said to write to him at about the close of school next year about my work during vacation, or to come and see him.

Tonight for $.50 I got at Gill's a slide-rule book called "The Mannheim (Complete Manual) and the Duplex Slide Rules" by Wm. Cox and also the supplementary pamphlet called "The K. and E. Polyphase Duplex Slide Rule."

FRIDAY, OCTOBER 5, 1917

Here are my last term in High School examination marks.

English [7]	Matthew Linnehan	B
Math [8]	Virgil Earle	A
Math [7 tr]	" "	A
Latin [7]	Mr. Fenstermacher	B+
Physics Science [5]	Mr. Holloway	A+

Mr. Holloway read my examination paper (100+) to the class, and told them that it was the best he had ever read.

SUNDAY, OCTOBER 7, 1917

Arrived yesterday. Staying at Mrs. F. J. Carton with Mamma. She got weekend round trip tickets for $3.50.

I have a nice big room, much larger than two boys usually have. I will share it with a sophomore named Murhard, who has not yet arrived. Last night the two other boys and I killed about 50 yellow jackets there with a fly swatter. They are two rooks; one, a 20 yr. old talkative fellow, named Hofman, weight 175# and always talks about his girl, Millicent, nicknamed "Titter." The other, Henry, is a very quiet, small young man, but slightly deaf. He will take Commerce, and Hofman will take Forestry.

Last night at the train I met Mr. Johnson, and his small son. He asked me if I was new, and said he was the head of the math department. According to the catalogue he is: Charles Leslie Johnson, B.S., Professor of Mathematics. I intend to take every one of the courses offered in Mathematics.

OCTOBER 10, 1917

I'm getting along all right. Cleaned the fountain today and serpentined with a couple of hundred other rooks to the football field, where we yelled for O.A.C. and sung some songs. We then marched to Waldo Hall and sang "How green I am" to a crowd of the inmates. We were guarded by about 20 sophs.

This evening I went to see Paul Harvey at the Sigma Chi house, and met about twenty fellows. They were singing and playing on the piano and uke banjo.

MONDAY, OCTOBER 29, 1917

Am getting along all right. Have lots of beaver pep. Like Mr. Johnson, prof in math (calc.), Brodie, in chemistry. Room with Mervyn, junior, & Errol Alexander Murhard, soph. Still retain my hair.

Saturday (two days ago), I went to work at Kincaid's chopping wood. I saw Irene at 8 o'clock in morning. I saw her again once during morning. In afternoon she went to game. About 6:30 I called her up and asked her to go to the show. She consented, and I got up some speed getting ready.

He made me feel bad that he could do all that school work and not try one-tenth as hard as I was. I really noticed it. He was able to read fast and powerfully and absorb it, and it stayed with him.

Al Bauer, OAC roommate

Linus Pauling, lower right, at Intra-Fraternity Smoker, 1920

"The house had a rule that we had to have a date, they called it fussing in those days, and have a date once…once a month…or I don't know what the time was, anyway, and Pauling and I, both, were a little bit bashful, I guess, as far as that was concerned. Once in a while we'd get a paddling or sometime as a serious offense, they'd dunk us in the bathtub in cold water. His studies…the rest of the boys were kind of jealous of him. He seemed to have a lot of time to do things that the rest of us didn't have because he didn't do much studying. It just seemed like all he'd have to do was sit down at a table and look at a book and he'd absorb the knowledge without reading it…looking at it. And…he was…it was common comments among the students in the college that, you know, he was so damned sharp. And he was a chem engineer, I guess, and physics. He'd often argue with these professors and lots of times they'd say, 'Well, hell, he knew more than the profs anyway. He could conduct the class better than they did.' So he was regarded as quite a brain in those days always.

I do remember once we were practicing basketball, had a house team, you know, and the fella that was supposed to take charge of the team, he was out playing and he kicked [Pauling] off the floor and said, 'We don't want the floor cluttered up with players like you.' So he wasn't too active, I guess, but he didn't go in for sports at all, he was interested in learning more than that. I do remember a picture of him … at some party…that Pauling was dressed up as a…it was four of the boys, I think, dressed as women. And uh, that was interesting. Pauling was a good-looking little gal."

Ed Larson, OAC fraternity brother

We went to show and to A's & K's. Sunday I stayed away all day, then called her up about 6 and went to Presbyterian church with her. I do not know whether she likes me or not. I hope she will go to Lyceum with me Sat. night. I must remember to reserve seats for it. Then we will have reserved seats together for all Lyceums this year. She is the girl for me. She is 17 years old and is about 5' 5" tall. She is rather light and fragile. On account of lack of strength she is taking a special course in Dom. Sc., together with stenography. She lives with her uncle and aunt, Mr. & Mrs. Kincaid. They have been in Corvallis about 4 months, having lived in Eugene before. She said she had never gone with anyone for over six months, but I will show her. I must not, however, monopolize her. She has pretty curly hair. Her last name is Sparks. I must be as nice as possible to her.

INTERVIEW WITH DR. LINUS PAULING

On November 11, 1990 by Wayne Reynolds,
Executive Director, American Academy of Achievement,
at the home of Dr. Pauling, Big Sur, California.

INT: *Was there an event or person who inspired you most as a young person? Let's talk first about the person who inspired you most, who was a big influence on you as a young man?*

LP: Well, by the time I got to graduate school, there were people who had a great influence on me. One was Roscoe Gilkey Dickinson. He had got his doctorate in physical chemistry, x-ray crystallography, in 1920. He was the first person to get a Ph.D. from the California Institute of Technology. And he was continuing with x-ray crystallography, determining the structure of inorganic crystals. A.A. Noyes, the head of the division of chemistry and chemical engineering at the California Institute of Technology, after I had accepted appointment as a graduate student, wrote to say that he had decided that I should work with Roscoe Dickinson on determining the structure of crystals. This was really extremely fortunate for me, in my opinion. I don't think that there was any field that was more suited to my interests, and I don't really know why Dr. Noyes selected me out of eight or ten new graduate students to do x-ray crystallography. Dickinson had a remarkable mind. He was a very careful investigator and thinker, a very logical thinker. When he was teaching me x-ray crystallography, he also taught me to ask at each stage in the argument, what assumptions are being made? How reliable is the conclusion that you draw? What chance is there that one of the assumptions you have made is not correct? "You should recognize," he said to me, "that there is in almost every investigation a lack of complete rigor. You should understand just how reliable the arguments are that you are presenting."

Then starting immediately when I became a graduate student, there was a professor of physical chemistry and mathematical physics in the California Institute of Technology who had just come at that time, and who was very influential with me. He was Richard Chace Tolman, who had been at MIT and at Berkeley, and then came to the California Institute of Technology. He immediately began giving a course of the basis of science, a very interesting course in which he discussed the question of how science is in fact prosecuted. He introduced some new ideas about physics which turned out not to be right. He also began giving a course on quantum theory and atomic structure, using the book, *The Origin of Spectra*, by Foote and Mohler.

The next year I studied quantum theory (this was the old quantum theory of course in those years). I studied quantum theory with Tolman in a seminar in which [Arnold] Sommerfeld's book on quantum theory and atomic structure was used as the text. One year the German edition, because there was no English edition, and the next year the English translation. Tolman had made a great impact on me in regard to physical and chemical theory, so those two people, I think, were probably most important in the early period of my career.

INT: *They not only imparted knowledge to you, but also helped you understand the tools that you would need to work with for the rest of your scientific career.*

LP: Yes, the experimental work that I did in x-ray crystallography was not especially complicated in the way that some modern experiments are. But I was at least a passable experimenter, and I was good in the laboratory, making chemical compounds and crystallizing them. So I got

…[I]n my first year as a graduate student, when I was in Pasadena and writing a letter every day to my future wife in Corvallis, I happened to say in one letter something about the acidic acid in sauerkraut. I got back a letter saying "—any damned fool knows that there's no acidic acid in sauerkraut; it's lactic acid!"

Linus Pauling

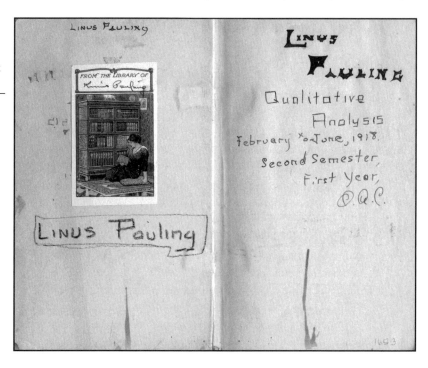

Linus Pauling's chemistry textbook, freshman year at OAC

along all right. My work as a whole has been about half experimental and half theoretical. Which I think is a good combination.

INT: *I thought it is very interesting that you learned to check your assumptions at every stage of the process. It seems like a critical faculty to maintain when you are doing research. One may be tempted to run off and follow a train of thought because you think it may lead you somewhere.*

LP: Yes, going to Cal Tech for graduate work led to my understanding that it is possible to make progress in science. To get a better... to get increased knowledge about the nature of the world. When I was a senior still at Oregon Agricultural College I tried to carry out an experiment, a rather difficult one for me, to answer a question that I had formulated for myself. I had for years already mulled over the tables of properties of substances, magnetic susceptibility, hardness, and of course in the case of minerals, cleavage, color and other properties. One property that interested me was magnetism. I was also very much interested in metals and alloys, so when I was a senior I had the idea of carrying out an experiment to check on a hypothesis that I had formed. I knew that one could, by electrolysis, convert the salt of iron into iron crystals, and the idea I had was that if I would deposit crystals of iron electrolytically in a magnetic field, the interaction of the magnetic field with the crystals should orient the crystals. Though I didn't know enough about this field to... this whole field of research, to formulate a good experiment, but I did attempt to carry out this experiment during my senior year, and I wasn't successful. There were practical problems, about the electrolysis that caused difficulty for me. However, when I got to Pasadena, Cal Tech, in the fall of 1922, I soon recognized that the scientists were working very vigorously on research problems to get additional information about the nature of the universe, and this really appealed to me very strongly.

INT: *That is one thing that seems to be fascinating about the fields you have worked in. You discovered all sorts of new relationships in the physical world. The structure of the atom, the nuclei, that sort of thing. For the layman, for someone who doesn't really understand these things, what did those kinds of things tell us about the world and the way the world works? Can you summarize that for the non-scientist?*

LP: The chemists of the middle nineteenth century, about 140 to 120 years ago, had made an astonishing discovery about the nature of the world. Thousands of different chemical substances, elements and compounds were known. The compositions were becoming known. The question was why do these compounds have certain compositions: the number of atoms of each element, the molecules, and why are the properties what they are? So the chemists formulated the ideas that we call the chemical structure theory, old fashioned molecular structure theory. That, for example, hydrogen atom forms one chemical bond. The carbon atom forms four chemical bonds. So the methane molecule, the same methane that you can buy to build a methane air torch, for example, for soldering, this methane molecule, they said, consists of one carbon atom forming it's four bonds with four hydrogen atoms, thus it is CH_4. Then they had the idea that carbon atoms, this was around 1850, that carbon atoms could form carbon-carbon bonds. So that one could build up a framework of atoms corresponding to many different elementary compositions.

[In] 1873 the idea was developed that the bonds of the carbon atom are not flat in a plane, but arranged in space pointing toward the directions of a tetrahedron. And this meant that there are certain molecules that you can say are right-handed, and others that are very similar, with the same elementary composition, are left-handed. They are mirror images of each other. Now without knowing what the nature of the chemical bond was, this idea, that there are bonds between pairs of atoms, was enough to permit the whole field of chemistry and the pharmaceutical field, composition of drugs, and many other fields, practical fields, to be developed. Then, of course, after the electron had been discovered in 1896, and the nucleus of the atom as an extremely small part of the center of the atom had been discovered in 1911, it became possible to determine many properties of molecules, such as how far apart the atoms are, that hadn't been available for experimental study before. X-ray diffraction was one of the methods. I was fortunate then in being able to use this essentially new experimental technique discovered in 1914, eight years before I became a graduate student, in attempting to answer many questions that I had formulated about chemical substances and their properties. And yet, they had only experimental answers to them.

The next important development was that the theory of quantum mechanics was discovered in 1925 and 1926. This was an improvement on the old quantum theory. The old quantum theory was an approximate theory which sometimes worked in a very remarkable way, and sometimes failed. But quantum mechanics—so far as chemistry is concerned—quantum mechanics is the basic theory and there is nothing wrong with it; it works. I realized in 1926 already that quantum mechanics could be applied to answer many additional questions about the nature of the chemical bonds, about the structure of molecules and crystals. So, during the next ten years I was able to apply quantum mechanics to chemical problems in very productive ways, changing the whole basic nature of chemistry in such a way that essentially all chemists make use of these new ideas, along with the old structural chemistry that had been developed much earlier.

INT: *It must be very exciting to be in something that you realize, at least later, is in a sense a turning point, or the opening of a door for scientists and researchers to walk through into a new area of discovery.*

LP: Yes, someone asked me not long ago, what was the discovery I made that excited me the most. And I answered that it was the basic discovery about directed chemical bonds that I made in January of 1931. I had in fact published a paper in 1928 already, two years after I began learning quantum mechanics, in which I said that from quantum mechanics, by a treatment that I call the resonance theory, I could explain the tetrahedral nature of the bonds of the carbon atom. And that I would publish details later. Nearly three years went by before I published the details. In 1928, I was working with the quantum mechanical calculations which were very complicated mathematically, and I managed to derive the result that the carbon atom would form four bonds in tetrahedral directions, but it was so complicated that I thought people won't believe it. It is so hard to see through this mass of symbols and equations and relationships, that they won't believe it. And perhaps I don't believe it either. [laughs] Oh, I published a statement about it – it took a long time for me to simplify the quantum mechanical equations so that they were very easily applied to various problems. So the day, probably January 19... I may have a record of it, but January of 1931, late in the day I had this idea – I can use a simple method of simplifying, a powerful method of simplifying these equations. Then I can apply these simplified equations to various chemical problems. So I worked, I think, nearly all night, very excited about applying this idea. I not only can easily derive the tetrahedral arrangement of the bonds of the carbon atoms, but also various other arrangements of atoms around a central atom, not only tetrahedral, but also octahedral ligation and square planar ligation, which do occur with certain substances. And I did make predictions about relationships between magnetic properties and the arrangements of the atoms around each other. I considered that paper, which was published 17th of March, 1931, as my most important paper, and I believe I am right in saying that it is the one that developed the greatest feeling of excitement in me.

INT: *What experience or event... we talked about the people who influenced your life, but was there an experience or event that also had a major impact on you?*

LP: Well, I think that meeting the young woman whom I married a year and a half later was the event that had the greatest effect on my life. She, I can see in retrospect, she felt that her duty was to see to it that her husband lived as good a life as possible. And in particular, that she would handle the problems and stresses associated with family, leaving me free to devote all of my time and effort to working on the problems that I wanted to work on, the scientific problems.

INT: *And having that concentration was a great advantage in your work, no doubt.*

LP: Yes, I'm sure. I've been asked from time to time how does it happen that you have made so many discoveries –are you smarter than other scientists? And my answer has been that I am sure that I am not smarter than others. I don't have any precise evaluation of my IQ, but to the extent that psychologists have said that my IQ is about 160, I recognize that there are one hundred thousand or more people in the United States that have IQs higher than that. So I have said that I think I think harder, think more than other people do, than other scientists do. For years, almost all of my thinking was about science and scientific problems that I was interested in. So I owe much of this to my wife.

INT: *Who kept you from having to worry about anything other than your science?*

LP: Yes, that's right.

INT: *I'm fascinated by what you say in the sense that there are indeed many people who are well-educated, who are very smart, who are doing research. And yet a few people make the great discoveries, write the books that influence the rest of the research in their field. Do you think there is a role in there for luck?*

LP: Well, I'm sure there is. Those two events I mentioned, first being selected as a graduate student teaching fellow at Cal Tech. I don't think there was any institution in the world in 1922 that would have provided a better opportunity for me to be educated for the career that I have had. I was fortunate that I didn't receive the Rhodes Scholarship two years earlier - Oxford was pretty backwards, so far as science was concerned at that time. And well, I doubt that I could have accepted the scholarship anyway, because it didn't cover all the expenses and we didn't have any money. Then the second good luck was Dr. Noyes saying that I should work on x-ray diffraction. That, that was really fine.

INT: *One of the things that has also stood you in good stead all these many years is that you were a very good student. If I remember correctly, you read an enormous amount as a young boy.*

LP: Yes, my father, when I had just about reached my ninth birthday, wrote a letter to the Portland *Oregonian* asking for advice as to what books to get for me. He said that I seemed to have an unusual interest in reading, especially history. Then he went on to say - "And don't say the Bible and Darwin's *Origin of Species* because he has already read them." Well, I think I can remember reading the Bible at an early age, but I don't remember, that is the only evidence I have that I had read Darwin's *Origin of Species* before I was nine years old. So I did like to read, and I became, without anyone, well my father had some influence on this way of thinking because I used to watch him compounding prescription drugs in the back room of his drug store, and he was interested in teaching me a little medical Latin and other things, so he may have influenced me somewhat, but I early developed a great curiosity about the nature of the world, the nature of the Universe. So as time went on, I became more and more interested to learn more by reading about the universe, the world, but also to discover something new.

INT: *What did your parents first think? Did they have a notion about what they wanted you to be?*

LP: My father died when I was nine, shortly after he had written this letter, and my mother was not very interested in ideas, I think, in intellectual matters. I don't remember any general discussions held in the family with my mother. The aunt and uncle of Lloyd Jeffress, this young fellow who was my best friend for many years, in fact all of his life essentially, were, I would say, intellectuals. They weren't university people, but they were interested in ideas, and I learned something about ideas from them. Also, they were influential in my life in that when I was sixteen, in June I got a job in a machine shop. And every time I received my paycheck, my salary had been increased. So by the end of the summer I was getting pretty good pay for a sixteen-year-old. My mother was having so much financial trouble as a widow with three children that she was hoping that I would continue in the machine shop, and continue to bring a salary. Lloyd Jeffress' aunt and uncle, however, were determined that I should go on to college, and they convinced me, I suppose, that it was my duty that I go on to college. It didn't require much money; there was no tuition at Oregon Agricultural College. My mother, for six

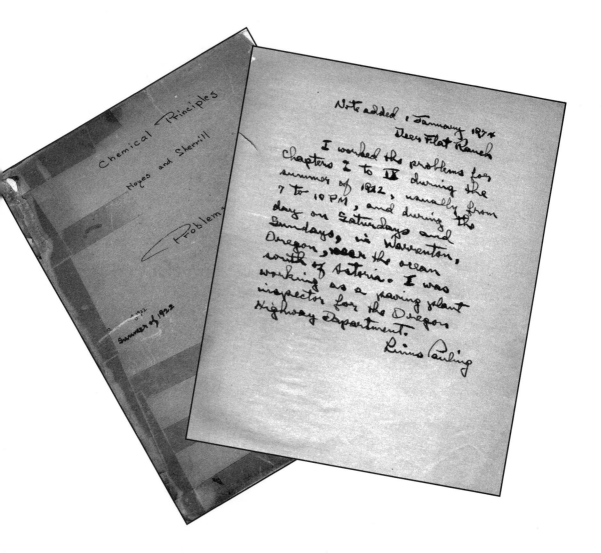

months at any rate, sent me twenty-five dollars a month that I was able to live on, and then she couldn't send it and I had some trouble the next three months getting by. But from then on I was able to earn my living and even help my mother out somewhat.

INT: *You talk about reading books about natural science and history and so forth. Did you read any fiction as a young man? Was there anything that captivated you in other ways?*

LP: Oh, yes. I read almost any book that I could get hold of. I mentioned to the people in the library at Oregon Agricultural College, Oregon State University, when I was up in Corvallis just recently, that in a sense I owed my general education to the library at Oregon Agricultural College. I can remember many of the books that I read. I got from the library in succession, I think, all of the plays that George Bernard Shaw had written. I can remember reading Voltaire's poems, I studied French in college, and there were many other books. I read romances; there was one while I was still in high school that came out, *The Girl of the Limberlost* or something about some region of the mountains in a southeast country. Just a love story. I rather liked those. I bought the *Saturday Evening Post* nearly every week if I had a nickel that I could spare, and read the stories in the *Saturday Evening Post*. One of them, I realized later, had been written by an author who collaborated with a well-known American physicist. It was called, "The Man Who Rocked the World." It was about radioactivity. The physicist was R. W. Wood, professor of physics at Johns Hopkins [University]. Someone had discovered a way to make a substance radioactive, to induce radioactivity. And there was a cliff in Greenland, I think, containing the substance that could be made radioactive by this method. So the plot involved a man having the idea that he would illuminate this cliff in such a way that the radioactive particles were shot out and that could shift the axis of rotation of the earth. So he was using this to blackmail the countries, the people of the whole world into paying tribute to him. [laughs] And I remember a series of stories about a boy who had an extraordinary memory. He apparently could recall memories in such a way that he saw the scenes that he had viewed at some earlier time. So he was called in to help solve problems such as discovering a criminal by recalling a scene and pointing out some features that weren't in his conscious memory before. This sort of eidetic... I learned later this is called eidetic memory, when you can see a scene as though it were on a television screen in your mind. Well, I read everything I could get my hands on about it. Early science fiction, *Argosy* magazine, mainly sort of adventure stories, but some of them could be called early science fiction. And of course Jules Verne and [H.G.] Wells, …

INT: *Which of the Wells stories did you like the most?*

LP: Well, I can't say which I liked the most at the time I read them. I probably liked all of them, but of course I've re-read them since then. *The War of the Worlds,* for example, I think that was the one in which these flying machines came over at the tremendous height of four hundred feet above the ground, and dropped bombs or threatened to drop bombs. And of course I can remember one of his stories where there were large speakers at the street corners, and advertising saying "Buy Glaxo cold medicine and control your cold" and things like that [laughs] so he anticipated many developments just as did the other writers of science fiction.

INT: *Let me go back and ask you about the love stories we were talking about. Why were you drawn to those? Why did you like the romantic stories that you were reading?*

LP: I suppose I am romantic by nature. The... well I read almost everything. Every once in a while when I was around eleven, twelve years old, my mother would have me go the fourteen miles to Oregon City at the invitation of my uncle, who had a small daughter, little Mary, perhaps four years younger than I, in order to give her some companionship. She was a rather odd little girl, in fact. So my uncle, who was a judge and became Chief Justice of the Oregon Supreme Court later, had a copy of the Encyclopedia Britannica, 1911 edition. I entertained little Mary by lying on the floor and reading the encyclopedia while she lay on the floor beside me. I don't think I read it out loud, I just read page after page in the encyclopedia.

INT: *What about the story about the boy with eidetic memory? Why did that intrigue you so much? Something to do with your curiosity about the world?*

LP: Yes, the boy was called Marcus Aurelius Fortunatus Tidd, and I suppose I identified somewhat with him, that is being the hero in providing the solution to a problem. But it's something like reading detective stories, which I like to do. Not the British women author's detective stories, I never have cared for them. But good detective stories. Novels, I have given up reading novels, romantic novels, because it seems to me there is nothing new. I have read it all before, and I am no longer very interested anyway. And the same thing is true of science fiction stories. It seems to me that the plots of the modern, the new science fiction stories are all plots that I have run across before.

INT: *In working yourself through school, I know it was a necessity, but were there some things that you learned in those jobs? Did you get a perspective that you would have missed had your family been more fortunate financially?*

LP: Well, I'm sure that I got in the habit of working and not being lazy, not wasting my time. In the third term of my freshman year, when my mother was no longer sending me money, I was able to make twenty-five dollars a month, which was barely enough for me to get by with, by working one hundred hours a month chopping wood and cutting quarters of beef for the girls' dormitory. And mopping the kitchens every night. And in order to do this, to work one hundred hours a month for twenty-five cents an hour, and to keep up with my studies, it was necessary that I not waste any hours during the day. So I think I developed the habit of working.

INT: *I'm sure that is a habit that helped you out enormously as you spent years and years and years in a laboratory, where it seems to me it would be easy to waste time, to go off and putter.*

LP: Well, maybe. My success in solving scientific problems I think is the result in part of a quality, or two qualities that I have. One is that of being able to formulate or discover problems. The other is that of being able to make a decision as to which problems I might be able to solve, and which I probably would not be able to solve, so that I don't waste time on those.

INT:: *Do you have any idea how you developed those traits?*

LP: No, I can't... well I have some idea. As the years have gone by, starting quite early I have, I realized, tried to formulate a picture of the universe. In a sense, a theory of everything. Whenever I hear something new, I try to fit it into the picture that I have already formed of the universe. If it fits, well and good, I don't need to worry about it. But if it doesn't fit in, then I ask, why doesn't it fit in with my ideas about how the universe ought to be operating? I would better try to find the answer to that. So then I can ask, well, is my background of knowledge and experience such that I have a reasonable chance of finding the answer? And if it

Sketch for Pauling's work on rocket propellants during World War II

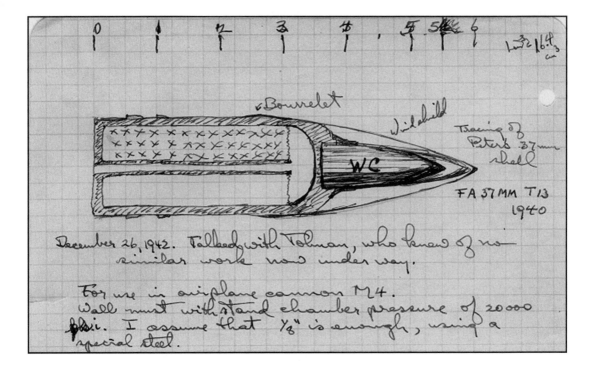

isn't, then I would say, well perhaps someone else will make some progress with that idea, but I better go on with the others. So I have lots of ideas. I do a lot of scientific reading, and quite often, every week perhaps, I read about something that someone is reporting that puzzles me. So I have a big pile of questions of this sort that I would like to settle down to work on.

INT: *Is it hard to think of any obstacles that you have encountered along the way?*

LP: So far as my scientific career goes, of course there was the decision that I made in 1945, '46 perhaps, but starting in 1945 and that may have been made by my wife rather than me, to sacrifice part of my scientific career to working for the control of nuclear weapons and for the achievement of world peace. So, for years I devoted more than half my time, perhaps, to giving hundreds of lectures and to writing my book, *No More War!* But in the earlier years, especially to studying international affairs and social, political and economic theory to the extent that enabled me ultimately to feel that I was speaking with the same authority as when I talked about science. This is what my wife said to me back around 1946, that if I wanted to be effective, I'd have to reach the point where I could speak with authority about these matters, and not just quote statements that politicians and other people of that sort had made.

INT:: *What was it that first got you interested in becoming an activist in the social and political sense?*

LP: When the atomic bomb was dropped at Hiroshima and then at Nagasaki, I was immediately asked, within a month or two, by the Rotary Club, perhaps in Hollywood, to give a talk, an after dinner talk, about atomic bombs. My talk, as I recall, was entirely on what the atom is, what the atomic nucleus is, what nuclear fission is, how it is possible for a substance to be exploded liberating 20 million times more energy than the same amount of dynamite or TNT could liberate. A couple of days after my talk, there was a man in my office from the FBI saying, "Who told you how much plutonium there is in an atomic bomb?" And I said, "Nobody told me, I figured it out." And he went away and that was the end of that. But I kept giving these talks, and I realized that [the] more and more I was saying, it seems to me that we have come to the time war ought to be given up. It no longer makes sense to kill 20 million or 40 million people because of a dispute between two nations, who are running things, or decisions made by the people who really are running things. It no longer makes sense. Nobody wins. Nobody benefits from destructive war of this sort and there is all of this human suffering. So... and Einstein was saying the same thing, of course. So, that is when we decided, my wife and I, that first I was pretty effective as a speaker. Second, I had better start boning up, studying these other fields so that nobody could stand up and say, well the authorities say such and such...

I know that you would bring an independent and conscientious spirit to the task of our enquiry and I should greatly value your participation.

Bertrand Russell, March 6, 1967 (Russell had invited Pauling to join an investigation team for the International War Crimes Tribunal. Pauling refused on the grounds of his overwhelming commitments elsewhere.)

INT:: Do you think the scientist in particular has an obligation to be engaged in those kinds of activities?

LP: Well, yes. I have said this for many years. Almost every problem in the modern world has some scientific content, sometimes very great scientific content. For example, the argument going on now about the ozone layer, the destruction of the ozone layer, or the nuclear winter if there were to be a nuclear war. That seems no longer to be an important matter. I think the chance of having a nuclear war is much less than it was before. Or, the greenhouse effect with an increase in temperature of the earth. But all minor problems, too, the ecological problems... they are largely scientific problems. And while scientists may not be able to decide what the best course is to follow, nevertheless, I think their judgment has to be a little better about these problems than that of the non-scientist. So I have said that the scientist has an obligation to his fellow citizens to help them to understand the problems and to make the right decisions.

Linus Pauling speaks for peace, Germany, 1960

INT: You took the information that you saw, and the concerns that you had, and you organized scientists. Tell me about the petition that you got back in 1958 and why you began that?

LP: I had been talking about the need to control nuclear weapons to prevent a nuclear war and to make treaties for world peace for, oh, a dozen years by 1957. Of course I was often asked to speak at various affairs. In particular I was asked to speak at the honors convocation at Washington University in St. Louis. During the preceding months there had been additional information released about damage done by radioactivity from testing of nuclear weapons, and by the Hiroshima and Nagasaki bombs. So, my talk was about that. It got a tremendous response from the audience when I said we have to stop the testing of nuclear weapons in the atmosphere because hundreds of thousands of unborn children and people now living are being damaged. So with two other professors, Barry Commoner and Ed Condon, I decided to write a petition. The next day we met, each of us had written a version of the petition and I think mine was essentially the one selected by the three of us. We mimeographed it and sent it out to twenty-five scientists that we knew.

They all sent it right back, signed. So then I got back to Pasadena and my wife and I and some of our students and others in the lab got busy and sent out hundreds of copies with the names of these first twenty-five signers. And within a month or two I had two thousand signatures from American scientists which I presented to Dag Hammarskjöld. I think that was later, scientists from all over the world began signing this petition. Originally it was a petition by American scientists, but eventually it became a petition by world scientists. I think it was about nine thousand that I gave, my wife and I gave to Dag Hammarskjöld, and ultimately about thirteen thousand scientists all over the world had signed this petition. So that had a great effect, and I think even on President Kennedy. Because a few years later he gave a speech about a need for a treaty limiting bomb testing and of course pretty soon this treaty was made.

INT: *Did you have some specific goal such as that in mind when you started, or did you simply begin with the idea of making a statement?*

LP: Well, back in 1945, my first talks, these were just pedagogical. I was just explaining nuclear fission. Then I began rather gradually expressing the opinion that the time had come to work for international treaties and international law to settle disputes rather than to use the barbaric method of war, made especially barbaric by the nuclear weapons. So, I was working toward the goal of a world without war. But I didn't ever think that I would obtain the sort of prominence that I have obtained. The McCarthy period came along, of course, 1950, '51, '52, and the others, many of the other people, scientists who had been working on these same lines, gave up. Probably saying why should I sacrifice myself, I am a scientist, I am supposed to be working on scientific things, so I don't need to put myself at risk by talking about these possibilities. And I have said that perhaps I'm just stubborn. I don't like the idea, I have said, I don't like anybody to tell me what to do or to think, except Mrs. Pauling. I ran across this statement in some testimony I was giving before a Senate committee.

INT: *What was it that you said?*

LP: I said nobody tells me what to think, except Mrs. Pauling. [laughs]

INT: *As you mentioned, many shared your views about nuclear testing and other concerns, those were the days, it was the height of the cold war. There were a lot of other political subcurrents that went the other way. Your views and actions, then, came under a great deal of scrutiny during that period, and a great deal of suspicion. Would you talk about that period?*

LP: Well, it was a difficult period. For example, my scientific work was in part supported, a considerable part, supported by grants from the National Science Foundation and the National Institutes of Health. So I got a communication that these grants were not going to be made - despite the letter I received two months before that the grants were

Dearest Paddy,
   …I suppose you think you are pretty smart don't you? Guggenheim Advisory Board. Phooey! They ought to know who the Paddy Advisory Board is….

Ava Helen Pauling, 1937, in response to a letter from Linus informing her that he had just been appointed as a member of the Advisory Board to the John Simon Guggenheim Memorial Foundation.

going to be made - they were not to be made. For a while I didn't understand what it was about, and I telephoned the National Institutes of Health and the man that I talked to said, "Well, you have associates, why don't you split up the application and you apply for part of the work, and your two associates, Dr. Corey and Dr. Campbell, apply for other parts." So we did that. Within a week we sent in these revised applications. In another week Dr. Corey and Dr. Campbell had their grants approved, and even the amount increased and the period extended, and they never acted on my application.

So I was fortunate that this political action by the National Institutes of Health, who were worried about McCarthyism, didn't really seriously interfere with my researches. But there were, I understand, forty, or I understood at the time, forty scientists who had their grants cancelled at this time. I remember talking with one of them at Columbia University. He was despondent. He didn't know what to do. The university wouldn't support him and his work, was more closely knit, he didn't have an associate who could apply for the grant. So there were scientists who were really very hard hit in their scientific work by this political action. Oveta Culp Hobby from Texas, who was Secretary of [the Department of] Health, Education and Welfare, was frightened enough by McCarthy to have the people go over the list and select people they thought might be attacked by McCarthy, and cancel their grants.

That was one thing that happened. Also, the State Department prevented me from traveling for two years. The first time, when the Royal Society of London was holding a two-day conference to discuss my work, I was to be the first speaker [to discuss] work on the structure of protons. An international conference just to discuss these discoveries that I had made. And I couldn't go to the conference because I couldn't get the passport. So, for two years, the State Department caused trouble for me. They wouldn't tell me why - they said not in the best interest of the United States, or your anti-Communist statements haven't been strong enough. I was having a scrap with the Communists, the Russians and the Soviet Union at the time, and I was critical of the Soviet Union, but they used that as an excuse, saying they weren't strong enough, my statements. I'm sure this interfered seriously with my work. When I was awarded the Nobel Prize in chemistry, the *New York Times* had an article saying "Will Professor Pauling be Allowed to Go to Stockholm to Receive the Nobel Prize?" So I received the passport, which had been turned down only a short time before. It was sent to me. Some years later, Senator [Thomas C.] Hennings of Missouri was chairman of a committee in the Senate, investigating the State Department's passport division. The assistant Secretary of State was testifying after I testified. Senator Hennings said, "How did Pauling happen to get his passport then? Was there an appeal?" "Well," he said, "A sort of self-generating appeal." So Senator Hennings said, "Do you mean to sit there and tell me that the State Department of the United States of America allows some committee of foreigners in a foreign country to decide which Americans will be allowed to travel?" Well, he didn't have any answer to that question.

INT: *We were talking about the difficulties during this period. You mention some problems for other academics. If I remember correctly, you had some difficulties in the academic world, too. Cal Tech didn't look kindly on some of your activities.*

LP: The trustees, of course, were mainly business men and conservative and supporters of the Cold War, and they seemed to consider that working for peace between the U.S. and the Soviet Union was in some way subversive, as compared with preparing for a war that would rid the world of the menace of communism. Probably, really, socialism worried them rather than communism. So, the trustees tried to get the Institute to fire me, and a committee was set up, I didn't know about it at the time, learned only later, that [it was] reported that they couldn't find a way by which I could be fired. I wasn't guilty of moral turpitude in the usual sense which was one way in which a professor could lose his job. So, they began sort of harassing me. Well, I was chairman of the Division of Chemistry and Chemical Engineering. The president [had] said, well, that's one job they could take away from me which would mean a decrease in salary. I didn't mind. I had served in that position for twenty-two years, and had felt that I had done my duty, with respect to that administrative job. But they began interfering with my research projects, and I decided that I was going to have to leave the Institute.

When I received notice of the award of the Nobel Peace Prize to me, I found, when I returned to Pasadena, that the president had stated to the *Los Angeles Times*, published there, that it was pretty remarkable for any person to receive two Nobel Prizes, but there was much difference of opinion about the value of the work that Professor Pauling had done. So I decided that the time had come for me to resign and I did. I didn't like that. I had been at the California Institute of Technology for forty-one years then, and I thought it was really the best institution in the world. Of course my opinion of it is still a very high one. With respect to science it comes close to being the best university in the world. So, I wasn't happy about leaving the Institute, but I did leave.

INT: *Did anyone express any regrets at all, or was it just time for the move?*

LP: The Division of Chemistry and Chemical Engineering did not hold a party to celebrate my getting the Nobel Peace Prize, whereas they had held one when I got the Nobel Prize in chemistry. But the biology division did hold a party for me, and in a sense the biological scientists, I think, in general were more sympathetic to what I was saying about damage done by fallout radioactivity and carbon-14 than the physical scientists. So this was understandable. I was, I think, to some extent disappointed that my colleagues in the Institute did not express sympathy with me in this situation.

INT: *I would think so, after you had colleagues for many years, even if they disagreed with you. Did you have any discussions with any of them on a one-on-one basis about that?*

LP: I'm not sure that I can remember. Beadle, the chairman of the biology division, had been a member of the committee to recommend to the trustees whether they could fire me or not, and he told me about it some years later. I don't remember when it was that he told me about it. I note that he was in a sense sympathetic to me. Well, there were many people at the Institute that I considered my friends, and perhaps if they are still alive, still consider them my friends. But it was a difficult period, so I can't complain about their not being open in expressing sympathy for me.

INT: *In spite of the fact that there has been a lot of acceptance of your views on the use of vitamins and many positive responses, there are still many skeptics. Including many people in the scientific community. To what do you attribute that skepticism?*

LP: Well, first I would say I don't think that there are many skeptics in the scientific community. Scientists know me from way back. And they are in a position to appreciate the significance of anything that I say. It is the M.D.'s, the physicians that constitute the problem, with a few exceptions. A few oddball scientists who say that I am wrong, it is mainly just the medical establishment that supplies the opposition to orthomolecular medicine. And we can ask why. In fact, many articles, two books have been written discussing just this problem. One of them is called, one of them just in the process of publication, by Dr. Evelleen Richards, is called *Vitamin C and Cancer*. Another by Ralph Moss, which is available now, is called *The Cancer Industry*. Each of them suggests that the profit motive plays an important part. The drugs that are used to treat cancer and heart disease and other diseases often are sold at very high prices, they run hundreds of millions, hundreds of billions of dollars every year spent on medicine. Much of it, the cost of the drugs which may be several thousand dollars per year per patient, and the cost of paying physicians for their time and paying for the very expensive diagnostic instruments that are used, and so on. And I can understand concern about opposition coming through the treatment of diseases or prevention of diseases by substances that cost almost nothing. Vitamins are very cheap, you know. So the profit motive probably is operating here, even though the medical authorities might deny it.

INT: *I gather from what you are saying, you don't feel that there is as much danger of people getting a toxic level of vitamins, as there is a danger of them not having enough in their system to prevent disease.*

LP: Well, there is essentially no danger of damage from overdosage by vitamins. Even the damage from vitamin A, which is always mentioned as the dangerous one, is very small compared with overdoses from drugs. Such over-the-counter drugs as aspirin cause hundreds of deaths per year. Nobody has ever died, possibly one person is known to have died from an overdose of vitamin A. So, there is no danger from overdoses of vitamins, essentially. There is a limitation on the amount of vitamin A that is recommended. I have said I think people shouldn't take more than twenty-five times the recommended RDA of vitamin A. Now it is said you shouldn't take more than eight times or ten times the RDA of vitamin A. But some people develop headaches if they take forty thousand units of vitamin A per day for long periods of time. That's all right. You can take beta-carotene, which is a precursor of vitamin A, and changes into vitamin A in the human body, without limit; no toxic dose is known for beta-carotene. For vitamin C, I knew a man who took 130,000 milligrams of vitamin C a day for thirteen years to control his cancer. That's a quarter of a pound of vitamin C a day. So, he wouldn't need to eat so much starch. He could rely to some extent on burning the vitamin C in the cells of his body to provide energy, as well as controlling the cancer. So, I take now three hundred times the RDA of vitamin C per day. I have been doing that for years. And I take eighty times of the RDA of vitamin E. I take about ten times the RDA of vitamin A plus a good slug of beta-carotene. And I take about twenty-five times the RDA of the other B vitamins. And I take the

Dustjacket for Cameron and Pauling's book on cancer and vitamin C

Ewan Cameron and Linus Pauling

Ewan Cameron
Linus Pauling

CANCER AND VITAMIN C

CANCER AND

VITAMIN C

A
Discussion
of the Nature,
Causes,
Prevention,
and Treatment of Cancer,
with Special Reference
to the Value of
Vitamin C

Ewan Cameron

Linus Pauling

recommended amounts of minerals too—not large amounts, the recommended amounts. I drink milk every day.

INT: *Is it terribly frustrating for you to feel that you know what is right, and still hear people either dismissing it or saying there are dangers from it, or somehow pooh-poohing the idea, of doing what you think is an excellent way to good health?*

LP: Yes it bothers me. For seventeen years, for sixteen years starting in 1973 I tried to get the National Cancer Institute to carry out some studies of vitamin C in the prevention and treatment of cancer, without success. They gave us some money once for animal studies, but only once. They turned us down eight times and then I stopped applying to NCI. Last year I went to see the new director of the National Cancer Institute. He didn't want to talk to me at first, but he agreed and said that he could spare an hour. He listened to me for three hours. The first two hours he was incensed by my saying that I thought it was criminal that the authorities were not paying attention to this really important possibility of controlling cancer. He didn't like that but he continued to listen to what I had to say. Finally, after he had said the Mayo Clinic has shown that vitamin C has no value in the treatment of cancer, I said that Mayo Clinic study was a fraud. And I can explain just how. The Mayo Clinic people didn't follow the procedure that Dr. [Ewan] Cameron used at all. They say that they did, but they didn't. We know that they didn't. So you can't rely on that. Finally, he became interested. The National Cancer Institute, together with the National Institute of Diabetes and digestive and kidney diseases, sponsored jointly an international conference held in the fall of 1990 in Bethesda in the National Medical Library Building, at which forty scientists presented papers on vitamin C and cancer. Basic scientific studies bearing on the question of the use of vitamin C in the control of cancer. The National Cancer Institute has now set up a panel of physicians to examine the case histories of the patients that my associate Dr. Cameron has sent into them as having remarkable responses to vitamin C. So it looks hopeful in this respect. The National Cancer Institute is also carrying out studies on the value of increased intake of vitamin C in preventing cancer, [an] epidemiological study. So, things are moving along. I regret that it took sixteen years to get the National Cancer Institute [interested], but I am pleased now that they are moving ahead.

INT: *Do you finally feel vindicated, at least to some extent, that people are even taking an interest?*

LP: Well, people have taken an interest for a long time. Millions of Americans - it is estimated that 40 percent of American families take high doses of vitamin C regularly. A few years ago the amount of vitamin C used in the United States had increased five fold, a factor of five, and it may be ten fold now. I get, can say [have received] over the years, many hundreds of letters from people thanking me for suggesting

---

Ten years ago, after my book *Vitamin C and the Common Cold* came out, the assistant dean of the [Stanford] medical school invited my wife and me to a party where there were about 25 other doctors. The assistant dean said practically all of them take vitamin C but they don't let anybody know that they do.

Linus Pauling, 1986

vitamin C to control colds, saying they no longer get these colds. And I have gotten hundreds of letters from people, including physicians, asking for more information about vitamin C for controlling cancer, but also sending information about how long they have been able to control their cancer by taking perhaps thirty-six grams a day, day after day. Or in the case of this one man, a chemist in San Jose working for IBM, taking 130 grams a day.

INT: *It must be very rewarding to you, in spite of the controversy, and some skeptics, to know that people everywhere, when they think of having a cold, they think of vitamin C.*

LP: Yes, it is. So, as I say I'm sure that most scientists accept what I have been saying these years. I wasn't the first to say it either. Other people had been advocating vitamin C for controlling the common cold, and cancer, and other diseases back starting fifty years ago. The... well I do feel satisfaction in thinking that I have been able to contribute to this, what I think is a great step forward in the control of disease and the decrease in the amount of suffering. If you can keep people living to be one hundred years old, we know from experience that death of very old people is not in general accompanied by so much suffering as death in younger people. If we can control cancer, cancer is a terrible, horrible way of dying that involves so much suffering, and of course often young people in the period of the teens, cancer and automobile accidents are the principal causes of death for these young people.

INT: *Let me ask about cancer. I have often wondered whether we are more sensitive to it, or there is actually an increase? It seems that so many people these days are dying from cancer or suffering from cancer. Has something changed in our world?*

LP: Well, we don't have good evidence in that up to forty years or fifty years ago, people suppressed the fact that someone had died of cancer. When Arthur Amos Noyes, the head of our chemistry department, died of cancer in 1936, the death certificate said pneumonia. Well, many cancer patients develop pneumonia, because they are so debilitated they no longer have any resistance. So in the old days, cancer was not put down as the cause of death. There were some.... it was a stigma for a person to develop cancer and die of cancer. So the old statistics are not of much value. The more recent statistics indicate that the incidence of cancer, the age standardized incidence has not changed much. Despite all the hullabaloo about the anti-cancer drugs and other new methods, the death rate stays essentially the same.

❦❦❦

INT: *If you were a young person now in the sciences and chemistry, what would you want to go into? What would you suggest people go into?*

LP: Well, I continue to think that I was fortunate in having started out, at least by the time I got my doctor's degree, by getting a good

Interviewer: To what extent can we understand a living organism by investigating its isolated pieces, in contrast to trying to study processes in whole cells or organisms?
Pauling: Well, I think you have to do both. Life is too complicated to permit a complete understanding through the study of whole organisms. Only by simplifying the problem—breaking it down into a multitude of individual problems—can you get the answers.

1980 interview

understanding of physics, basic physics and advanced physics and of chemistry as a whole. And here, I had one short course in organic chemistry, but I am considered to have made great contributions to organic chemistry. I had no courses in biochemistry, but I am considered to, I'm usually described as the great biochemist Linus Pauling. You see, I have made contributions to biochemistry. There were no courses in molecular biology, I had no courses in biology at all, but I am one of the founders of molecular biology. I had no courses in nutrition or vitaminology. Why? Why am I able to do these things? You see, I got such a good basic education in the fields where it is difficult for most people to learn by themselves. Very few people are able to study mathematics by themselves, they need to have it taught. I learned a lot of mathematics, a lot of physics, a lot of chemistry. The chemistry, much of it I might have learned by myself, but when it comes to these other subjects, I can... I was able to learn enough about these other fields just by reading because my basic understanding was so great that I could interpret the sentences that I read. I can read, if I become interested in cardiology say, or in general, I can read books, medical books about heart disease and understand what the authors are saying. So my recommendation to young people, which I have been making for fifty years, is that if you want to go into biology, biochemistry, molecular biology, why don't you start out by majoring in physics and chemistry and mathematics and then move on, later. I've even recommended fifty years ago to students interested in biology to take the Ph.D. in chemistry, rather than biology, and then get a job with... well, start doing work in some field - plant physiology or some other field. With your basic understanding you will be able to be successful in this field.

Even fifty years ago I was recommending to students in the California Institute of Technology who came to me for advice, to do graduate work in chemistry rather than in biology, even if they were interested in biology. They could take some courses in biology, but they could do reading by themselves to learn most of biology. Genetics was already a good science in biology, I recommended taking a course in genetics. So ever since then, I have said to students - if you are interested in science, I think a good thing for you to get is as much training as possible in the basic sciences - mathematics, physics, chemistry including physical chemistry. And then you can move on into these more applied fields. Many of these fields I consider to be just applied chemistry. Molecular biology is a branch of chemistry, just as biochemistry is a branch of chemistry. Astronomy in some respects is, because the astronomers are studying the molecules in interstellar space that show up on the spectrographic studies that they make. And the geologist of course, much of geology depends on minerals, and that essentially is a branch of chemistry.

INT: *Let me ask you something that applies to both vitamin C and your efforts against nuclear testing. Those were both areas in which you took controversial stands, which there was a good deal of criticism of your views. It is one of those things, and I think it is interesting for young people, because I wonder how you look at those two parts of your life, and what they say about how much impact an individual can have.*

LP: Sometimes I say you shouldn't think that your efforts, your demonstration, participation in peace walks or writing letters to members of Congress or to the local newspaper, are wasted efforts. You can contribute and you can't be sure how great your contribution is, but you can contribute, so do it. From time to time, I have done something that led to my being criticized by some people. I brought out in the 1930s the theory of resonance in chemistry. And then around 1949, there was issued an attack on me in the Soviet Union saying that the theory of resonance is incompatible with dialectical materialism. There was a meeting of eight hundred chemists in Moscow where they got up one after the other, many of them, and said "I've used Professor Pauling's theory of resonance in my teaching, or my publications in the past, though I now see the error of my ways and I promise that I shan't do it in the future." So, I was involved at an international meeting in chemistry in Stockholm, where the newspaper said "Battle between American and Soviet Chemical Giants", where one chemist from the Soviet Union attacked the theory of resonance and I supported it. And after, so here I presented a chemical theory and it was at first accepted. My book, *The Nature of the Chemical Bond,* was translated into Russian. The professor … who translated it lost his job, was fired, and for several years … well, I visited the Soviet Union in 1957 for the first time, and at a small seminar in physics, in fact, the physicist who was presenting his ideas said that, "in the old fashioned nomenclature, which we don't use anymore, we would say this is an example of resonance." So he was able to present his argument the way I would present it, but he protected himself by saying he was using an old fashioned nomenclature. So this was a surprise to me. A little later when I was having trouble getting my visa for my trip to the Soviet Union, the people, some Russians who were at a meeting in Yugoslavia where my wife and I were at a chemical meeting, they said they would telephone Moscow and find out why they don't have permission to give you a visa. They called back, they came a couple of days later to the meetings and said they found out what the trouble was. "In Paris, when you went to the embassy, you said that you were 'LEE-nus' Pauling." I was accustomed to using that pronunciation after being in Germany for a year and a half. "Lee-nus" Pauling. "Lee-nus" Pauling is the idealistic representative of the capitalistic West who has developed theories in chemistry that are incompatible with dialectical materialism such that no patriotic Soviet scientist will use them. You should have said that you were "LIE-nus"

Pauling. Linus Pauling is the great friend of the Soviet Union and worker for world peace. So it is all straightened out now, the visa is being issued to "LIE-nus" Pauling.'

So then, of course, I wrote my book *Vitamin C and the Common Cold* in 1970, August 1970. I thought, you know, everybody will be happy to have this book that tells about how to keep from suffering with the common cold. The doctors will be happy, they won't be pestered with patients with this minor problem the way they are now. They can concentrate on more serious diseases. And what happened? A month later, the *Medical Letter* published an attack on me for having written this book. And all the other medical... *Modern Medicine* published an attack on me for a whole lot of things. I wrote to the man, the editor of *Modern Medicine* and said, "You remember that *Modern Medicine* gave me the *Modern Medicine Award* four or five years ago for my work on sickle cell anemia? And here you are attacking me". And then I went up and said I want you to publish this retraction. And I wrote a very abject retraction on all the points and they published it just the way I had written it, retracting. I had been astonished by the medical profession, the response of the medical profession to orthomolecular ideas.

INT: *Do you find it annoying? I know its irritating, but do you ever get just downright angry about it?*

LP: I don't think so. It's not in my nature. I left out, of course, the response by the American government to the Institute to my efforts for world peace. It didn't occur to me back in 1946 for me to be saying what I thought was a completely logical way - that the time had come to give up wars between the great nations. They are counter-productive now, nobody benefits. They are so destructive that nobody benefits so we better be sensible. And here I would get attacked. So every time, you'd think I'd learn after awhile to not be surprised.

INT: *Back in those days when your efforts against nuclear testing and so forth got you into trouble and forced you to resign ultimately, did you feel betrayed in any way by those around you, that they didn't stand up for you, that they looked the other way?*

LP: Well, there was one time when I felt betrayed. I had been participating in four days of hearings, when I was a member of the executive council at Cal Tech, and it was decided that the members of the executive council ought to have clearance at a very low level, not secret or top secret. I had a top secret clearance before, but.... so I said OK, and I signed the application for clearance for restricted documents, the first level of secrecy, and was turned down. I was irritated enough by being turned down, that I appealed. So for four days there were hearings held by the appeal board. I asked a couple of my associates who had known me for twenty years or more, professors, and one of them refused to testify as a character witness for me. This was a shock to me. The other one did testify. Then I asked one of my best friends, who was at the time working for the Department of Defense in Washington, on leave from the Institute. And my lawyer talked with him and asked him certain various questions. How would you answer these questions if they were asked? Then he came and testified for me, or testified anyway, and he was asked, "Would you hire Dr. Pauling to work under you in this job?" and he said "No". My lawyer was very angry. I was really thoroughly disappointed. The lawyer said that he had told him that he would say yes to that question. So, that was one episode that caused me real concern. So I never spoke to this man from then on. I just found difficulty in seeing him.

INT: *Well, how did the hearing turn out?*

LP: Toward the end of the fourth day I said it seems to me that this is a lot of fuss to go to just for someone who wants to be cleared for the lowest level of classified material, and the chairman said, "But it says here 'top secret'. Somebody had written top secret on the application and it wasn't until the end of these four days that I realized that. So they said, "Well, no use going on." I gave up the idea of being cleared for restricted material. It wasn't important anyway. So I sent my lawyer's bill to Cal Tech, and they paid it. Someone there had made the mistake of putting down top secret. So that was a nuisance to have to spend these four days, and all the effort I involved.

INT: *As you talk about the security clearance issue, it reminds me of all the controversy surrounding Oppenheimer and the dispute with Teller and over who said what about whom and all that sort of thing. You were a bit outside that because you declined to work on the Manhattan Project.*

LP: That's right. And I had known Teller from 1930, and of course had much respect for him as a scientist. A very smart fellow. Too emotional. I debated with him for an hour on KQED [a TV station], quite a formal debate, you know, with a stop watch and so on. And it was somewhat unsatisfactory in the same way that a professor at Stanford remarked. This professor at Stanford debated with him, and afterward he was very angry with Teller. He said, "Here, Teller, [Pauling] made a statement", and Teller said that he had access to classified documents that showed that what I [Pauling] said was not true. [Teller] doesn't have any more knowledge about these matters than I have, so this was a dirty trick in a debate.

INT: *Do you have strong feelings from that era when Oppenheimer lost his security clearance, when there was that whole debate over who is and who isn't a "real" American?*

LP: Yes, I think it was shocking that the United States government authorities should show so little gratitude to Oppenheimer the way they did in these hearings. Teller wasn't the only one who testified against Oppenheimer. There were two or three other scientists too. And of course the main person involved was Strauss. Strauss, a banker, began thinking of himself as a theoretical physicist, and began to be jealous. Strauss was the chairman of the Atomic Energy Commission. He began to be jealous of Oppenheimer. Oppenheimer of course could be caustic in his criticisms, and I was told the story about a seminar that Teller gave at Los Alamos and Oppenheimer said, "Here, how could you have made such an elementary mistake as the one you made back in some of your equations." Teller felt that he was demeaned by this. I don't know exactly what occurred, but this is the story that went around. Oppenheimer was unhappy with Teller in that Teller was brought to do a part of the job connected with making the atomic bomb, and he just refrained from doing it or refused to do it, so that Oppenheimer had to get someone else in to do the job that Teller was supposed to do.

INT: *There are a number of people who are great physicists who say that they would have been chemists but found it too difficult.*

LP: Well, Einstein, for example. Well, Einstein, of course, was very smart. In 1931 perhaps, I've forgotten which year, Einstein was visiting at Cal Tech, and I gave a physics seminar on quantum mechanics and chemical structure. And Einstein was there sitting in the front row in the physics lecture room. There were reporters there, of course, as usual wherever Einstein was. And at the end, the reporters asked him, "What did you think of Professor Pauling's talk?" And he said, "It was too complicated for me." This was published in the *Pasadena Star News*. Well, it may be that I should have presented it more simply and perhaps I did include too much detail for a physicist. Chemists are more interested in the details than the physicists are.

INT: *How do you feel about the contributions you have made? You talked to some extent earlier about some of the things. Do you, all modesty aside, what do you think are your greatest contributions?*

LP: I have answered that question in the past by saying that I think my 1931 paper was the most important of the papers that I have written. There were others, too, that all together they contributed to making a great change in the way that essentially all chemists think – changed the science of chemistry. It's hard to say what practical effect there is of that. How many people have benefited from the fact that chemists are able to work more effectively now than they were before 1930? I don't know. In a practical sense, stopping the bomb test. I was not alone responsible for that, but if for the sake of argument we might say, as in fact the chairman of the Norwegian Nobel Committee said, that there probably would not have been a bomb test treaty if there hadn't been somebody doing what I was doing for those years. If the bomb testing had gone on at the same rate for a few more years, it would have meant that millions of children, according to my calculations, which seem to have been essentially right, millions of children, infants, would have been born with gross physical and mental defects that otherwise would not have had the defect, and millions of people would have died of cancer at an earlier age than otherwise. So that, to the extent that I was involved, that was I think pretty important. Also, the ideas about orthomolecular medicine, I think, have already affected millions of people. So, I feel much surprise to think that I have contributed something to the well-being of human beings.

INT: *In all this time, did you ever worry about failing?*

LP: I don't think so. I never got involved in a race. You know, I have said I wasn't in a race with Watson and Crick. They thought they were in a race with me. My feeling was that it wasn't a race. I wasn't working very hard on the DNA problem, I was doing other things too. And I probably did have a sort of feeling that sooner or later I would work out the DNA puzzle. I never had been involved in the sort of race that we read about from time to time. The race for a Nobel Prize when there are two groups, each struggling to get ahead of the other one in making a discovery that they think will bring them the Nobel Prize. For one thing, my work that brought me the Nobel Prize for chemistry, I didn't think myself was of Nobel caliber, in that Nobel, in his will, referred to the greatest single discovery or invention made in the preceding year. I thought that the discoveries that I made in the period 1927 to 1937, say, altogether constituted a considerable advance in our understanding, but I couldn't think of a single discovery that was most important. Well, actually other people had trouble too. Albert Szent-Gyorgyi wrote to me, this is, I think, [what] people are not supposed to do. He wrote to me saying that he was going to nominate me for the Nobel Prize in chemistry, so what should he say was the discovery that I had made? And I thought about it for a while and I wrote back and said I thought he should say the discovery of the hybridization of bond orbitals. That's the one thing in the 1931 paper that I would say is more important that any of my other ideas. And I don't know what he did, if he did nominate me. But the Nobel Committee apparently decided they could lump all of my discoveries together and say, "For his work on the nature of the chemical bond."

INT: *In a more general sense and more personal sense, including your professional life, how much control does a person have over his or her future?*

LP: Well, I think life is apt to be full of surprises. My feeling is, first, about a young person... How can a young person be happy? I think a good way of increasing the probability of leading a happy life is to do two things. First, to think about what you like to do, whoever you are, what you like to do, and then see if you can make your living doing it. Second, look around, keeping your eyes open and your brain working and find somebody of the opposite sex with whom you enjoy talking and with whom you can get along. Get married young and stay married. So those are the two ways in which I believe young people can be doing something wise to determine, to some extent at any rate, the nature of their future lives.

SUMMER EMPLOYMENT

Linus Pauling

❦❦❦

*Pauling worked odd jobs from an early age. He set pins in a bowling alley,
delivered newspapers, operated the projector at a movie theater, even tried to
start his own photographic developing business. This short, previously
unpublished piece describes some of the summer jobs he undertook. It
highlights both the necessity of employment—without summer jobs, Pauling
could not have attended college—and the variety of work he attempted. It is
important, too, that in addition to demonstrating his versatility and
entrepreneurial streak, Pauling's jobs helped him learn some practical
chemistry, from investigating methods of testing asphalt to developing an
interest in metalworking that would later yield many homemade metal
molecular models.*

When I was fifteen years old, summer of 1916, I worked in
Portland for the Post Office, delivering special delivery letters.
The special delivery headquarters was in the main Post Office,
about 5th and Morrison streets. As the newest special delivery boy, I got
the letters for outlying parts of Portland. Usually I delivered them by riding
my bicycle.

The next summer, when I was sixteen, summer of 1917, I worked for
Mr. Schweizerhof in a small machine shop, with about ten employees. I did
odd jobs, operated a drill press, and assisted in other ways in making the
machines that were used for lifting sacks of wheat and so on to a height of
12 or 15 feet. Mr. Schweizerhof raised my salary every month, and tried to
get me to stay on, instead of going to Oregon Agricultural College in
September.

In June 1918 I went with Mervyn [Stephenson, a cousin] to San
Francisco, where we spent one month in the Presidio, Reserve Officers
Training Corps camp. Then we returned to Oregon, and went to
Tillamook, where Aunt Goldie and her husband were operating a hotel.
My mother was there at least part of the time, with Mr. Bryden, whom she
had married at some earlier time, possibly while I was in San Francisco. Mr.
Bryden was in the Army. He had been a lumberman and I think that he
was continuing work as a lumberman while in the Army—he wore his
uniform. I saw him a few times during the summer, and I think once
during the later months, when I came home from Corvallis to Portland for

Paving inspector Linus Pauling on bridge in Sutherlin, Oregon, 1922

a visit. I had very little information about my mother's marriage to him. I think that they were divorced after a few months of marriage.

During the rest of the summer of 1918 I worked in a shipyard in Tillamook—that is, on Tillamook Bay, a few miles from the small city. Mervyn and I, with other workers, were taken on a small boat from the dock at Tillamook to the shipyard. The ship being built in the shipyard was 4,000 tons, a wooden ship with steel band reinforcement. I believe that it was abandoned, half built, when the war came to an end. I did odd jobs, carrying lumber, making treenails with use of a machine, heating rivets for a riveter, helping hold an air hammer for driving the treenails into the holes that had been drilled for them and so on. The treenails were about an inch and a quarter in diameter and three feet long.

In 1919, at the end of my sophomore year, I saw an advertisement by a chemical engineer who had a contract with the State of Oregon to inspect pavement that was being laid. I answered the advertisement, was interviewed by the man in Portland, and rejected as being too young (eighteen). I then was given a job by Mr. Ecklemann, owner of the Riverside Dairy, who was one of my mother's roomers. My job was to deliver milk to about six hundred customers, between 8 p.m. and 4 a.m. each night, seven nights a week. The milk was carried in a milk wagon drawn by a horse who knew the route to follow pretty well, and would keep jogging along while I ran back and forth from the wagon to the houses, delivering the various amounts of milk and cream that had been ordered. I rather liked the job during the first week, while I was learning it, but I got very tired of it, and I told Mr. Ecklemann that I was going to quit the job at the end of the thirty days that I had agreed to stay.

I then went back to the chemical engineer, applying again for the job as paving plant inspector, and was given the job, and sent to Wolf Creek in southern Oregon. I was there for five months, living in a tent, with other workers for the paving contractor, and eating in the mess tent. At the end of five months I received a telegram offering me a job, at reduced salary, as assistant instructor in chemistry at Oregon Agricultural College, and I quit the paving plant job and went to Corvallis.

I then worked for four more summers as a paving plant inspector. For three of these summers I was employed by the State of Oregon, which was doing its own inspecting from 1920 on, and in 1923, after my wife and I were married, I worked for the summer for the Warren Construction Company of Portland, Oregon.

CHILDREN OF THE DAWN

Linus Pauling

❧❧❧

While a student at Oregon Agricultural College, Pauling became interested in the art of public speaking. During his junior year, he competed in a schoolwide oratorical contest as his class's representative, readying himself by seeking out coaching in diction and delivery from a former minister. The speech he delivered, reprinted below, demonstrates that Pauling's optimism, wide-ranging approach, and belief in the scientific method were all a part of his character an early age. Pauling's faith in progress appears to have been too upbeat for the judges, however. He lost to the senior speaker, whose topic was "House Divided Against Itself," and tied with the sophomore speaker, who spoke of the dangers of "Closing our National Door" to immigrants.

My body slept. My mind soared. From infinite distance, attainable only by the flight of thought, I saw in the midst of the limitless universe the solar system—its sun, a pigmy amidst other pigmy suns, dimly visible as a minute radiating point—our earth, revolving about the sun, hardly to be differentiated from the myriads of other planets. That hour a thought was born in me: "The earth is not the center of the universe, but merely a tiny part of the Great Design."

As I gazed, entranced, the vapors about the earth condensed, and oceans were born. Aeons passed. Plant and animal life appeared, simple forms at first, then more complex. Other aeons passed, and prehistoric man came into existence. He learned the use of fire. With it he smelted ores, and fashioned tools of copper, bronze, and iron. He tilled the soil, domesticated animals, constructed substantial swellings, developed his language. The first faint rays of civilization pierced the darkness.

Progress became rapid. Man learned to draw, to write, to think. Art, literature, and science flourished. Civilization advanced, with ever-accelerated speed. Within my mind another thought was born: "Man is not the ultimate goal of the evolutionary process, but only the present phase of a long development."

But yesterday, the part of this development that had taken place was unrealized. The genius of Darwin enlightened the world, so that now it is generally believed that man is an evolutionary product, with lineage extending back to the lowest forms of life. But though we know that man is immeasurably superior now to what he once was, we do not realize the marvelous changes to come, the splendid improvements yet to be made.

Physical changes in man are the result of changes in his physical environment. Efficiency is Nature's goal. As conditions changed on this earth, so did the forms of life change, until man, the highest of the animals, has approached physical perfection.

Similarly, physical changes in man are the result of changes in his mental environment. "The conditions under which men live are changing with an ever-increasing rapidity, and, so far as our knowledge goes, no sort of creatures have ever lived under changing conditions without undergoing the profoundest changes themselves." A young man now may know more of geometry than Euclid, and more of calculus than Newton. He has the advantage of knowledge which required years of arduous toil for them to discover. The mental environment in which he lives has changed. Their work changed it. In science, literature, and industry, the same improvements have been made. Is it not evident that the great mental development which has characterized the last few thousand years is still taking place? Man has merely started on the journey towards great intelligence. We occupy the same position mentally to the beings to come that our slimy amphibious ancestors of the Mesozoic age bore physically to us.

Hundreds of thousands of years have been required for the evolution of man to his present state. During the last few thousand years only has mental development outstripped the physical. Yet the intellectual changes that have taken place in that short time are prodigious. Psychically speaking, the distance between civilized man and his half-human ancestor of a relatively short while ago is so great as to dwarf into insignificance the entire distance traversed in the process of evolution up to that time. The improvements wrought by the last century are greater than those of the thousand years before it. Steam and electricity, on which modern industry is dependent, have grown from infants to giants in the last one hundred years. The sciences are swiftly following the road to knowledge on which they had merely started in 1800. Organic chemistry was born in 1828, with Wohler's synthesis of urea. Today the food we eat, the clothes we wear, the books we read, have all been bettered by this one branch of science. The twentieth century has brought not a retardation, but an acceleration of this growth. From the progress of science and invention during the first twenty years of the present century, we can without hesitancy prophesy that the closing years of the century are to bring changes that will dwarf those of the nineteenth as those of the nineteenth dwarfed those of the eighteenth. Civilization is progressing at an ever-increasing rate.

True it is that there have been retrogressions. Greece and Rome waxed and waned, yet out of the ruins of those ancient civilizations has grown ours, incomparably better. Egyptian, Assyrian, Chaldean—each soared to its peak and descended; but each was followed by a greater. So the major trend of civilization is upward. The fall of an empire is but an infinitesimal jog on the rising curve of progress.

Compare the conditions under which men live now and under which they lived only a few generations ago. Then the great mass of humanity labored almost incessantly for a livelihood. Education was a closed door. Enlightenment, culture, refinement—they touched not at all the lives of the multitude. But as his scientific knowledge progressed, and labor-saving devices were introduced, man lived more and more by harnessing the inexhaustible forces of nature, and less through the sweat of his brow. As less time was needed to gain a living, more time was available in which to develop his cultural and spiritual life. But even now the millennium has not come. Social conditions have improved marvelously; yet the improvements which have been made are but the first step in scaling the towering mountain of reformation that is ahead of us.

The scholarly John Fiske, even when the theory of evolution was derided, saw this. "The future is lighted for us with the radiant colors of hope," he contended. "Strife and sorrow shall disappear. Peace and love shall reign supreme. The dream of poets, the lesson of priest and prophet, the inspiration of the great musician, is confirmed in the light of our modern knowledge; and as we gird ourselves up for the work of life, we may look forward to the time when in the truest sense the kingdoms of the world shall become the kingdom of Christ, and he shall reign forever and ever, king of kings and lord of lords."

It is impossible for us to imagine what developments in science and invention will be witnessed by the next generation. No man has an imagination so vivid as to conceive of the world as it will be a century hence. How, then, can we hope to know specifically the human race as it will be when thousands of years have rolled by? All we know is that we have climbed a

Linus Pauling, early OAC years, 1917-18

long way out of the depths from which we came, and that dazzling heights are before us. We believe in the greatness of human destiny. Knowing that we are progressing now at a greater rate than ever before, we have no reason to conclude that man himself is man's destiny. We are forced instead to believe that man is but the child that is father of the superman that is to be.

John Fiske, advancing the conclusion of other able scholars besides himself, insists that "the production and perfection of the higher spiritual attributes of humanity" have from the beginning been the aim of the long cosmic process. But why should we believe that even perfected man is God's final handiwork? We cannot, realizing the many creatures through which he was evolved in the countless ages of the past. We cannot, knowing the mental developments of the past few thousand years. We cannot, observing the great changes taking place around us, even within the span of our individual personal memories. We see instead that we are in the midst of a progress that will never cease, will never reach perfection, and that man himself, one link in the great chain of evolution, will eventually be forgotten.

We are not the flower of civilization. We are but the immature bud of a civilization yet to come. We are children of the dawn, witnessing the approach of day. We bask in the dim prophecies of the rising sun, knowing, even in our inexperience, that something glorious is to come; for it is from us that greater beings will grow, to develop in the light of the sun that shall know no setting.

"All this world is heavy with the promise of greater things, and a day will come, one day in the unending succession of days, when beings, beings who are not latent in our thoughts and hidden in our loins, shall stand upon this earth as one stands upon a foot-stool, and shall laugh and reach out their hands amid the stars."

LINUS PAULING, THE TEACHER

David P. Shoemaker

❧❧❧

One thing that differentiated Pauling from many other great scientists was his ability to impart his knowledge in the classroom with a certain amount of showmanship. David Shoemaker (1920-1995), a notable crystallographer, studied under Linus Pauling at Caltech in the 1940s. He later went on to become chairman of the Chemistry Department at Oregon State University. The following essay is from a talk given by Dr. Shoemaker in 1975 at the 75th Anniversary meeting of the American Chemical Society.

Linus Pauling is not only a great scientist, whose name is known to nearly every educated person. He is a great teacher of science.

It is impossible to deal adequately with Linus Pauling as a teacher without reference to the science that he taught, much of which is of his own discovery. In Linus Pauling, scientist and teacher are inextricably interwoven. This is particularly well illustrated by the establishment and wide acceptance of the marvelous collection of principles and insights under the name "The Nature of the Chemical Bond." The development of this body of knowledge and understanding was itself an immense scientific achievement. However its wide, well-nigh universal acceptance is due not only to its scientific merit *per se*, but also to Linus Pauling teaching it to graduate students, weaving it into his lectures to freshmen, putting it into his very successful text books, attracting and inspiring visiting scholars, and to Linus Pauling himself, as well as his former students, lecturing on the principles, insights, and applications far and wide.

The teaching of Linus Pauling was of course by no means limited to that particular body of knowledge. As a teacher of chemistry he was as much a universalist and generalist as any person I have ever known. You could not type-cast Linus Pauling the teacher as a physical chemist, an inorganic chemist, an organic chemist, a biochemist, a nuclear chemist, etc. He was all of these at various times, and the students who went out from

Linus Pauling teaching a class, early 1940s

Caltech with the benefit of his teaching show this in the variety of their accomplishments. Certainly the success of Pauling the Teacher is measured by the careers of these students, and I propose to dwell on this by doing some name-dropping here. I will concentrate here mostly on those who received their Ph.D. degrees at Caltech under his influence, although there are thousands of others who can rightfully claim membership in the body of his students for having taken his freshman course in General Chemistry and perhaps other courses as well. As to the Ph.D. students, not all I will name had Linus Pauling's signature on the title pages of their theses in the official role of Research Supervisor; such was the power of his intellectual influence and the informality of interactions between and among graduate students and faculty in the Caltech Chemistry Division that Linus Pauling was often an effective collaborator in thesis research work being conducted under the formal direction of any of several other faculty members, particularly Verner Schomaker, Eddie Hughes, Holmes Sturdivant, and Robert Corey, but including a number of others at various times. I give notice now that in this essay I will pay little or no attention to whether Ph.D. students were or were not Pauling's own; for present purposes it does not matter much. I, for example, was formally a student of Robert B. Corey, but I owe much to Verner Schomaker and to Linus Pauling in my graduate research and I do not hesitate to claim both of them as among my teachers of scientific research, quite apart from courses I took from them. Also among those who can claim Linus Pauling as their teacher in this broad but real sense are postdoctorals and visiting scientists who became absorbed into the research community of which he was the leader. Although they similarly distinguished themselves in their careers since leaving Caltech I will not deal with them individually.

Linus Pauling received his own Ph.D. at Caltech in 1925, only five years after that degree began to be given at that institution. In his early years of teaching at Caltech he already was inspiring students to reach beyond themselves. He interested a freshman named Edwin McMillan, a physics major, into doing some research with him. Puzzling inconsistencies existed in thermal and electrical literature data concerning the thallium-lead phase diagram; the prediction of a compound PbT_{12} ran contrary to other indications. Edwin McMillan and Linus Pauling established by x-ray powder photography that the predicted compound does not exist at room temperature and that a mixture of that composition consists at equilibrium of two solid solution phases having the room-temperature structures of the separate elements. This resulted in Edwin McMillan's first published research paper, which, with Linus Pauling as co-author, appeared in the *Journal of the American Chemical Society* in March 1927, a year before Edwin McMillan graduated in physics. McMillan went on to build a brilliant career in nuclear physics, and was co-recipient in 1951 (with Glenn Seaborg, President of the American Chemical Society) of the Nobel Prize in Chemistry for the discovery of the chemical element Plutonium.

Ed McMillan is not the only Caltech undergraduate who received inspiration from Linus Pauling. Others include Robley Evans, class of '28, who is now Professor of Physics at MIT, an authority on radioactivity, isotopes, and health physics, and William Shockley, class of '32, Pontiatoff Professor of Engineering Science at Stanford, co-recipient in 1956 (with John Bardeen and Walter Brattain) of the Nobel Prize for the discovery of the transistor principle. Kenneth Pitzer, former President of Rice University and later Stanford University, now Professor at the University of California, Berkeley, graduated in Chemistry from Caltech in 1935, I am sure under Linus Pauling's strong influence.

Linus Pauling's early research interests were heavily concentrated in the direct elucidation of the atomic structure of matter by the only method then available, namely x-ray diffraction. Perhaps his first graduate student in that field was James Holmes Sturdivant, who got his Ph.D. degree in 1930. Holmes Sturdivant, who died a very few years ago, made his career at Caltech, doing research in crystal structure, training many graduate students in structural crystallography, and serving the department in many ways including organization of splendid x-ray diffraction and other instrumental facilities. Two lecture rooms in the Arthur Amos Noyes Laboratory of Chemical Physics at Caltech are dedicated to his memory.

In 1932, J. Lynn Hoard received his Ph.D. degree under Linus Pauling, and went on to establish himself in the structural chemistry of boron and of tetra-pyrrhole systems, especially metalloporpharins, as a Professor of Chemistry at Cornell University. He was recently elected a member of the National Academy of Sciences. Ralph Hultgren finished the following year. His career, which began with crystal structure work, led him into metallurgy and mineral engineering, ultimately at the University of California, Berkeley.

X-ray diffraction did not very long remain the only available research tool for direct elucidation of the geometrical arrangement of atoms in molecules; gas-phase electron diffraction early established itself at Caltech as the first U.S. site with a machine constructed by Lawrence O. Brockway under the leadership of Linus Pauling. Lawrence Brockway received his Ph.D. degree in 1933 and has been for a long time Professor of Chemistry at the University of Michigan, Ann Arbor. The same year E. Bright Wilson received his Ph.D. He went on to Harvard and collaborated with Linus Pauling on the famous textbook, *Introduction to Quantum Mechanics*, on which a whole generation of chemists have cut their quantum-mechanical teeth. Bright Wilson, who has had a long career in quantum mechanics and infrared and microwave spectroscopy, is a member of the National Academy of Sciences, and two years ago was recipient of the Pauling Award of the Oregon-Puget Sound Sections of the ACS.

Charles Coryell received his Ph.D. in 1935, and collaborated with Linus Pauling in the famous magnetic work on hemoglobin. During the war, on the Manhattan Project, Charles Coryell participated in the discovery of the up-to-then missing lanthanide element, Promethium. He was a long-time

---

Pauling's lecture style was brilliant. His ability to capture the attention of his audience left them with the feeling that they shared his understanding of the subject.

Alexander Rich, Pauling's student and colleague

member of the faculty of MIT, and an esteemed colleague of mine during my nineteen years there. At MIT and everywhere else he went, Charles Coryell was a devoted, loyal, and vocal disciple of Linus Pauling until cancer claimed him in 1970.

In the middle thirties another distinguished group of scientists finished their Ph.D. work under Linus Pauling's direction or strong influence. David Harker, now one of the senior scholars of crystallography, was a pioneer in protein structure work and with his group at Roswell Park Memorial Institute elucidated the detailed structure of the enzyme ribonuclease. Henri Levy has dealt with a wide variety of structure problems with both x-ray and neutron diffraction at Oak Ridge National Laboratory.

In 1940 David Pressman received his Ph.D. During the war years he stayed at Caltech to work with Dan Campbell and Linus Pauling in immunology. He went on to Roswell Park Memorial Institute where he is Research Professor and Assistant Director. The late Robert E. Rundle finished the following year and went on to Iowa State University. Among his interests there was the physico-chemical nature of starch, and he succeeded in elucidating the nature of the blue starch-iodine complex. Over his career until his untimely death in the early sixties, he attacked many structural problems including rare earth compounds, coordination compounds, and metals and alloys. In the same year as Rundle, Austin Wahrhaftig (now at Utah) and the late Richard M. Noyes (who taught at the University of Oregon at Eugene) also finished. Within the next year or two were Stanley Swingle, who worked with Linus Pauling on proteins with electrophoresis and unfortunately died in the early fifties; Jürg Waser who did structural work with Pauling and Schomaker, taught for a while at Rice Institute, and returned to Caltech where he wrote a couple of textbooks and assumed an important role in the teaching of General Chemistry; and Bill Eberhardt, now at Georgia Tech. Dick Noyes and Bill Eberhardt were not as close to Linus Pauling in their degree research as many I have mentioned but they served importantly as Teaching Assistants under Pauling, as did John O'Gorman (now at Pratt Institute) who finished a few years later.

In the later forties came my own generation. William Lipscomb, now a National Academy member and Nobel laureate, went to University of Minnesota and later Harvard. He determined many boron hydride structures and wrote an important book on boron chemistry. He has since been involved in protein structure, among other things. Jerry Donohue went to USC and then to University of Pennsylvania. In addition to working on a wide variety of structural problems he has made a reputation of keeping other crystallographers honest. Among many substantial contributions to structural chemistry he has earned a footnote in the history of molecular biology, for James Watson credits him with facilitating the discovery of the base-pairing scheme in DNA by pointing out that it is the keto rather than the enol forms of guanine and thymine that should be involved in the hydrogen bonding.

You could listen to [Linus' chemical bond course] year after year, because every year, the lectures were different. He was an incredibly marvelous lecturer. . . The first third of the lecture someone off the street could understand. The next third was what every graduate student could understand, and the last third was the research socket, which was new.

William Lipscomb,
Pauling's student and
Nobel laureate

Arthur Pardee, a National Academy member, is at Princeton University and has done a great deal of enzyme chemistry and microbiology. Kenneth Hedberg, an electron diffraction student of Verner Schomaker and Linus Pauling, has established an outstandingly successful gas electron diffraction laboratory at the Oregon State University, where he is a colleague of mine. Kenneth Trueblood received his degree in organic chemistry, but surely under the influence of the Pauling school he began a very successful career in x-ray structure determination and structural chemistry at UCLA. Perhaps Kurt Mislow of Princeton University and Kent Wilson of the National Science Foundation, although their Caltech thesis work was not as close to Linus Pauling's immediate interests, would admit to considerable inspiration and influence from him.

In the fifties Harvey Itano, now Professor of Pathology at San Diego, collaborated with Linus Pauling on the characterization of sickle-cell anemia as a truly molecular disease. Bill Sheehan, now at Santa Clara, is author of a well-known physical chemistry text. Walter Hamilton had an impressive career in the making at Brookhaven, where he established a program of combined neutron and x-ray diffraction in studies of amino acids and other hydrogen-bonded systems, and was rapidly becoming established as one of the ranking crystallographic theoreticians, but his career was tragically cut short by cancer. James Ibers was for a while a colleague of Walter Hamilton at Brookhaven but he moved to Northwestern University, where he and his group have determined the crystal structures of many very complicated coordination complexes and other molecules. Others finishing in the forties and fifties are George Guthrie, Fred Ordway, Heinz Pfeiffer, Philip Vaughan, Vert Keilin, Adam Schuch, Harry Yakel, Al Soldate, Yu-chi Tang, Gunnar Berman, Richard Goldberg, Martin Karplus and Matthew Meselson of Harvard, Joe Kraut, William Sly, Elihu Goldish, and myself. No doubt there are some later ones who should merit mention; unfortunately I do not know them all that well.

I am sure I have made some important omissions, and if so I apologize to them, with the reminder, however, that it is not them but Linus Pauling we are honoring here. I may also be guilty of some inadvertent errors of fact, for which I apologize, blaming a hazy memory. Such omissions and errors aside, these individuals I have mentioned are ones who, among many others, would acknowledge Linus Pauling as the one teacher, or one of a very few (like two or three), who most influenced the direction of their careers as scientists. For establishing Linus Pauling as one of the great teachers of our time I could, on that evidence, rest my case.

However it must be of interest to all to know how Linus Pauling actually functioned as a teacher. A description of his teaching technique will bear no significant relation to the gimmickry of which the present-day chemical education establishment is so fond—audio visuals, programmed and self-paced instruction, and the like—valuable as some of these things might be. Linus Pauling had his own basics and resources within himself.

First, and this needs no elaboration at all, he has always had superb command of the subject matter he was lecturing about.

Second, as far as I have ever been able to tell, he was always intensely interested in his subject matter. Without that you cannot really inspire.

Third, he loved his students, at all levels. He could communicate with them and share their interests.

The above are the basics. The rest come out of the personality that is Linus Pauling. His lectures rarely or never appeared to be tied to a rigidly organized outline. If a sideline interested him he would pursue it, following like a bloodhound a trail laid by his own enthusiasm. Thus it is that his freshmen lectures often contained digressions into molecular structure, immunology, magnetochemistry, molecular biology, physics of metals, and structure of the nucleus, at a level considerably beyond anything the textbook might contain. This resulted frequently, I believe, in some bewilderment on the part of many of the freshmen, and indeed in not a few of the teaching assistants attending the lectures. Speaking of bewilderment, I suffered from a fair share of that while I was taking Linus Pauling's quantum mechanics course, and was about as bewildered to receive from him grades of A in the course. So what? The occasional bewilderment was part of the challenge, as was the electric atmosphere of scientific excitement that was always present in Linus Pauling's teaching.

Pauling being filmed in the classroom ca. 1957

Together with spontaneity, vigor, and excitement, there was an ever-present sense of humor, and what a great many people have called "showmanship." Some have called one aspect of it "classroom calisthenics"—leaps from the classroom floor to a sitting position on the lecture desk with legs dangling, or parallel bar exercises with one hand on the chalk tray and the other on the lecture podium, the body swinging back and forth while the lecture was going on at the same time. His sense of timing and of the dramatic is illustrated by a story told me by Dick Noyes, one of his teaching assistants, concerning a lecture-table demonstration as prosaic as a titration with permanganate. He started the permanganate running full blast from the burette into the initially colorless reductant in the titration flask and turned his back to it to balance the relevant stoichiometric equation at the blackboard, while the contents of the flask were seemingly being overwhelmed by opaque purple as the students sat squirming in their seats. The blackboard work done, he casually turned back to the burette, closed the stopcock, swirled the flask, and the purple color faded and disappeared. With only one or two more drops he was at the end-point. To my regret, I never was a teaching assistant in that course, but I often happened to be at the doors of 22 Gates as students and TAs were streaming out of the lecture, and sometimes I had the impression that they were in a kind of daze, as if something had hit them between the eyes. Probably something had, and they would be thinking about it for a while.

Linus Pauling's teaching was not all in the classroom or laboratory or seminar room or colloquium, nor was it all about science. Some of it was about integrity, intellectual freedom, and personal courage. Linus Pauling spoke his mind on science and on public affairs, without evidence of fear or timidity, even when his expressed views were highly unpopular, as often they were, with University trustees, state and federal legislators, and much of the general public. He would have been justified in being fearful, if indeed he ever was, as his outspoken views produced frightening reactions. He lost his passport for a time, and was threatened with real trouble at the hands of legislative investigating committees. A recent President of the United States, whose name I do not wish to mention, twice struck his name from a list of those to be awarded the National Medal of Science. I am glad to say that he was awarded that honor.

Linus Pauling never wavered or recanted, and today, curiously enough, many of his expressed views of a generation ago are not all that unpopular anymore. I do not wish on this occasion to take the responsibility of defending the views themselves as right and condemning his critics as wrong. I do think, however, that Linus Pauling gave the country a generation-long lecture course in forthrightness, steadfastness of conviction, and personal courage, and that by exercising his freedom of speech under trying circumstances he has strengthened that freedom for all of us. I believe that his persistent agitation on one important and controversial subject constituted an important and perhaps critical motivation toward the eventual conclusion of an important international treaty with tremendous implications to public health: there is now much less strontium 90 in the milk our children drink.

In assembling material for this essay I am indebted to Verner Schomaker and Dick Noyes for valuable discussions. I am also indebted to Linus Pauling himself for the same, but I am infinitely more indebted to him for something else: that he was my teacher.

THE INCIDENT ON THE CLIFF

Linus Pauling

After Pauling won the Nobel Prize for Chemistry in 1954 he and Ava Helen looked for a place near the ocean in which they could be alone and escape the pressures of Caltech. They bought a hundred and twenty-two acre spread on an isolated stretch of rugged seashore in Big Sur. Pauling often took long walks on the property where he could concentrate on various problems. During one of these trips, an incident occurred which would have frightening and dramatic consequences. The account below is in the form of a letter which Pauling wrote to his children after the event.

I am writing to tell you what happened to me on Saturday 30 January. I have been rather upset during the days since then, so that only now have I felt that I could settle down to writing to you.

On Wednesday 27 January Mama and I drove to Asilomar. We stopped in King City at the ranger station to see Alex Campbell, but found that, because of a misunderstanding about our visit, he was away. He had suggested that we have a talk about the possibility of making a trade of some of our land for some of the Los Padres National Forest land. I left word that we would be at the ranch on Saturday and Sunday, in case that he were to come to see us.

The meeting at the Asilomar was a meeting of the Western Spectroscopy Association. I gave a talk on aging and death at the banquet Thursday night, and a talk on theory of the hydrogen bond Friday morning. Then on Friday afternoon Mama and I drove to the ranch.

On Saturday morning we planned to have a lunch on the beach. We also discussed the possibility that Alex Campbell would come in, probably a little before noon, as he had done a couple of months ago. I told Mama that I wanted to check some of the lines representing the bounds of the ranch, and I started off, somewhere between half past nine and ten. I said that I probably would try following a contour, but I realized that I had not told Mama exactly where I was going and I was not sure that she had seen me start off toward Salmon Cone. It turned out that she thought that I had gone up above the road, or perhaps toward Soda Springs Creek.

I walked over to China Camp and up the slope to the first ledge. I was interested to discover that this ledge is covered with a shell mound—I judge that the Indians lived here for a long period. Then I climbed up to the second ledge, elevation about a hundred feet—the horizontal pile of big rocks, on which there is a small monument of rocks.

I continued walking toward the east, along the south side of Salmon Cone. I stayed at a level approximately one hundred feet above the beach. I had tried a couple of years ago to get to the mouth of Salmon Creek by following along the beach, and I found that there is a place where the waves beat against the cliff, so that it is not possible to get around the bluff to the mouth of Salmon Creek except perhaps at extremely low tide. I had in mind a possibility that water from Salmon Creek might be brought over to China Camp at about the hundred-foot level, without having to be pumped up to three hundred or four hundred feet to get it over Salmon Cone.

After clambering across some rather big rocks I came to the place where there is a cliff about three hundred feet high rising rather steeply from the beach toward the top of Salmon Cone. I followed a deer trail for a couple of hundred feet. When the deer trail came to an end I saw what looked to be a continuation some twenty or thirty feet higher up, and I scrambled up to it, traversing some loose rock on the way. In this way I got onto a little ledge. I saw that it would be impossible to continue east from this point, because there is a very steep cliff in that direction, without much vegetation. When I looked back, I was unable to see a way of getting back safely. I was afraid to retrace my steps, because I felt that it would be dangerous to go down the slope up which I had scrambled. The loose rock seemed to me to be especially dangerous. I thought about going back and continuing upward, but it seemed to me that I was apt to be stranded in a worse place than the ledge that I was on and it turned out that I was not able to make the effort.

The ledge that I was on was about three feet wide and five or six feet long. There was a rock face behind me, and the ledge was made by a big rock below. There was some loose material on the ledge, dirt and small rock, causing it to slope down. I sat on this ledge for a couple of hours, thinking that Mama would miss me and would probably come along to the beach looking for me, and that she could then get the ranger to help get me off the ledge. After a couple of hours I discovered that I could stick my walking stick, which was about four feet long, into the dirt and rock beneath me, and I felt safer when had done this and held onto it. I then had the idea of making a seat for myself, by digging away some of the dirt and loose rock. Later in the afternoon, when I thought that there was the possibility that I might have to stay there all night, I began digging out the dirt and loose rock to a depth of about a foot, making a little hole, about two feet wide and three feet long. I piled the dirt and loose rocks up around the edge of the hole, so that the rim was about eighteen inches above the bottom of the hole.

I went on a hiking trip with another graduate student, Prescott, in the Mount Wilson area and we got lost in the wilderness there, and wandered around with no trails, finally ending up at Owens Camp after crawling through brush. This taught me a lesson about just following along with someone else. In fact, he crawled out on a cliff, and I crawled out on this cliff too and then I realized this was a foolhardy thing to do. It was loose rock, not hard rock climbing, and here he came from the east, from Yale. He didn't know anything about the mountains. He might well have killed both of us, so I stopped and sort of froze and said we'd have to go back, and with his encouragement I gradually worked my way back. There was a big drop of five hundred feet perhaps from this mountain, but he might have killed himself. In fact, I guess he did kill himself some years later in an explosion in his laboratory. I can still remember how frightened I was when I realized what was going on.

Linus Pauling, early 1920s

At about four o'clock I decided that it was necessary for me to leave and to get home, because I was sure that Mama would be very upset by my absence. I was sufficiently frightened so that it was difficult to me to stand up on the ledge, but I succeeded in standing up and taking the first step off the ledge, to a place where a rock about twelve inches in diameter was stuck. The next step would have been on some loose material, and the third step onto a place where the material on the face of the cliff was compacted by a growing bush. I found that it was impossible for me to take the second step, onto the loose material. I judge that I had been frightened by the realization that I had got myself into a place that was not very safe, and that for this reason I was immobilized. About every fifteen minutes, from then on until dark, I stood up and attempted to leave the ledge; but each time I found that I was unable to do so, and when it began to get dark I decided that I would have to stay on the ledge overnight.

The dirt in the bottom of the hole that I had dug was somewhat damp, and I pulled up several bushes that were growing near the ledge. I stopped pulling up bushes when I pulled on one that I could just reach, directly above me, and dislodged a large rock, about a foot in largest diameter, which then caught in the bush and remained there from then on. I broke up some of the bushes into twigs, to make a sort of mattress underneath me, and kept two or three to put over me. They turned out to be unsatisfactory, however, because they were in the main bare of leaves, and later in the night I broke them up and put them under me. During the night parts of the bushes got inside my clothes, and I pulled out some handfuls of twigs.

I decided that I should stay awake all night. I was afraid that if I went to sleep then wakened suddenly I might fall off the ledge. Also, I decided that I should keep moving, in order to keep warm. From that time on I kept moving one arm or one leg all of the time. It was not a very cold night, and I did not get really chilled.

I lay on my back or one side in this little hole, at first with a couple of bushes over me. Then I unfolded my map of the Burro Mountain quadrangle, about twenty-four by twenty-seven inches, and place it over me. It seemed to help considerably in keeping me warm.

Time went by very slowly. I put in much of my time watching the motion of the stars, during a period of about five hours when the stars were visible. It was cloudy or foggy from sundown until about 10 P.M. and from 3 A.M. until perhaps noon the next day.

In the meantime Mama had not got worried until late afternoon. At about 5:30 P.M. she went to the ranger station and telephoned Barclay. The ranger made a tour around Salmon Cone at about 7 P.M. He was perhaps a hundred fifty feet above me. I saw his light [inserted written text "on the fog"] and could hear him shout, but he did not hear my shouts. I did not have matches with me, nor any tool except my Swiss knife. I had slacks, a cotton shirt, and a light corduroy jacket on, also my corduroy cap.

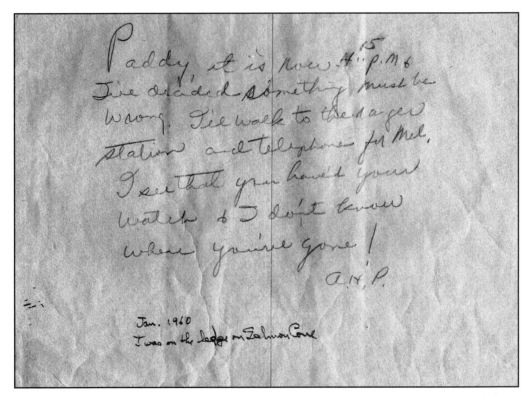

Paddy, it is now 4:15 P.M.
I've decided something must be
wrong. I'll walk to the ranger
station and telephone for Mel.
I see that you have your
watch & I don't know
when you've gone!

A. H. P.

Jan. 1960
I was on the ledge on Salmon Cone

Note hastily written on a paper bag by Ava Helen to Linus Pauling when he was stranded on the cliff

At 11:30 P.M. Lieutenant E. R. Thornburn, deputy sheriff from Monterey, came. He said that nothing should be done until the next morning. There were some men whom the ranger had got who were looking about, but they stopped at that time. Barclay came at 2:30 A.M., and immediately looked along the cliff toward Soda Spring Creek. Then he slept from 4 to 6 A.M., and then looked along the beach toward Soda Spring Creek, and Later went to the upper ranch. I did not see or hear any of the dozen men looking about until 9:45, when a young man named Terry Currence came along the beach below me. When I called to him he scrambled up to the ledge, and called to the deputy sheriff, who was coming around Salmon Cone at a level perhaps fifty feet higher than the ledge. He came over to the ledge, and sent Mr. Currence on up the cliff, to take word to Mama that I was all right. He also said to have some ropes brought over.

Then, after a few minutes, he said that he thought that we should try to get out without the aid of ropes, because the cliff continues for perhaps a hundred fifty feet above the ledge. I was skeptical, but agreed to try. We moved toward the west and up the face of the cliff, following a course that I would have been afraid to tackle alone. This brought us out near the top of Salmon Cone, and we then cut across toward the cabin.

I found that Mama was very much upset by her long wait, and the uncertainty as to what had happened to me. We stayed at the cabin that day, and then drove back to Pasadena Monday. I thought that I was in good shape, and on Tuesday I went to the laboratory, with the intention of giving my lecture on the nature of the chemical bond. I found, however, that I was unable to talk to my secretary when I arrived, and unable to give the lecture. I went home, and stayed in bed for several days. I apparently was suffering from slight shock, the after-effect of my fright on the cliff. I also began to suffer from a very severe case of poison-oak dermatitis, which is still bad, two weeks after the episode.

I made several mistakes. One of them was to have rushed forward in an over-exuberant and light-hearted way, across a somewhat dangerous stretch of cliff, onto a ledge, without having considered the question of how to get back from the ledge. A second was that I did not tell Mama exactly what I was planning to do. I do not think that my staying on the ledge overnight was a mistake, because it seems to have been beyond my decision; I had got frightened enough so that I was unable to leave the ledge. I am very sorry that I caused you and Mama so much anguish and concern.

II

LINUS PAULING

Photograph by Phil Stern

THE SCIENCE

←←←

THE SCIENTIFIC CONTRIBUTIONS
OF LINUS PAULING

Jack Dunitz

❧❧❧

The distinguished chemist Jack Dunitz, now retired from his position as professor of chemical crystallography at the Swiss Federal Institute of Technology, Zurich, held positions twice as a postdoctoral researcher at Caltech between 1948 and 1954. During his Caltech years, Dunitz worked with Linus Pauling, and came to know him, his research, and his colleagues well. In the following overview, adapted from an appreciation published originally in the Biographical Memoirs of Fellows of the Royal Society, Dunitz reviews the many high points of Pauling's long scientific career, including important areas that have been underappreciated by many Pauling observers.

Linus Pauling is widely considered the greatest chemist of his century. Most scientists create a niche for themselves, an area where they feel secure, but Pauling had an enormously wide range of scientific interests: quantum mechanics, crystallography, mineralogy, structural chemistry, anesthesia, immunology, medicine, evolution. In all these fields and especially in the border regions between them, he saw where the problems lay, and, backed up by his speedy assimilation of the essential facts and by his prodigious memory, he made distinctive and decisive contributions. He is best known, perhaps, for his insights into chemical bonding, for the discovery of the principal elements of protein secondary structure, the alpha–helix and the beta–sheet, and for the first identification of a molecular disease (sickle–cell anemia), but there are a multitude of other important contributions. Pauling was one of the founders of molecular biology in the true sense of the term. For these achievements, he was awarded the 1954 Nobel Prize in chemistry. Pauling's name is probably best known among the general public through his advocacy, backed up by personal example, of large doses of ascorbic acid (vitamin C) as a dietary supplement to promote general health and prevent (or at least reduce the severity of) such ailments as the common cold and cancer. Indeed, Albert Einstein and Linus Pauling are probably the only scientists in our century whose names are known to every radio listener, television viewer, or newspaper reader.

Linus did well at school. He collected insects and minerals and read omnivorously. He made up his mind to become a chemist in 1914, when a fellow student, Lloyd A. Jeffress, showed him some chemical experiments he had set up at home. With the reluctant approval of his mother he left school in 1917 without a diploma and entered Oregon Agricultural College at Corvallis as a chemical engineering major, but after two years his mother wanted him to leave college to earn money for the support of the family. He must have impressed his teachers, for in 1919, after a summer working as a road-paving inspector for the State of Oregon, he was offered a full-time post as instructor in qualitative analysis in the chemistry department. The eighteen-year-old teacher felt the need to read current chemical journals and came across the recently published papers of Gilbert Newton Lewis and Irving Langmuir on the electronic structure of molecules. Having understood the new ideas, the "boy professor" introduced them to his elders by giving a seminar on the nature of the chemical bond. Thus was sparked the "strong desire to understand the physical and chemical properties of substances in relation to the structure of the atoms and molecules of which they are composed," which determined the course of Pauling's long life.

Pauling came to the California Institute of Technology as a graduate student in 1922 and remained there for more than forty years. He chose Caltech because he could obtain a doctorate there in three years (Harvard required six) and because Arthur Amos Noyes offered him a modest stipend as part-time instructor. It was a fortunate choice both for Pauling and for Caltech. As he wrote towards the end of his life, "Years later...I realized that there was no place in the world in 1922 that would have prepared me in a better way for my career as a scientist." When he arrived, the newly established institute consisted largely of the hopes of its three founders, the astronomer George Ellery Hale, the physicist Robert A. Millikan, and the physical chemist Arthur Amos Noyes. There were three buildings and eighteen faculty members. When he left, Caltech had developed into one of the major centers of scientific research in the world. In chemistry Pauling was the prime mover in this development. Indeed, for many young chemists of my generation, Caltech meant Pauling.

Pauling's doctoral work was on the determination of crystal structures by x-ray diffraction analysis under the direction of Roscoe Gilkey Dickinson (1894-1945), who had obtained his Ph.D. only two years earlier (he was the first person to receive a Ph.D. from Caltech). By a happy chance, Ralph W. G. Wyckoff (1897-1994), one of the pioneers of x-ray analysis, had spent the year before Pauling's arrival at Caltech and had taught Dickinson the method of using Laue photographic data (white radiation, stationary crystal; a method that fell into disuse but has newly been revived in connection with rapid data collection with synchrotron radiation sources). Wyckoff taught Dickinson, and Dickinson taught Pauling, who soon succeeded in determining the crystal structures of the mineral molybdenite MoS_2 and the MgSn. By the time he graduated in

1925 he had published twelve papers, most on inorganic crystal structures, but including one with Peter Debye (1884-1966) on dilute ionic solutions and one with Richard Tolman (1881-1948) on the entropy of super-cooled liquids at 0°K. Pauling had already made up for his lack of formal training in physics and mathematics. He was familiar with the quantum theory of Planck and Bohr and was ready for the conceptual revolution that was soon to take place in Europe. Noyes obtained one of the newly established Guggenheim fellowships for the rising star and sent him and his young wife off to the Institute of Theoretical Physics, directed by Arnold Sommerfeld (1868-1951), in Munich.

Pauling at Yale-Silliman lecture, October 1947

They arrived in April 1926, just as the Bohr-Sommerfeld model was being displaced by the "new" quantum mechanics. It was an exciting time, and Pauling knew he was lucky to be there at one of the centers. He concentrated on learning as much as he could about the new theoretical physics at Sommerfeld's institute. Pauling had been regarded, and probably also regarded himself, as intellectually outstanding among his fellow students at Oregon and even at Caltech; however, he must have become aware of his limitations during his stay in Europe. The new theories were being made by men of his own generation. Wolfgang Pauli (1900-58), Werner Heisenberg (1901-76), and Paul Dirac (1902-84) were all born within a year of Pauling and were more than a match for him in physical insight, mathematical ability, and philosophical depth. Pauling was not an outstanding theoretical physicist and was probably not particularly interested in problems such as the deep interpretation of quantum mechanics or the philosophical implications of the uncertainty principle. On the other hand, he was the only chemist at Sommerfeld's institute and saw at once that the new physics was destined to provide the theoretical basis for understanding the structure and behavior of molecules.

The year in Europe was to have decisive influence on Pauling's scientific development. In addition to Munich, he visited Copenhagen in the spring of 1927 and then spent the summer in Zurich. In Copenhagen it was not Bohr but Samuel A. Goudsmit (1902-78) who influenced Pauling (they later collaborated in writing *The Structure of Line Spectra*, New York: McGraw-Hill, 1930). And in Zurich it was neither Debye nor Schrodinger but the two young assistants, Walter Heitler (1904-81) and Fritz London (1900-54), who were working on their quantum-mechanical model of the hydrogen molecule in which the two electrons are imagined to "exchange" their roles in the wave function—an example of the "resonance" concept that Pauling was soon to exploit so successfully.

One immediate result of the stay in Munich was Pauling's first paper in the *Proceedings of the Royal Society of London*, submitted by Sommerfeld himself. Pauling was eager to apply the new wave mechanics to calculate properties of many-electron atoms and he found a way of doing this by using hydrogen-like single-electron wave functions for the outer electrons with effective nuclear charges based on empirical screening constants for the inner electrons.

THE NATURE OF THE CHEMICAL BOND

In 1927 Pauling returned to Caltech as assistant professor of theoretical chemistry. The next twelve years produced the remarkable series of papers that established his world-wide reputation. His abilities were quickly recognized through promotions (to associate professor, 1929; full professor, 1931), through awards (Langmuir Prize, 1931), through election to the National Academy of Sciences (1933), and through visiting lectureships, especially the Baker lectureship at Cornell in 1937-38. Through his writings and lectures, Pauling established himself as the founder and master of what might be called structural chemistry—a way of looking at molecules and crystals.

Pauling's way was first to establish a solid and extensive collection of data. By means of x-ray crystallography, gas phase electron diffraction (installed after Pauling's 1930 visit to Europe, where he learned about Hermann Mark's pioneering studies), and infrared, Ramen, and ultraviolet spectroscopy, interatomic distances and angles were established for hundreds of crystals and molecules. Thermochemical information was already available. The first task of the theory, as Pauling saw it, was to provide a basis to explain the known metric and energetic facts about molecules, and only then to lead to prediction of new facts. At this stage of his development Pauling was attracting many talented co-workers, undergraduates, graduate students, and postdoctoral fellows, and their names read like a Who's Who in the structural chemistry of the period: J. H. Sturdivant, J. L. Hoard, J. Sherman, L. O. Brockway, D. M. Yost, G.W. Wheland, M. L. Huggins, L. E. Sutton, E. B. Wilson, S. H. Bauer, C. D. Coryell, V. Schomaker, and others. Here are the major achievements.

Pauling's ionic radii: Once the structures of simple inorganic crystals began to be established, it was soon seen that observed interatomic distances were consistent with approximate additivity of characteristic radii associated with the various cations and anions. Among the several sets that have been

In my own case, I tried to fit knowledge that I acquired in to my system of the world—my understanding of the world. And much of the new information that I learned—discoveries that have been made—seemed to me to be compatible with my existing understanding of the world. When something comes along that I don't understand, that I can't fit in, that bothers me: I think about it, mull over it, and perhaps ultimately do some work with it. And that's perhaps the reason that I've been able to make discoveries in molecular biology, for example, in the early days when the subject didn't exist. Often I'm not very interested in something new that's been discovered, because even though it's new, it doesn't surprise me and interest me.

Pauling to Dan Campbell, 1980

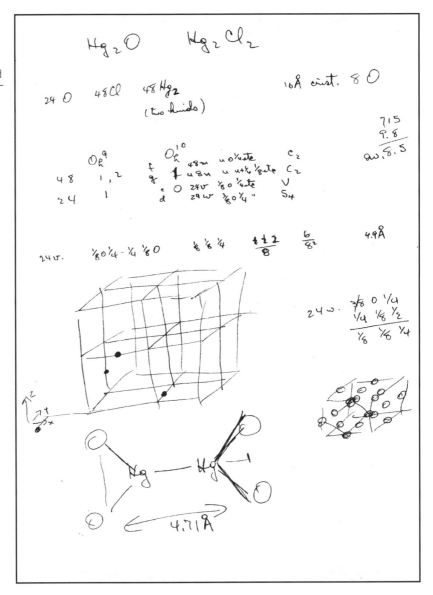

Pauling sketches for his work on the chemical bond

proposed, Pauling's are not merely designed to reproduce the observations but, typical for him, are derived from a mixture of approximate quantum mechanics (using screening constants) and experimental data. His values, derived almost seventy years ago, are still in common use, and the same can be said for the sets of covalent radii and nonbounded (van der Waals) radii that he introduced.

Pauling's rules: Whereas simple ionic substances, such as the alkali halides, are limited in the types of crystal structure they can adopt, the possibilities open to more complex substances, such as mica, $KAl_3Si_3O_{10}(OH)_2$, may appear to be immense. Pauling (1929) formulated a set of rules about the stability of such structures, which proved enormously successful in testing the correctness of proposed structures and in predicting unknown ones. As

Pauling himself remarked, these rules are neither rigorous in their derivation nor universal in their application; they were obtained in part by induction from known structures and in part from theoretical considerations. His second rule states essentially that electrostatic lines of force stretch only between nearest neighbors. In the meantime, as structural knowledge has accumulated, this rule has been modified by various authors to relate bond strengths to interatomic distance, but it seems fair to say that it is still the basis for the systematic description of inorganic structures. W. L. Bragg, who may have felt somewhat beaten to the post by the publication of these rules, wrote (1937): "The rule (the second one) appears simple, but it is surprising what rigorous conditions it imposes upon the geometrical configuration of a silicate...To sum up, these rules are the basis for stereochemistry of minerals."

Quantum chemistry: In 1927 O. Burrau solved the Schrodinger equation for the hydrogen molecule ion H_2^+ in elliptic coordinates and obtained values for the interatomic distance and bonding energy in good agreement with experiment. Burrau's wave function fails, however, to yield much physical insight into the stability of the system. Soon afterwards, Pauling (1928) pointed out that although an approximate perturbation treatment would not provide any new information, it would be useful to know how well it performed: "For perturbation methods can be applied to many systems for which the wave equation cannot be accurately solved..." Pauling first showed that the classical interaction of a ground state hydrogen atom and a proton is repulsive at all distances. However, if the electron is not localized on one of the atoms, and the wave function is taken as a linear combination of the two ground state atomic wave functions, then the interaction energy has a pronounced minimum at a distance of about 2 a.u. This was the first example of what has come to be known as the method of Linear Combination of Atomic Orbitals (LCAO). For the hydrogen-molecule ion, the LCAO dissociation energy is only about 60% of the correct value, but the model provides insight into the source of the bonding and can easily be extended to more complex systems. In fact, the LCAO method is the basis of modern molecular orbital theory.

A few months earlier Heitler and London had published their calculations for the hydrogen molecule. This was too complicated for an exact solution, and their method also rested on a perturbation model, a combination of atomic wave functions in which the two electrons, with opposite spins, change places. More generally, the energy of the electron-pair bond could now be attributed to "the resonance energy corresponding to the interchange of the two electrons between the atomic orbitals." As developed by Pauling and independently by John C. Slater (1900-76), the Heitler-London-Slater-Pauling (HLSP) or Valence Bond model associates each conventional covalent bond with an electron pair in a localized orbital and then considers all ways in which these electrons can "exchange."

Much has been made of Pauling's preference for Valence Bond (VB) theory over Molecular Orbital (MO) theory. The latter, as developed by Fritz Hund (born 1896), Erich Huckel (1896-1980), and Robert S. Mulliken (1896-1986), works in terms of orbitals extended over the entire molecule, orders these orbitals according to their estimated energies, and assigns two electrons with opposite spin to each of the bonding orbitals. Electronic excited states correspond to promotion of one or more electrons from bonding to antibonding orbitals. Nowadays, MO theory has proved itself more amenable to computer calculations for multicenter molecules, but in the early days, when only hand calculations were possible, it was largely a matter of taste. The main appeal of the MO model was then to spectroscopists. Chemists, in general, were less comfortable with the idea of pouring electrons into a ready-made framework of nuclei. It was more appealing to build molecules up from individual atoms linked by electron-pair bonds. The VB picture was more easily related to the chemist's conventional structural formulas. Both models are, of course, drastic simplifications, and it was soon recognized that when appropriate correction terms are added and the proper transformations are made they become equivalent. In particular, the MO method in its simplest form ignores electron–electron interactions, while the VB method overestimates them.

Pauling was fully acquainted with the early MO theory—there is at least one important paper on the theory of aromatic substitutions. But he clearly preferred his own simplified versions of VB theory and soon became a master of combining them with the empirical facts of chemistry. A remarkable series of papers entitled "The Nature of the Chemical Bond" formed the basis for his later book with the same title. In the very first paper Pauling (1931) set out his program of developing simple quantum mechanical treatments to provide information about

> *the relative strengths of bonds formed by different atoms, the angles between bonds, free rotation, or lack of free rotation about bond axes, the relation between the quantum numbers of bonding electrons and the number and spatial arrangements of bonds, and so on. A complete theory of the magnetic moments of molecules and complex ions is also developed, and it is shown that for many compounds involving elements of the transition group this theory together with the rules of electron pair bonds leads to a unique assignment of electron structures as well as a definite determination of the type of bonds involved.*

To a large extent Pauling developed his own language to describe his new concepts, and of the many new terms introduced, three seem indelibly associated with his name: hybridization, resonance, and electronegativity.

Hybridization: Only the first of these truly originates from him. In the first paper on the series, Pauling took up the idea of spatially directed bonds. By a generalization of the Heitler-London model for hydrogen, a normal chemical bond can be associated with the spin pairing of two electrons, one from each of the two atoms. While an s orbital is spherically symmetrical, other atomic orbitals have characteristic shapes and angular distributions. It was not difficult to explain the angular structure of the water molecule H_2O and the pyramidal structure of ammonia H_3N. But the quadrivalency of carbon was a problem. From its ground state ($1s^2 2s^2 2p^2$) carbon ought to be divalent; from the excited state ($1s^2 2s^1 2p^3$) one might expect three mutually perpendicular bonds and a fourth weaker bond (using the s orbital) in some direction or other. As a chemist Pauling knew that there must be a way of combining the s and p functions to obtain four equivalent orbitals directed to the vertices of a tetrahedron. Atomic orbitals can be expressed as products of a radial and an angular part. Pauling solved the problem by simply ignoring the former. The desired tetrahedral orbitals are then easily obtained as linear combinations of the angular functions. Pauling called these hybrid orbitals and described the procedure as hybridization. Other combinations yield three orbitals at $120°$ angles in a plane (trigonal hybrids) or two at $180°$ (digonal hybrids). With the inclusion of d orbitals other combinations become possible. In his later years Pauling stated that he considered the hybridization concept to be his most important contribution to chemistry (Kauffman and Kauffman, 1996).

Resonance: In attempting to explain the quantum-mechanical exchange phenomenon responsible for the stability of the chemical bond, Heitler and London had used a classical analogy originally due to Heisenberg. In quantum mechanics a frequency $v=E/h$ can be associated with every system with energy E. Two noninteracting hydrogen atoms are thus comparable to two classical systems both vibrating with the same frequency v, for example, two pendulums. Interaction between the two atoms is analogous to coupling between the pendulums, known as resonance. When coupled, the two pendulums no longer vibrate with the same frequency as before but make a joint vibration with frequencies $v + \Delta v$ and $v - \Delta v$, where Δv depends on the coupling. Going back to quantum mechanics, it is as if the system now has two different energies, one higher and one lower than before. Heitler and London interpreted the combination frequency Δv as the frequency of exchange of spin directions.

Pauling first used the term resonance more or less as a synonym for electron exchange, in the Heitler-London sense, but he went on to think of the actual molecule as "resonating" between two or more valence-bond structures, and hence lowering its energy below the most stable of these. Thus, by resonating between two Kekule structures, the benzene molecule is more stable than these extremes, and the additional stability can be attributed to "resonance energy." Through his resonance concept Pauling reconciled the chemist's structural formulas with simplified quantum mechanics, thereby extending the realm of applicability of these formulas, and he proceeded to reinterpret large areas of chemistry with it.

In the mid-years of the century resonance theory was taken up with enthusiasm by teachers and students; it seemed to be the key to understanding chemistry. Since then, its appeal has declined. It has now a slightly old-fashioned connotation. Certainly, it had some failures. Resonance theory would lead one to expect that cyclobutadiene should be more stable as a symmetric square structure than as a rectangular one with alternating long and short bonds, whereas the contrary is true. (It seems ironic that in the 1935 classic *Introduction to Quantum Mechanics* by Pauling and E. Bright Wilson Jr., qualitative MO theory was applied to only one example, four atoms in a square. In contrast the Valence Bond method, which gave a typical "resonance energy" to this system, the MO model gave none. Of course, cyclobutadiene was then still only a synthetic chemist's dream.) Similarly, it does not explain the stability of the cyclopentadienyl anion compared with the corresponding cation; in these and other cases simple molecular orbital theory provided immediate and correct answers. In the index of a modern textbook on physical chemistry "resonance" is likely to appear only in an entry such as "resonance, nuclear magnetic." It does not fare much better in textbooks on inorganic and organic chemistry; a few pages on resonance formalism are usually followed by a more extensive account of simple molecular orbital theory.

Electronegativity: The third concept associated with Pauling's name is still going strong. It emerged from his concept of partially ionic bonds. The energy of a bond can be considered as the sum of two contributions—a covalent part and an ionic part. The thermochemical energy of a bond D(A—B) between atoms A and B is, in general, greater than the arithmetic mean of the energies D(A—A) and D(B—B) of the homonuclear molecules. Pauling attributed the extra energy Δ(A—B) to ionic resonance and found he could assign values xA, etc., to the elements such that Δ(A—B) is approximately proportional to $(x_A - x_B)^2$. The x values form a scale, the electronegativity scale, in which fluorine with $x=4$ is the most electronegative element, cesium with $x=0.7$ the least. Apart from providing a basis for estimating bond energies of heteropolar bonds, these x values can also be used to estimate the dipole moment and ionic character of bonds. Other electronegativity scales have been proposed by several authors, but Pauling's is still the most widely used—it is the easiest to remember. According to Pauling, electronegativity is the power of an atom *in a molecule* to attract electrons to itself. It therefore differs from the electron affinity of the free atom although the two run roughly parallel. Many other interpretations have been proposed.

These and many other topics were collected and summarized in the book based on Pauling's Baker lectures, *The Nature of the Chemical Bond*, probably the most influential book on chemistry this century. In my opinion the 1940 second edition is the best; the 1939 edition was short-lived, and the 1960 edition, although it contains much more material, did not evoke the same feeling of illumination as the earlier ones.

Like so many others, I first encountered Pauling through this book, which I discovered sometime in my second year as an undergraduate at Glasgow University. It came as a revelation. Setting out to offer an introduction to modern structural chemistry, it explained how the structures and energies of molecules could be discussed in terms of a few simple principles. The essential first step in uderstanding chemical phenomena was to establish the atomic arrangements in the substances of interest. To try to understand chemical reactivity without this information or with dubious structural information was a waste of time. This was just what I needed to help me make up my mind that my future was to be in structural chemsitry.

PAULING AND MOLECULAR BIOLOGY

The Nature of the Chemical Bond marks perhaps the culmination of Pauling's contributions to chemical bonding theory. There were achievements to follow, notably an important paper (1947) on the structure of metals, but the interest in chemical bonding was being modified into an interest into the structure and function of biological molecules. There are intimations of this in the chapter on hydrogen bonds. Pauling was one of the first to spell out its importance for biomolecules:

> *Because of its small bond energy and the small activation energy involved in its formation and rupture, the hydrogen bond is especially suited to play a part in reactions occuring at normal temperatures. It has been recognized that hydrogen bonds restrain protein molecules to their native configurations, and I believe that as the methods of structural chemistry are further applied to physiological problems it will be found that the significance of the hydrogen bond for physiology is greater than that of any other single structural feature.*

Like many of his comments it seems so obvious, almost a truism, but it was not obvious then. Essentially the same idea had been expressed in a 1936 paper by Mirsky and Pauling, but hydrogen bonds are not even mentioned, for example, in Bernal's 1939 article on the structure of proteins.

Two remarkable observations from 1948 deserve to be mentioned here. One is a forerunner of the 1953 Watson-Crick DNA double-helix structure and explains what had not yet been discovered:

> *The detailed mechanisms by means of which a gene or a virus molecule produces replicas of itself is not yet known. In general the use of a gene or a virus as a template would lead to the formation of a molecule not with identical structure but with complementary structure... If the structure that serves as a template (the gene or virus molecule) consists of, say, two parts, which are themselves complementary in structure, then each of these parts can serve as the mold for the production of a replica of the other part, and*

the complex of two complementary parts thus can serve as the mold for the production of duplicates of itself.

And in the same vein, although nothing whatsoever was known about the structure of enzymes, the other announced what became clear to biochemists in general only many years later:

I think that enzymes are molecules that are complementary in structure to the activated complexes of the reactions that they catalyze, that is, to the molecular configuration that is intermediate between the reacting substances and the products of reaction for these catlyzed processed. The attraction of the enzyme molecule for the activated complex would thus lead to a decrease in its energy, and hence to a decrease in the energy of activation of the reaction, and to an increase in the rate of reaction.

The message seems to have laid in oblivion until well after "transition-state binding" had become popular; it is not mentioned, for example, in Jencks's classic work on enzyme catalysis.

Both of these prescient statements depend on the concept of complementarity, which arose out of Pauling's early work on proteins and antibodies. This started because, in the search for funding during the Depression, Pauling obtained a grant from Warren Weaver, director of the Rockefeller Foundation Natural Science Division, but only for research in life sciences. With his knowledge of inorganic structural chemistry, hemoglobin was the first target, and within a few months he solved an important problem. By magnetic susceptibility measurements it was shown that, whereas hemoglobin contains four unpaired electrons per heme and the oxygen molecule contains two, oxyhemoglobin (and also carbonmonoxyhemoglobin) contains none. This result showed that in oxygenated blood, the O_2 molecule is attached to the iron atom of hemoglobin by a covalent bond—that it was not just a matter of oxygen being somehow dissolved in the protein. Magnetic susceptibility measurements could also yield equilibrium constants and rates for many reactions involving addition of molecules and ions to ferro- and ferrihemoglobin. It is interesting that Pauling had introduced the magnetic susceptibility technique at Caltech in connection with the prediction and identification of the superoxide radical anion, a molecule whose biological significance was recognized only many years later.

In 1936 Alfred E. Mirksy (1900-74) and Pauling published a paper on protein denaturation, which was known to be a two-stage process, one under mild conditions partially reversible, the other irreversible. Pauling associated the first stage with the breaking and reformation of hydrogen bonds, the second with the breaking of covalent bonds. The native protein was pictured as follows:

The molecule consists of one polypeptide chain which continues without interruption throughout the molecule (or, in certain cases, of two or more

Talk about an antithesis... Corey was... modest, is one word. Cautious. I don't think that on a personal basis he ever was close to Pauling, just because they were so different. Pauling would come up with an idea, and at that time he had funding, I guess, from the National Foundation of Infant Paralysis. Talked to Corey and Corey would kind of take it from there. He had all these great ideas about putting molecules together and peptides, what they looked like, and Corey pursued the ideas, but very quietly and careful[ly], perhaps, and slow[ly]. He had none of this flair, or perhaps, intuition. Well, the ideas, I think, were 95% Pauling. The hard work and putting things together and proving that the idea was correct... a lot of that was Corey. Probably...well, in terms of the man work, it was mostly Corey. He was a wonderful foil for Pauling just because of his, "Now, lets make sure this is right."

Richard Marsh, Pauling's research associate

such chains); this chain is folded into a uniquely defined configuration in which it is held by hydrogen bonds… The importance of the hydrogen bond in protein structure can hardly be overemphasized.

Loss of the native conformation destroys the characteristic properties of the protein. From the entropy difference between the native and denatured froms of tryspin, about 10^{20} conformations were estimated to be accessible to the denatured protein molecule. On heating, or if the pH of the solution was near the isoelectric point of the protein, unfolded segments of acidic or basic side-chains would get entangled with one another, fastening molecules together, and ultimately leading to the formation of a coagulum. This was perhaps the first modern theory of native and denatured proteins.

Complementariness enters the picure in 1940, when Max Delbruck (1906-81) and Pauling published their refutation of a proposal of Pascal Jordan, according to which a quantum-mechanical stabilizing interaction between identical or nearly identical molecules might influence biological molecular synthesis in such a way as to favor the formation of molecular replicas in the living cell. After dismissing this proposal, the authors went on to say that complementariness, not identity, should be given primary consideration. They continued:

The case might occur in which the two complementary structures happened to be identical; however, in this case also the stability of the complex of two molecules would be due to their complementariness rather than their identity. When speculating about possible mechanisms of autocatalysis it would therefore seem to be most rational from the point of view of the structural chemist to analyze the conditions under which complementariness and identity might coincide.

The use of the word "complimentariness" instead of the more usual "complementarity" is striking. According to Delbruck, his only role in the publication, apart from suggesting a few minor changes, was to have drawn Pauling's attention to Jordan's proposal, and it seems quite likely that "complementariness" was one of these minor changes, introduced in order to aviod the epistemological connotations that Delbruck associated with "complementarity" in Bohr's sense.

By this time Pauling was thinking about antibodies. In 1936 he had met Karl Landsteiner (1868-1943), discoverer of the human blood groups and instrumental in establishing immunology as a branch of science. According to Pauling, Landsteiner asked him how he would explain the specificity of interaction of antibodies and antigens, to which he replied that he could not. The question set Pauling thinking about the problem, and it was not long before he had a theory that guided his research on antibodies for years to come. Eventually, it turned out to be wrong, or at least only half right.

The correct part was that the specificity of antibodies for a particular antigen is based on complementarity: "Atoms and groups which form the surface of the antigen attract certain complementary parts of the globulin

Pauling in his Caltech office, 1957. (Photograph by Phil Stern)

chain and repel other parts." The wrong part was his assumption "that all antibody molecules contain the same polypeptide chains as normal globulin and differ from normal globulin only in the configurations of the chain." Pauling was clearly not too happy about this assumption, which he adopted only because of his inability "to formulate a resonable mechanism whereby the order of amino-acids residues would be determined by the antigen." He could not know then about the genetic basis of amino-acid sequence. So he was right about how antibodies work and wrong about how they are produced. It was still a long time before a better theory emerged, based not on instruction but on selection, and involving hypervariable regions of the amino-acid chain and shuffling genes. In retrospect, then, it is not surprising that Pauling's immunochemistry program, carried out mainly by his Caltech collaborator Dan Campbell, never achieved the successes he had hoped for. During World War II there was a brief flurry of excitement when they claimed to have made "artificial antibodies" from normal globulins, but the claim proved to be ill founded and was soon retracted.

In 1941 Pauling's intense work schedule was temporarily stemmed when he was diagnosed as having Bright's disease, regarded then by many doctors as incurable. Under the treatment of Dr. Thomas Addis, he slowly recovered. Addis, a controversial figure, put Pauling on a low-protein, salt-free diet, which was effective in healing the damaged kidneys. After about six months Pauling was more or less back to normal, but he kept to Addis's diet for many years afterwards. Pearl Harbor brought further distractions when Pauling's energies were diverted to war work, mainly on rocket propellants and in the search for artificial antibodies. Earlier he had used the paramagnetism of oxygen to design and develop an oxygen meter for use in submarines.

By the end of the war Pauling felt well enough to travel abroad again. In late 1947 he came as Eastman visiting professor with his family to England, where he gave lectures to packed audiences in Oxford and elsewhere, received medals, and suffered from the climate. In 1948, confined to bed with a cold, he began thinking again about a problem that had briefly occupied him a decade earlier—the structure of α-keratin. By this time, thanks to the x-ray crystallographic work of Robert B. Corey and his associates, the detailed structures of several amino acids and simple peptides were known, and although the interatomic distances and angles did not differ much from the values derived earlier by resonace arguments, Pauling could now take them as facts rather than suppositions—especially the planarity of the amide group. With the help of paper models he then set himself the problem of making a polypeptide chain, rotating round the two single bonds but keeping the peptide groups planar, repeating with the same rotation angles from one peptide group to the next, and searching for a helical structure in which each N-H group makes a hydrogen bond with the carbonyl oxygen of another residue. He found two such structures, one of which also fulfilled the condition of tight packing down the central hole. The structure in question repeated after 18 residues in 5 turns at a distance of 27 Å, hence 5.4 Å per turn, whereas x-ray photographs of α-keratin seemed to show that the repeat distance was 5.1 Å. The discrepancy could not be removed by minor adjustments to the model and was large enough for Pauling to put the problem aside.

It was taken up again after his return to Pasadena, with the help of Corey and a young visiting professor, Herman Branson, who checked details of the model and searched for alternatives, but without coming up with anything really new. Then came a paper from the Cavendish Laboratory by Bragg, Kendrew, and Perutz who described several possible helical structures for α-keratin, all unacceptable in Pauling's view because they allowed rotation about the C-N bond of the amide group. This paper provoked Pauling to publish his ideas in a series of papers that described the now famous α-helix (essentially the one modeled in Oxford with 3.7 residues per turn), the so-called γ-helix (disfavored on energetic grounds), and the parallel and anti-parallel pleated sheets with extended polypeptide chains. By this time x-ray photographs of synthetic polypeptides had clarified the apparent discrepency concerning the repeat distance along the helix; it was 5.4 Å after all. Max Perutz has vividly described his consternation on first reading Pauling's proposed structure and how he managed to corroborate it by observing the 1.5 Å reflection corresponding to the step distance along the α-helix, which everyone had missed until then.

Very soon evidence began to accumulate that the α-helix is indeed one of the main structural features and that the two pleated sheets structures are also important elements of the secondary structure of globular proteins. Just as a few rules concerning the regular repetition of simple structural units had sufficed twenty years earlier to successfully predict the structures of minerals, now a few simple principles derived from structural chemistry were enough to predict the main structural features of proteins.

I regret that I did nothing on anesthesia after about 1942, and not much then.
I have to think seriously about your crystallization hypothesis. I do not know how the concentration of an anesthetic needed to narcotize an animal depends on its temperature. This seems a possibly decisive method of disproving your hypotheses. However you have no doubt collected data on such matters.

J.B.S. Haldane to Pauling

Pauling's next essay in model building was not so successful. In the summer of 1952 he learned about the Hershey-Chase experiment proving that genetic information was carried not by protein but by DNA, deoxyribonucleic acid, a polynucleotide. Pauling felt it should be possible to decipher the structure of this substance by model building along lines similar to those in the protein work. The available x-ray diffraction patterns showed a strong reflection at about 3.4 Å, but nothing much else. Having convinced himself that a two-stranded helical structure would yield too low a density, he went on to the assumption of a three-stranded helical structure held together by hydrogen bonds between the phosphate groups of different strands—that is, the structure rested on the tacit assumption that the phospho-diester groups were protonated! They were closely packed about the axis of the helix with the pentose residues surrounding them and the purine and pyrimidine groups projecting radially outward. When this structure was presented at a seminar, Verner Schomaker is credited with the remark, "If that were the structure of DNA, it would explode!" Nevertheless, the structure was published, a pre-publication copy having been sent to Cambridge, where it stimulated Watson and Crick into their final spurt, culminating in their base-paired structure, which was immediately acclaimed as correct by everyone who saw it—including Pauling. The Watson-Crick structure conformed to the self-complementarity principle that Pauling had enunciated many years earlier and then apparently forgotten.

Linus Pauling holding molecular model, 1954

Much has been written about this spectacular failure. Why was his model-building approach so successful with the polypeptides and so unsuccessful (in his hands) with DNA? First was the time factor. Pauling had thought about the polypeptide strutures for more than a decade before he risked publishing his conclusions; he thought for only a few months about DNA.

Secondly, the available information: for the polypeptide problem, precise metrical and stereochemical data for amino acids and simple peptides, mostly from Pauling's own laboratory, were at hand; for DNA almost nothing was known about the detailed structures of the monomers or oligomers. The x-ray photographs available to Pauling were obtained from degraded DNA specimens and were essentially noninformative (they were later recognized to be derived from mixtures of the A and B forms of DNA), and he made a bad mistake in neglecting the high water content of the DNA specimens in his density calculations.

Yet Watson and Crick succeeded with Pauling's methods where Pauling failed. There is no doubt in my mind that if Pauling had had access to Rosalind Franklin's x-ray photographs, he would immediately have drawn the same conclusion as Crick did, namely, that the molecule possesses a twofold axis of symmetry, thus pointing to two chains running in opposite directions and definitely excluding a three-chain structure. Then there were Chargaff's data about base ratios; Pauling later admitted that he had known about these but had forgotten. It seems clear that Pauling was in a hurry to publish, although, according to Peter Pauling's entertaining account twenty years later, he never felt he was in any sense "in a race." Finally, as described in the next section, he was by this time under severe harassment from the FBI and other agencies for his political views and activities. This must have taken up much of his mental and emotional energies during these months.

Pauling's standing as a founder of molecular biology rests partly on his identification of sickle-cell anemia, a hereditary disease, as a molecular disease—the first to be recognized as such. The red blood cells in the venous systems of sufferers adopt sickle shapes which tend to block small blood vessels, causing distressing symptoms, whereas the cells in the more oxygenated arterial blood have the normal flattened disc shape. When, towards the end of the war, Pauling heard about this, it occurred to him that it could be due to the presence of hemoglobin molecules with a different amino acid sequence from normal. The abnormal molecules, but not the normal ones, could contain self-complementary patches such as lead to end-to-end aggregation into long rods that twist the blood cells out of shape. Oxygenation could cause a conformational change to block these sticky patches. It took several years to confirm the essential correctness of what was no more than an intuitive guess. In the preliminary studies, attempts to identify any differences between the hemoglobins of normal and sickle-cell blood were unsuccessful, but with the advent of electrophoresis it could be shown that molecules of sickle-cell and normal hemoglobin moved at different rates in the electric field; the two molecules have different isoelectric points and must indeed be different. When, much later, it became possible to determine the amino-acid sequence in a protein, sickle-cell hemoglobin was found to contain valine instead of glutamic acid at position 6 of the two β chains. A single change in a single gene is responsible for the disease.

A decade later the further study of mutations in hemoglobin led to yet another fundamental contribution to molecular biology—the concept of the "molecular clock" in evolution. By this time, amino-acid sequencing of proteins had become standard. Hemoglobins obtained from humans, gorillas, horses, and other animals were analyzed. From paleontological evidence the common ancestor of man and horse lived somewhere around 130 million years ago. The α-chains of horse and human hemoglobin contain about 150 amino acids and differ by about 18 amino-acid substitutions, that is, about 9 evolutionary effective mutations for each of the chains, or about one per 14 million years. On this basis the differences between gorilla and human hemoglobin (two substitutions in the α- and one in the β-chain) suggest a relatively recent divergence between the species, on the order of only 10 million years. On the other hand, differences between the hemoglobin α- and β-chains of several animals suggest divergence from a common ancestor about 600 million years ago, in the pre-Cambrian, before the apparent onset of vertebrate evolution. From this work it became clear that comparison of protein sequences (now replaced by comparison of DNA sequences) is a powerful source of information about the origin of species. Evolution of organisms is bound with the evolution of molecules.

MOLECULAR MEDICINE

In the mid-1950s Pauling had become interested in phenylketonuria (mental deficiency due to inability to metabolize phenylalanine) as a further example of a molecular disease arising from the lack of a specific enzyme. At about this time he was also developing his theory that xenon acts as anesthetic because it forms crystalline polyhedral hydrates; microcrystals of such hydrates in the brain could interfere with the electric oscillations associated with consciousness. He obtained a $450,000 grant from the Ford Foundation to study the molecular basis of mental disease and turned his laboratories more and more away from traditional chemistry, not to the unanimous approval of his colleagues. In 1958 he resigned from his position as department chairman, a position he had held for more than twenty years, and found himself under pressure to give up research space to a new generation of researchers. In these years he devoted a great deal of time to anti-nuclear activity and world travel, so he was in any case spending less and less time with his own research group and in keeping up with new developments in chemistry. In 1963, angered by the lukewarm response of Caltech administrators to his Nobel Peace Prize, he announced that he was leaving the school.

The next few years were not the happiest in Pauling's life. Not only did he sever his connection with Caltech, he resigned from the American Chemical Society as well. A move to Santa Barbara was not a success. He turned to theoretical physics, but his close-packed spheron theory of the atomic nucleus met with little acceptance. He became engaged in actual and threatened libel suits. He moved briefly to the University of California at San Diego (1967-69) and then on to Stanford University (1969-72), where he was closer to his ranch at Big Sur, but he had no stable position in which to continue his planned research into "orthomolecular" psychiatric therapy. Meanwhile, he was deeply unhappy about the American involvement in Vietnam and about American politics in general.

One consolation was that after he passed his sixty-fifth birthday Pauling's health took a sudden turn for the better. Thanks to Dr. Addis's unconventional low-protein diet, he had recovered well from the kidney disease that had laid him low in his forties, but he had always suffered from severe colds several times a year. In 1966, following a suggestion from Dr. Irwin Stone, the Paulings began to take three grams of ascorbic acid per day each. Almost immediately they felt livelier and healthier. Over the next few years the colds that had plagued him all his life became less severe and less frequent. This experience made Pauling a believer in the health benefits of large daily amounts of vitamin C. It was not long before he was enthusiastically promulgating this belief in lectures and writings, which, not too surprisingly, brought on him the displeasure of the American medical establishment. After all, the then recommended daily allowance (RDA) of vitamin C was 45 mg; it was well known that there was no known cure for the common cold, and, in particular, previous studies had shown conclusively that vitamin C had no effect. Nevertheless, the NAS Subcommittee on Laboratory Animal Nutriton was then recommending daily intakes around 100 times that of the human RDA (adjusted for body weight) to keep laboratory primates in optimal health.

In his 1970 book *Vitamin C and the Common Cold*, Pauling gave evolutionary arguments why much larger amounts of vitamin C than the RDA may be conducive to optimal health. He cited studies supporting its efficacy in preventing colds or at least in lessening their severity. He criticized studies that claimed the opposite and he argued that since vitamin C is not a drug but a nutrient there is no reason why a large daily intake should be hamful. Pauling's arguments did not win the approval of the medical profession, but they caught on with the general public. The book rapidly became a best seller. As a result, in America and later in other countries, millions of people have been persuaded that a daily intake of 1-2 g of ascorbic acid has a beneficial effect on health and well being, essentially agreeing with Pauling that "we may make use of ascorbic acid for improving health in the ways indicated by experience, even though a detailed understanding of the mechanisms of its action has not yet been obtained."

One result of the book was a collaboration with a Scottish surgeon, Ewan Cameron, from Vale of Leven, who had observed beneficial effects of high doses of vitamin C in treating terminal cancer patients. Cameron thought that vitamin C might be involved in strengthening the intracellular mucopolysaccharide hyaluronic acid by helping to inhibit the action of the enzyme hyaluronidase produced by invasive cancerous cells. A paper by Cameron and Pauling advocating vitamin C therapy in cancer was submitted to the *Proceedings of the National Acadamy of Sciences (PNAS)*, which, in an unprecedented move, rejected the paper (it was then published in the specialist journal *Oncology*). During the next few years Cameron continued his trials. Since a double-blind trial was ethically unacceptable, he compared results obtained with one hundred ascorbate-treated terminal patients and one thousand other cases, ten controls for each patient, matched as closely as possible, and found that the ascorbate-treated patients lived longer and felt better subjectively. A paper describing these results was eventually published in *PNAS* but only after long arguments with referees. The Cameron-Pauling collaboration culminated in their 1979 book *Cancer and Vitamin C*, which was again more popular with the public than the medical profession, which continued to regard claims about the effectivenes of vitamin C in treating or preventing cancer as quackery. But by this time several important changes had occurred in Pauling's life.

At Stanford, Pauling's demands for more laboratory space for his orthomolecular medicine studies had been turned down. A solution was found by a younger colleague, Arthur B. Robinson, who had left a tenured position at San Diego to work with Pauling at Stanford. Instead of working in cramped quarters at the university they would set up their own research institute nearby. A building was rented, initial financial help was forthcoming, and the Insititute for Orthomolecular Medicine was founded in 1973. Once the initial funding ran out the institute found itself in financial straits. Soon it was renamed the Linus Pauling Institute of Science and Medicine with Pauling as president.

Personal and scientific difficulties between Robinson and Pauling led to Robinson's departure in 1979 and to lawsuits that dragged on for years. Meanwhile, Pauling continued to defend his unorthodox views and became once again a controversial figure, regarded by some as a crackpot, by others as a sage. In 1986 he wrote another popular book, *How to Live Longer and Feel Better*, which, based on his own experiences, gave advice about how to cope with aging.

In July 1976 Ava Helen underwent surgery for stomach cancer. Instead of post-operative chemotherapy or radiation treatment she adopted vitamin C therapy to the tune of 10 grams per day. She was soon well enough to accompany Pauling on his various travels, but she finally succumbed five years later, in December 1981. Pauling continued to travel, appear on television, write, and receive honors—his energy seemed unabated. When quasi-crystals with forbidden fivefold symmetry were discovered in 1984, Pauling took a contrary position and argued that the fivefold symmetry seen in Al/Mn alloys resulted merely from twinning of cubic crystallites. He was probably wrong, but the resulting controversy was nevertheless useful in forcing the proponents of quasi-crystals to seek better evidence for their view.

He even became reconciled with Caltech, where his eighty-fifth and ninetieth birthdays were marked by special symposia in his honor. In 1991 he was diagnosed with cancer. Surgery brought temporary relief, and megadoses of vitamin C kept up his spirits. He spent his last months at the ranch at Big Sur and died there on August 19, 1994.

EARLY YEARS OF PHYSICAL CHEMISTRY
AT CALTECH

Linus Pauling

*Pauling's first years at Caltech, as a graduate student and young professor, were among the most important and stimulating of his life. As he later put it, "There was a general feeling of the excitement of discovery in those days." In 1965, in preparing an article for the **Annual Review of Physics and Chemistry**, he described the atmosphere, the researchers, and the tools (especially the pioneering use of x-ray crystallography) that made Caltech, small as it was, an extraordinary place to pursue science.*

Arthur Amos Noyes suggested that my doctoral research be on the determination of the structure of crystals, under the supervision of Roscoe Gilkey Dickinson. I had read Irving Langmuir's 1919 papers on the electronic structure of molecules and had developed such an interest in the subject that I gave a seminar talk on molecular structure and the nature of the chemical bond in Corvallis in the fall of 1919. I borrowed the Bragg book on x-rays and crystal structure from the Oregon State Library, read it, and wrote Noyes that I accepted his suggestion.

I began my research on 1 October 1922. For years (since 1918) I had been speculating about the relation between the properties of substances and their molecular structure; the x-ray diffraction technique was beginning to provide the answers to many questions, and I was eager to get the answers to others. For three weeks I worked on the synthesis of LiH, with the idea of using x-ray intensities to test the presence of the hydrogen anions in the crystal; then I learned that this job had already been done, by Bijvoet and Karrssen in Holland. During the next month I made crystals of fifteen inorganic substances and subjected several of them to the first stages of x-ray investigation. None of them seemed to be suitable for a structure determination by the methods that were then in use. During the third month Dickinson carried me through the various steps in the complete structure determination of a crystal, the mineral molybdenite, MoS_2.

This achievement made a great impression on me. The process of structure determination involved a succession of logical arguments, which were presented to me by Dickinson in a meticulous way, with emphasis on rigor. Dickinson was an especially clear-headed and thoughtful scientist, strongly critical of carelessness and superficiality. I was pleased to learn that questions about the nature of the world could be answered by carefully planned and executed experiments. Also, I was pleased that the study of molybdenite should have led to a surprise: the molybdenum atom was found to be surrounded by six sulfur atoms at the corners of a trigonal prism, rather than of an octahedron, as might have been expected from the earlier structure determinations. This was the discovery of the trigonal prism as a coordination polyhedron around metal atoms.

Because of the small number of graduate students in Pasadena in 1922, it was possible for them to come into close contact with the members of the faculty. For example, together with two or three other graduate students and a faculty member, Ellis, I was taken by Noyes on some camping trips to the Palm Springs region, and all of the graduate students were the guests of Noyes in his oceanside house at Corona del Mar, 50 miles south of Pasadena, where a few years later the California Institute of Technology set up a marine laboratory. These occasions gave opportunity for the unhurried discussion of scientific and practical problems. Dickinson also took me with him on a number of trips to the desert during my first year as a graduate student. Moreover, the members of the staff were not overloaded; in 1922-23 I was the only graduate student being supervised by Dickinson.

In addition to inspiring them with the desire to carry on research, it is necessary in the training of young scientists to give them a good background of the knowledge that has already been obtained. The California Institute of Technology, despite its small size, was already carrying out this function in an admirable way in 1922. Although Noyes, as Director of the Gates Chemical Laboratory and a member of the Executive Council, was primarily responsible for the development of the Institute as a leading teaching and research school in physical chemistry, it was Richard Chace Tolman who, in my opinion, made the greatest contribution to the achievement of this goal. Tolman, who had come to Pasadena in 1921, had a thorough understanding of the new developments in physics and the conviction that chemical problems could be solved by the application of physical methods. In my first term, the fall of 1922, I found his course Introduction to Mathematical Physics, in which he laid emphasis on the basic principles and their quantitative application to moderately simple problems, to be especially valuable. His courses on advanced thermodynamics and on statistical mechanics applied to physical and chemical problems were outstanding for their clarity and

Sometimes I have called myself a chemist or a physicist, but more recently I call myself a scientist.

Linus Pauling

thoroughness. But his greatest contribution to the training of the young physical chemists in Pasadena came, I believe, through the course called Seminar in Physical Chemistry. During the three years when I was a graduate student this seminar involved working through three books: first, *The Origin of Spectra*, by Foote and Mohler; second, *Atomic Structure and Spectral Lines*, by Arnold Sommerfeld; and third, *Atombau und Spektrallinien*, by Sommerfeld (new edition, available then only in German). The other courses that I studied during my graduate years were the following: advanced algebra (Van Buskirk); higher dynamics (C. G. Darwin); chemical thermodynamics (Noyes; this course, in the fall of 1922, was the last one that he taught); advanced thermodynamics (Tolman, spring of 1923; a newly published book by Lewis and Randall was the text); kinetic theory (Robert A. Millikan); thermodynamics (Millikan); vector analysis (Harry Bateman); Newtonian potential theory (Bateman); thermodynamics (P. S. Epstein); quantum theory (P. Ehrenfest); physical optics and quantum theory (Epstein); functions of a complex variable (Bateman); and integral equations (Bateman). These courses helped me to overcome the handicap of lack of knowledge of physics and mathematics. The course work of other graduate students in physical chemistry was similar, but on the average not so heavy.

I learned a great deal also from the research conferences. The chemistry research conference, held once a week, was made lively by Tolman's efforts to find out the extent of understanding that had been achieved by the graduate students.

Only rarely did a visitor speak at a chemistry conference. I remember that Fritz Haber was present at one, but did not speak. I do not remember any speaker from Berkeley, which is after all 420 miles away. The physics research conferences, on the other hand, often were held by visiting physicists, who sometimes also presented a series of special lectures. Among the visiting physicists in the early 1920s were H. A. Lorentz, C. G. Darwin, P. Ehrenfest, A. A. Michelson, R. C. Gibbs, S. Loria, A. Sommerfeld, M. Born, V. Bjerknes, C. V. Raman, J. Franck, and P. Langevin. There were two physics research conferences per week; often one was combined with the Physics and Astronomy Club, which met alternately at the Institute campus and the Pasadena laboratories of the Mt. Wilson Observatory.

Pauling photograph of the x-ray powder diffraction apparatus he built, 1923

The first three recipients of Ph.D. degrees from the Institute were chemists: Roscoe G. Dickinson (1920), Richard M. Bozorth (1922), and David F. Smith (1922). In 1924 six Ph.D. degrees were awarded in physics and three in chemistry (Richard M. Badger, R. Schumann, and Ernest H. Swift); in 1925 there were three in physics, one in mathematics, and four in chemistry (Paul H. Emmett, Linus Pauling, Albert L. Raymond, and Ernest C. White); and in 1926 nine in physics and six in chemistry (Gordon A. Alles, Sterling B. Hendricks, L. M. Kirkpatrick, C. H. Prescott, Oliver R. Wulf, and Don M. Yost).

Pauling photograph of his desk and x-ray apparatus in the basement of Gates Laboratory, 1923

By 1924 there were thirteen postdoctoral fellows at the Institute, of whom nine were National Research Fellows (four in chemistry—Arthur F. Benton, Philip S. Danner, George Glockler, and Maurice L. Huggins), and forty-three graduate students, of whom sixteen were in chemistry, fourteen of them in physical chemistry. The number of undergraduate students at this time was about five hundred; it had reached six hundred by 1937, and seven hundred by 1960. The number of graduate students was 220 (twenty-two in chemistry) in 1937 and 678 (eighty-seven in chemistry) in 1963. In the early 1920s, research in physical chemistry and physics received its main support from a five-year grant of $30,000 per year that had been made by the Carnegie Institution of Washington for the support of research on the structure of matter and radiation.

Six papers were published as contributions from the Chemical Laboratory of Throop College of Technology. These papers, published between June 1915 and January 1920, included three on the properties of aqueous solutions of strong electrolytes, two on the determination of the structure of crystals by the x-ray diffraction method, and one on the analysis of metal-organic compounds. The first contribution from the Gates Chemical Laboratory of the California Institute of Technology, Number 7 in the series of papers in chemistry, was on chromoisomeric silver salts of pentabromophenol and a theory of chromoisomerism of solid compounds, by Howard J. Lucas and Archie R. Kemp.

These first seven papers constituted the beginning of three of the principal fields of research in physical chemistry in the Institute. The first two, written by Professor Stuart J. Bates, were on the osmotic pressure of ions and of undissociated molecules of salts in aqueous solution (published in the *Proceedings of the National Academy of Sciences* and in the *Journal of the*

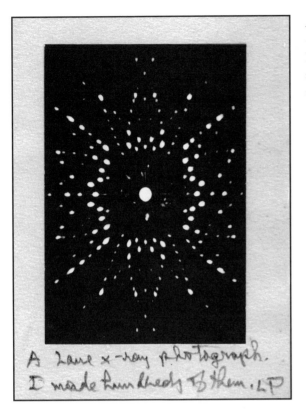

Laue x-ray
photograph by Linus
Pauling, 1922

American Chemical Society in 1915). The field of ionic solutions was of great interest to Noyes, who had carried out an extensive series of experimental investigations on these solutions over a period of three decades. Noyes continued for several years in the California Institute of Technology the experimental work in this field that had been initiated by him in the Massachusetts Institute of Technology. In 1904 he had pointed out that some of the properties of solutions of strong electrolytes, such as the dependence of absorption spectrum on concentration, indicate that many of the substances are completely ionized, even in concentrated solutions. By 1922 he had reached the conclusion that the dependence of thermodynamic activity and electric conductance of these solutions on concentration is determined by the electrostatic interaction of the ions, and he embarked upon an experimental test of these ideas, based upon the statistical mechanical treatment of the problem that had been published by Milner in 1912 and 1913. While he was preparing this work for publication, the paper by Debye and Hückel on the interionic attraction theory of ionized solutions was published. Noyes then published a detailed discussion of this theory, including especially the comparison with experiment. He concluded that the properties of ionized solutions are satisfactorily accounted for by the theory, and he brought his long series of researches in this field to an end. Fifteen of the early publications from the Gates Chemical Laboratory were on this subject.

During later years Noyes continued his work in the fields of qualitative inorganic chemical analysis, chemical thermodynamics, and inorganic chemistry. He was especially interested in the prosecution of research by undergraduate students, and in 1936 and 1937 he published four papers on strong oxidizing agents in nitric acid solution, including the formation of biposivite silver in nitric acid by the action of ozone. The work described in these papers was carried out under his supervision by Clifford S. Garner, Thomas J. Deahl, Charles D. Coryell, Fred Stitt, and Alexander Kossiakoff. In 1925 he became interested in the interpretation of chemical properties of elements on the basis of the electronic structure of their atoms, and he prepared two papers in this field, with the assistance of a graduate student, Arnold O. Beckman. He also brought Professor John J. Abel and Dr. E. M. K. Geiling for one year to the California Institute of Technology from the Department of Pharmacology of Johns Hopkins University, to work on insulin. Abel reported the crystallization in insulin in a joint communication from the Gates Chemical Laboratory and the Department of Pharmacology of Johns Hopkins University. The isolation of insulin and study of its properties were carried out in Pasadena by two graduate students, Albert L. Raymond and Gordon Alles, both of whom later made important contributions in the field of pharmacology. In 1926, Alles published an account of his research on the comparative physiological action of some derivatives of guanidine. This work may well have been the inspiration for his later investigations that led to the discovery of benzedrine and other physiologically active amines.

C. Lalor Burdick has stated that the development of x-ray crystallography in the California Institute of Technology was due entirely to the imagination, vision, and conviction of Arthur A. Noyes. In 1913 Burdick was a graduate student in physical chemistry under Noyes at M.I.T., and was

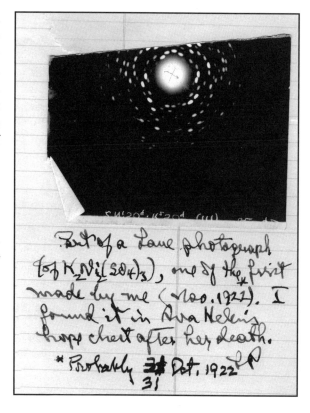

encouraged by him to go to Europe for doctoral work and postdoctoral study. After he had received his Ph.D. degree in Basel he was advised by Noyes to work for six months in the x-ray laboratory of W. H. Bragg at University College in London. Burdick collaborated there with Dr. E. A. Owen in studying carborundum with the use of the Bragg ionization chamber x-ray spectrometer. Noyes then invited him, in the latter part of 1916, to come to Pasadena. Burdick and James H. Ellis, a former M.I.T. student of Noyes who later became Associate Professor of Physical Chemical Research in the California Institute, built an improved spectrometer and used it to determine the crystal structure of chalcopyrite, $CuFeS_2$. The account of this work appeared in 1917 in both the *Proceedings of the National Academy of Sciences* and the *Journal of the American Chemical Society*. This work and the simultaneous work of Albert W. Hull on the structure of metallic elements, done in the General Electric Research Laboratory, were the beginning of x-ray crystallography in the United States.

In 1917 Dickinson came to Pasadena from M.I.T., at Noyes' request, and continued the x-ray work. Within a few years he had carried out several important investigations. He showed, with E. A. Goodhue, that in the crystals $NaClO_3$ and $NaBrO_3$ the chlorate ion and the bromate ion are pyramidal in structure, and he determined the bond lengths to within 0.03 Å. He also verified the octahedral configuration of the hexachlorostannate ion, the square planar configuration of the tetrachloropalladite and tetrachloroplatinite ions, and the tetrahedral configuration of the zinc tetracyanide and cadmium tetracyanide ions. He and Albert L. Raymond, who was beginning his graduate work, made the first crystal structure determination of an organic compound, hexamethylenetetramine, in 1922 (published in 1923). In 1923 Richard M. Bozorth reported his structure determination of KHF_2, which provided the first x-ray evidence for the hydrogen bond. Bozorth also made structure determinations of some other crystals, including As_4O_6 and Sb_4O_6, which were the first inorganic crystals shown to contain discrete molecules.

For several years x-ray diffraction was the principal field of research in chemistry in the Institute. Of the twenty papers that had been published by the end of 1922, fifteen were on the determination of the structure of crystals. As other fields of research began to be prosecuted the papers on the determination of the structure of crystals by x-ray diffraction dropped to about 20 per cent of the total, and then to about 10 per cent. During the last fifty years, about four hundred papers on x-ray diffraction have been published from the Gates and Crellin Laboratories of Chemistry of the California Institute of Technology, representing the determination of the structure of about four hundred crystals.

Dickinson spent the academic year 1924-25 in the Cavendish Laboratory, learning the techniques of radiochemistry. On his return to Pasadena he gradually dropped the crystal structure field. He did some work with Tolman on the theory of the rate of chemical reactions, and, together with Dillon and Rasetti, he obtained the first Raman spectra of polyatomic gases. In 1935, with Don M. Yost, he studied the diffusion and absorption of neutrons in paraffin. The major part of his work during the rest of his life was in the field of photochemistry.

In his researches, carried out in part with graduate students, Tolman, who was Professor of Physical Chemistry and Mathematical Physics, attacked problems that ranged over a wide field: the general theory of relativity, the application of the old quantum theory to systems with motion that is only an approximation to conditionally periodic motion, the theory of diatomic gases, rotational heat capacity, the experimental determination of the mass of the electric carrier in metals, the entropy of supercooled liquids at the absolute zero, the principle of microscopic reversibility, experimental determination of the rate of decomposition of nitrogen pentoxide and of the rates of other chemical reactions, and especially the theoretical attack on the problem of the rate of unimolecular reactions.

The problem of the rate of chemical reactions and the mechanism of activation was one of the liveliest problems in physical chemistry during the decade beginning forty years ago. The observed rates of some very rapid first-order reactions, such as the decomposition of nitrogen pentoxide, were so large that it seemed unlikely that the number of high-energy collisions between molecules was great enough to provide the

...[T]he first faculty member I saw at Caltech was Linus Pauling. And he asked me what I wanted to do, and I said I wanted to be a theoretical chemist....And Linus said "Well, if you want to be a theoretical chemist, you have to know everything there is to know about chemistry and physics and biology." And I said, "This guy is joking...maybe he's not joking."

Well, in fact, he was not joking and I took my own advice and went to work with Norman Davidson, because I felt [Linus] would be a pretty tough fellow to work for.

Harden McConnell, Pauling's student

equilibrium fraction of molecules with energy equal to the activation energy. Because of Tolman's interest in this problem, significant experimental contributions were made in this field by David F. Smith, Ernest C. White, Oliver R. Wulf, Martin E. Nordberg, Herman C. Ramsperger, William Ure, J. A. Leermakers, G. Waddington, Philip D. Brass, and William E. Vaughan. The attack on the theory of the rate of these reactions was made by Tolman in collaboration with R. G. Dickinson, Don M. Yost, and Herman C. Ramsperger, and the theoretical work was continued by Oscar K. Rice and Louis S. Kassel, as well as Ramsperger, during their stay in Pasadena as National Research Fellows. In the course of this work it was shown that the supply of activated molecules was not kept replenished in general through the absorption of infrared radiation, nor through individual bimolecular collisions of high energy, but rather, for molecules with several degrees of internal vibrational freedom, through a series of collisions of moderately high energy, such as to provide some molecules with an amount of internal energy equal to or greater than the activation energy.

Some branches of physical chemistry were taken up and then dropped. Arthur F. Benton came to Pasadena from Princeton in 1921, as a National Research Fellow. He worked on catalysis and surface chemistry, with Paul H. Emmett as a graduate student; but this field was dropped when they left in 1925. C.H. Prescott, Jr., made some measurements of chemical equilibrium at high temperatures; this field, too, was dropped at the end of the 1920s.

The work in physical chemistry became more and more the application of new physical techniques to the solution of chemical problems and the application also of the new physical theories, especially quantum theory and quantum mechanics. Richard M. Badger, who has been associated with the California Institute of Technology since 1918, presented an undergraduate thesis in 1921 with title *The Effect of Surface Conditions on the Intensity of X-ray Reflections From Crystal Plans,* describing work that he had done with the Bragg ionization spectrometer that had been constructed by Burdick and Ellis. Then, after some work on the free energy of hydrogen cyanide and other substances, he moved into the field of molecular spectroscopy, to which he has made many contributions. . . .

There was a general feeling of the excitement of discovery in those days. Quantum theory seemed to provide the answers to many puzzling questions, but it left others unanswered. For example, the moment of inertia and the vibrational frequency of the hydrogen molecule were thought to be known, and in fact were known, from the band spectrum of hydrogen, but the calculated values of the heat capacity of hydrogen gas at low temperatures could not be brought into agreement with experiment. Tolman and Badger compared the calculated heat capacity on the basis of many different assumptions about quantum weights of the rotational states with the experimental values, without finding a successful theory. The problem was not solved until 1927, when David M. Dennison, of the

University of Michigan, showed that the assignment of spin one-half to the proton coupled with the assumption that transitions do not occur between even and odd rotational states of hydrogen during the time of an experimental measurement of the heat capacity led to a satisfactory theoretical curve.

I remember that, as a graduate student and a young postdoctoral fellow, I felt that the time had come when it would be possible to make a successful attack on many chemical problems by applying quantum theory and quantum mechanics, but I did not feel that I might make a successful attack on some problems in physics itself. As I think back on those years, I conclude that I was not able to distinguish clearly between the unsatisfactory nature of the existing physical theories and the unsatisfactory nature of my own understanding of them, and I tended to assume that my understanding was at fault. For example, in 1924 I listened with great interest to Professor Arnold Sommerfeld's account of his work on the fine structure of x-ray spectral lines. In his theory, which accounted in what seemed to be a thoroughly satisfactory way for the x-ray energy levels of atoms, he assigned to an atom values of two kinds of azimuthal quantum numbers of the electron orbits. These two kinds of quantum numbers, called the inner quantum number and the outer quantum number, determined the s,p,d, ... splitting was accounted for as the result of a difference in penetration of the inner shells for orbits with different eccentricity, and the fine structure as the result of a difference in the relativistic change in mass of the electron in orbits of different eccentricity. Why the second effect could occur without the first effect is hard to understand; but, as I remember the lectures and their reception, Sommerfeld himself failed to mention this difficulty and no one in the audience commented on it. Later on Millikan and Bowen wrote a paper entitled "A Great Puzzle in the Theory of Spectra," in which they emphasized this point, and the puzzle was resolved, of course, by the discovery of the spinning electron, which produces a fine-structure splitting of spectral lines identical with that calculated by Sommerfeld for the relativistic change in mass.

I held a National Research Fellowship for seven months, and resigned in February 1926 in order to work in Europe for nineteen months as a Guggenheim Fellow. I wrote to Niels Bohr asking permission to come to work in his Institute in Copenhagen, and also to Sommerfeld, in Munich. Bohr did not answer the letter, but Sommerfeld did, and in this way the decision was made for me as to whether to go to Copenhagen or to Munich. Sommerfeld's lectures were outstanding, and I think it was good luck that led me to spend a year with him. I then spent a few weeks in Bohr's Institute and five months in Zurich, attending lectures by Schrödinger and Debye and working on the quantum mechanical theory of the chemical bond.

On my return to Pasadena in 1927 as Assistant Professor of Theoretical Chemistry, I presented a course on introduction to quantum mechanics,

I remember going to the dentist in Pasadena, when I shortly arrived there. And the dentist, on each wall, he had his little x-ray machine and came in and took x-rays and he said, 'you know that guy Pauling down at Caltech?' And I said, 'yes I know him.' And he said 'you know, they're gonna make us have lead aprons for everybody here and put the machines on the other side and they say that radiation's not good for you.' And of course, all of this has come to pass and it was Linus's words that started all of that.

Frank Catchpool, Pauling associate

with chemical applications. I gave this course every year for many years, and I also gave it, as well as a course on the nature of the chemical bond, in the University of California in Berkeley, where I spent one or two months each spring for five years, beginning in 1929, as Visiting Lecturer in Chemistry and Physics. Other graduate courses that I taught in Pasadena were on the structure of crystals, the nature of the chemical bond, and the theory of the electric and magnetic properties of substances.

I had a surprise in 1930. The relations between the divisions of the California Institute of Technology were very good, and when, in 1930, my first book was published (*The Structure of Line Spectra,* with S.A. Goudsmit, now editor of the *Physical Review,* as co-author), I planned to give a course on this subject. However, my proposal was, according to Noyes, vetoed by Millikan, who, Noyes said, felt that this subject should be left to the physics department. Later on I thought that Noyes himself might have made the decision to keep me from straying out of chemistry. In fact in early 1927, while I was in Munich, I received and accepted an offer of appointment as Assistant Professor of Theoretical Chemistry and Mathematical Physics, but when I arrived in Pasadena in October I found that Mathematical Physics had been dropped from my title.

In the spring and summer of 1930 I spent six months in Europe. I had been working on the structure of mica and other silicate minerals, and I first stayed for some time in the W. L. Bragg laboratory in Manchester, where I learned little except how to operate a Bragg x-ray spectrometer (the Pasadena spectrometer had been abandoned and replaced by photographic apparatus before my arrival in 1922). I then went to Munich, to continue my work on quantum mechanical problems. Fortunately I decided to visit Hermann Mark in his laboratory in Ludwigshafen. He showed me the electron-diffraction apparatus with which he and Wierl had determined the structure of gas molecules of carbon taetrachloride and benzene during the preceding year. I was overwhelmed by the possibilities of this new technique—for some time I had been looking for a diffraction method of determining the structure of molecules without having at the same time to determine the sometimes very complicated way in which the molecules are arranged relative to one another in a crystal. I asked Mark if he had any objection to my doing some electron-diffraction work in Pasadena. He said that he did not and that in fact he was not planning to continue the work much longer. On my return to Pasadena I asked a new graduate student, Lawrence O. Brockway, to build the apparatus, which he did, with the advice and help of Professor Badger.

The Nature of the Chemical Bond:

The Application of Results Obtained from the Quantum mechanics and from a New Theory of Paramagnetic Susceptibility to the Structure of molecules.

By Linus Pauling.

During the last four years the problem of the nature of the chemical bond has been attacked by theoretical physicists, especially by Heitler and London, by the application of the quantum mechanics. This work has led to the approximate theoretical calculation of the energy of formation and other properties of very simple molecules, such as H_2, and has also provided a formal justification of the rules set up in 1916 by G. N. Lewis for his electron-pair bond. In the following paper it will be shown that many more results of chemical significance can be obtained from the quantum mechanical equations, permitting the formulation of an extensive and powerful set of rules for the electron-pair bond, supplementing those of Lewis.

These rules provide information regarding the relative strengths of bonds formed by different atoms, the angles between bonds, free rotation or lack of free rotation about bond

THE ORIGINAL MANUSCRIPT FOR
THE NATURE OF THE CHEMICAL BOND

Linus Pauling

Historians of science are nearly unanimous in their agreement that the paper that Pauling wrote in early 1931 on the nature of the chemical bond could be construed as one of the more important papers in the history of chemistry. As such, one would think that the care given to this artifact would be of paramount importance. However, this was not necessarily the case.

During my early years as a scientist, beginning in 1919, I had a special interest in the problem of the nature of the chemical bond; that is, the nature of the forces that hold atoms together in molecules, crystals, and other substances. Much of my work during this early period was directed toward a solution of this problem, by application of both experimental and theoretical methods. As soon as quantum mechanics was discovered, in 1925, I began striving to apply this powerful theory to the problem. I published several theoretical papers in this field during the next few years, without, however, having been able to answer a number of important questions. Then one evening, in December 1930, while I was sitting at my desk in my study at our home on Arden Road and California Street in Pasadena, California, I had an idea about a way to simplify the quantum-mechanical equations in such a manner as to permit their easy approximate solution. I was so excited about this idea that I stayed up most of the night, applying the idea to various problems.

During the next two months I continued to work on this idea and to write a paper communicating the results of its application to the problem of the nature of the chemical bond. As I recall, the manuscript to which this statement refers was written in early February, 1931. A typescript was prepared from it, and the manuscript was put in the wastepaper basket, presumably by me, although I do not have a clear memory of this matter. Forty-seven years later, the manuscript was given to me by Professor Ralph Hultgren. In 1931 Ralph Hultgren was one of my graduate students, working for his Ph.D. in chemistry. He stated, when he gave me the manuscript, that he had removed it from the wastepaper basket and had kept it for the intervening forty-seven years.

I made some changes in the typescript, and the revised typescript was submitted to the editor of the *Journal of the American Chemical Society* on 17 February 1931. It was published in the April issue, which appeared on 6 April 1931 on pages 1367 to 1400 of the *Journal of the American Chemical Society*, Volume 53. The short time that elapsed between receipt of the article and publication in the *Journal* indicates that the editor of the *Journal*, Professor Arthur B. Lamb of Harvard University, did not go through the usual process of submitting the paper to referees for criticism, but instead decided that it was proper for it to be sent immediately to the printer.

There are a few differences between the manuscript and the published paper. The only major difference is that I removed the section on the single-electron bond, pages 4 to 7 of the manuscript, before submitting the typescript for publication. This section on the single-electron bond was later expanded and was published as a separate paper, with the title "The Nature of the Chemical Bond. II. The One-Electron Bond and the Three-Electron Bond," *Journal of the American Chemical Society* 53, 3225-3237 (1931). During the following two years five more papers were published with the title "The Nature of the Chemical Bond," III, IV, V, VI, and VII, in the *Journal of the American Chemical Society* and the *Journal of Chemical Physics.*

These seven papers, and especially the first one, for which the original manuscript has been preserved, constituted the principal basis of knowledge for my book, *The Nature of the Chemical Bond,* the first edition of which was published by Cornell University Press in 1939 (second edition 1940, third edition 1960). This 1931 paper may well be considered the most important part of the work for which I was awarded the Nobel Prize in Chemistry in 1954. The citation for the award states (in Swedish) "For his research on the nature of the chemical bond and its application in the elucidation of the structure of complex substances."

MODERN STRUCTURAL CHEMISTRY
NOBEL LECTURE, 1954

Linus Pauling

↞↞↞

Pauling had been spoken of as a potential Nobelist from the time he was thirty years old. But year after year went by without the Prize. By the early 1950s, Pauling himself had begun to doubt that he would win a Nobel, reasoning that the Prize was generally given for a single discovery while he had built a structural chemistry edifice of many parts. "That was the trouble," Pauling said. "What was the single great discovery that I had made?" In November 1954, he finally won; his citation said, "for research into the nature of the chemical bond." Nobel officials had broken precedent and given Pauling what was in effect a career award. Pauling reviewed that career in this, his 1954 Nobel Lecture.

A century ago the structural theory of organic chemistry was developed. Frankland in 1852 suggested that an atom of an element has a definite capacity for combining with atoms of other elements—a definite valence. Six years later Kekulé and Couper, independently, introduced the idea of valence bonds between atoms, including bonds between two carbon atoms, and suggested that carbon is quadrivalent. In 1861 Butlerov, making use for the fist time of the term "chemical structure," stated clearly that the properties of a compound are determined by its molecular structure and reflect the way in which atoms are bonded to one another in the molecules of the compound. The development of the structure theory of organic chemistry then progressed rapidly, and this theory has been of inestimable value in aiding organic chemists to interpret their experimental results and to plan new experiments.

A most important early addition to organic structure theory was made by the first Nobel Laureate in Chemistry, van't Hoff, who in 1874 recognized that the optical activity of carbon compounds can be explained by the postulate that the four valence bonds of the carbon atom are directed in space toward the corners of a tetrahedron.

The structure theory of inorganic chemistry may be said to have been born only fifty years ago, when Werner, Nobel Laureate in Chemistry in 1913, found that the chemical composition and properties of complex inorganic substances could be explained by assuming that metal atoms often coordinate about themselves a number of atoms different from their valence, usually four atoms at the corners either of a tetrahedron of a square coplanar with the central atom, or six atoms at the corners of an octahedron.

After the discovery of the electron many efforts were made to develop an electronic theory of the chemical bond. A great contribution was made in 1916 by Gilbert Newton Lewis, who proposed that the chemical bond, such as the single bond between two carbon atoms or a carbon atom and a hydrogen atom represented by a line in the customary structural formula for ethane, consists of a pair of electrons held jointly by the two atoms that are bonded together. Lewis also suggested that atoms tend to assume the electronic configuration of a noble gas, through the sharing of electrons with the other atoms of through electron transfer, and that the eight outermost electrons in an atom with a noble-gas electronic structure are arranged tetrahedrally in pairs about the atom. Applications of the theory and additional contributions were made by many chemists, including Irving Langmuir and Nevil Vincent Sidgwick.

After the discovery of quantum mechanics in 1925, it became evident that the quantum mechanical equations constitute a reliable basis for the theory of molecular structure. It also soon became evident that these equations, such as the Schrödinger wave equation, cannot be solved rigorously for any but the simplest molecules. The development of the theory of molecular structure and the nature of the chemical bond during the past twenty-five years has been in considerable part empirical—based upon the facts of chemistry—but with the interpretation of these facts greatly influenced by quantum mechanical principles and concepts.

The solution of the wave equation for the hydrogen molecule-ion by Ø. Burrau (*Det Kgl. Danske Vid. Selsk. Math.-fys. Meddelelser*, 7, 14 (1927)) completely clarified the question of the nature of the one-electron bond in this molecule-ion. Two illuminating quantum mechanic discussions of the shared-election-pair bond in the hydrogen molecule were then simultaneously published, one by Heitler and London (*Z. Physik*, 44, 455 (1927)). In the approximate solution of the wave equation for the hydrogen molecule by Heitler and London a wave function is used that requires the two electrons to be separated, each being close to one of the two nuclei. The treatment by Condon permits the electrons to be distributed between the two nuclei independently of one another, each occupying a wave function similar to Burrau's function for the hydrogen-molecule ion. Condon's treatment is the prototype of the molecular-orbital treatment that has been extensively applied in the discussion of aromatic and conjugated molecules, and Heitler and London's treatment is the prototype of the valence-bond method. When the effort is made to refine the two treatments they tend to become identical.

Perhaps, as one of the older generations, I should preach a little sermon to you—but I do not propose to do so. I shall, instead, give you a word of advice about how to behave toward your elders. When an old and distinguished person speaks to you, listen to him carefully and with respect—*but do not believe him. Never put your trust in anything but your own intellect. Your elder,* no matter whether he has gray hair or has lost his hair, no matter whether he is a Nobel Laureate—*may be wrong.* The world progresses, year by year, century by century, as the members of the younger generation find out what was *wrong* among the things that their elders said. So you *must always* be skeptical – always *think for yourself.*

Linus Pauling to students

These early applications of quantum mechanics to the problem of the nature of the chemical bond made it evident that in general a covalent bond, involving the sharing of a pair of electrons between two atoms, can be formed if two electrons are available (their spins must be opposed, in order that the bond be formed), and if each atom has available a stable electronic orbital for occupancy by the electrons.

The equivalence of the four bonds formed by a carbon atom, which had become a part of chemical theory, was not at first easily reconciled with the quantum mechanical description of the carbon atom as having one $2s$ orbital and three $2p$ orbitals in its outer shell. The solution to this difficulty was obtained when it was recognized that as a result of the resonance phenomenon of quantum mechanics a tetrahedral arrangement of the four bonds of the carbon atom is achieved. The carbon atom can be described as having four equivalent tetrahedral bond orbitals, which are hybrids of the s and p orbitals. Further study of this problem led to the discovery of many sets of hybrid bond orbitals, which could be correlated with bond angles, magnetic moments, and other molecular properties. In particular it was found that sp^3, dsp^2, and $d2sp3$ hybrid orbitals correspond respectively to the tetrahedral, square planar, and octahedral configurations of inorganic complexes that had been discovered by Werner. Conclusions as to the utilization of atomic orbitals in bond formation can be drawn from experimental values of magnetic moments. For example, the theory of the dsp^2 square complexes of bipositive nickel, palladium, and platinum requires that these substances be diamagnetic. The square complexes of bipositive palladium and platinum had been recognized by Werner and their structure verified by Dickinson (*J. Am. Chem. Soc.*, 44, 2404 (1922)); but the assignment of the square configuration to the complexes of nickel which are diamagnetic had not been made until the development of the new theory.

Further detailed information about the chemical bond resulted from a consideration of the energy of single bonds in relation to the relative electronegativity of the bonded atoms. It was found that the elements can be assigned electronegativity values such as to permit that rough prediction of the heats of formation of compounds to which chemical structures involving only single bonds are conventionally assigned, and that many of the properties of substances can be discussed in a simple way with the use of the electronegativity values of the elements.

The idea that the properties of many organic compounds, especially the aromatic compounds, cannot be simply correlated with a single valence-bond structure, but require the assignment of a somewhat more complex electronic structure, was developed during the period 1923 to 1926 by a number of chemists, including Lowry, Lapworth, Robinson, and Ingold in England, Lucas in the United States, and Arndt and Eistert in Germany. It was recognized that the properties of aromatic and conjugated molecules can be decried by the use of two or more valence-bond structures, as reflected in the names, the theory of mesomerism and the theory of intermediate states, proposed for the new chemical theory. In 1931 Slater,

Linus Pauling, Werner Kuhn, and Wolfgang Pauli during Pauling's European trip, 1926

E. Hückel, and others recognized that these theories can be given a quantum mechanical interpretation: an approximate wave function for a molecule of this sort can be set up as the sum of wave functions representing the hypothetical structures corresponding to the individual valence-bond structures. The molecule can then be described as having a structure that is a hybrid of the individual valence-bond structures, or as resonating among these structures, and the theory itself is now usually called the resonance theory of chemical structure. Very many quantitative calculations, approximate solutions of the wave equation, for aromatic and conjugated molecules have been made, with results that are in general in good agreement with experiment. Perhaps more important than the quantitative calculations is the possibility of prediction by simple chemical arguments. For example, the amide group, an important structural feature of proteins, can be described as resonating between two structures, one with the double bond between the carbon atom and the oxygen atom, and the other with the double bond between the carbon atom and the nitrogen atom.

General arguments about the stability of alternative structures indicate that the structure with the double bond between carbon and oxygen should contribute somewhat more to the normal state of the amide group than the other structure; experience with other substances and acquaintance with the results of quantum mechanical calculations suggest the ratio 60%: 40% for the respective contributions of these structures. A 40% contribution of the structure with the double bond between the carbon atom and the nitrogen atom would confer upon this bond the property of planarity of the group of six atoms; the resistance to deformation from the planar configuration would be expected to be 40% as great as for a molecule such as ethylene, containing a pure double bond, and it can be calculated that rotation of one end by 3° relative to the other end would introduce a strain energy of 100 cal/mole.

The estimate of 40% double–bond character for the C—N bond is supported by the experimental value of the bond length, 1.32 Å., interpreted with the aid of the empirical relation between double-bond character and interatomic distance. Knowledge of the structure of amides and also of the amino acids, provided by the theory of resonance and verified by extensive careful experimental studies made by R. B. Corey and his coworkers, has been of much value in the determination of the structure of proteins.

In the description of the theory of resonance in chemistry there has been a perhaps unnecessarily strong emphasis on its arbitrary character. It is true, of course, that a description of the benzene molecule can be given, in quantum mechanical language, without any reference to the two Kekulé structures, in which double bonds and single bonds alternate in the ring. An approximate wave function for the benzene molecule may be formulated by adding together two functions, representing the two Kekulé structures, and adding other terms, to make the wave function approximate the true wave function for the molecule more closely, or it may be constructed without explicit introduction of the wave functions representing the two Kekulé structures. It might be possible to develop an alternative simple way of discussing the structure of the amide group, for example, that would have permitted chemists to predict its properties, such as planarity; but in fact no simple way of discussing this group other than the way given above, involving resonance between two valence-bond structures, has been discovered, and it seems likely that the discussion of complex molecules in terms of resonance among two or more valence-bond structures will continue in the future to be useful to chemists, as it has been during the past twenty years.

The convenience and usefulness of the concept of resonance in the discussion of chemical problems are so great as to make the disadvantage of the element of arbitrariness of little significance. Also, it must not be forgotten that the element of arbitrariness occurs in essentially the same way in the simple structure theory of organic chemistry as in the theory of resonance—there is the same use of idealized, hypothetical structural elements. In the resonance discussion of the benzene molecule the two Kekulé structures have to be described as hypothetical: it is not possible to synthesize molecules with one or the other of the two Kekulé structures. In the same way, however, the concept of the carbon-carbon single bond is an idealization. The benzene molecule has its own structure, which cannot be exactly composed of structural elements from other molecules. The propane molecule also has its own structure, which cannot be composed of structural elements from other molecules—it is not possible to isolate a portion of the propane molecule, involving parts of two carbon atoms and perhaps two electrons in between them, and say that this portion of the propane molecule is the carbon-carbon single bond, identical with a portion of the ethane molecule. The description of the propane molecule as involving carbon-carbon single bonds and carbon-hydrogen single bonds is arbitrary; the concepts themselves are idealizations, in the same way as the concept of the Kekulé structures that are described as contributing to the normal state of the benzene molecule. Chemists have found that the simple structure theory of organic chemistry and also the resonance theory are valuable, despite their use of idealizations and their arbitrary character.

Other extensions of the theory of the chemical bond made in recent years involve the concept of fractional bonds. Twenty-five years ago it was discovered that a simple theory of complex crystals with largely ionic structures, such as the silicate minerals, can be developed on the basis of the assumption that each cation or metal atom divides its charge or valence equally among the anions that are coordinated about it. For example, in a crystal of topaz, $Al_2SiO_4F_2$, each silicon atom is surrounded by a tetrahedron of four oxygen atoms, and each aluminum atom is surrounded by a tetrahedron of four oxygen atoms, and each aluminum atom is surrounded by an octahedron of four oxygen atoms and two fluorine atoms. The valence of silicon, 4, is assumed to be divided among four bonds, which then have the bond number 1—they are single bonds. The valence of aluminum, 3, is divided among six bonds, each of which is a half bond. A stable structure results when the atoms are arranged in such a way that each anion, oxygen or fluorine, forms bonds equal to its valence. In topaz each oxygen atom forms one single bond with silicon and two half bonds with aluminum. The distribution of the valences hence then corresponds to the bivalence of oxygen and the univalence of fluorine. It was pointed out by W. L. Bragg that if the metal atoms are idealized as cations (Si^{+++++} and Al^{+++}) and the oxygen and fluorine atoms as anions (O^- and F^-), this distribution corresponds to having the shortest possible lines of force between the cations and the anions—the lines of force need to reach only from a cation to an immediately adjacent anion, which forms part of its coordination polyhedron. Occasionally ionic crystals are found in which there are small deviations from this requirement, but only rarely are the deviations larger than one quarter of a valence unit.

Another application of the concept of fractional valence bonds has been made in the field of metals and alloys. In the usual quantum mechanical discussion of metals, initiated by W. Pauli (*Z. Physik, 41* 84 (1927)) and Sommerfeld (*Naturwiss., 15*, 825 (1927)), the assumption was made that only a small number of electrons contribute significantly to the binding together of the metal atoms. For example, it was customary to assume that only one electron, occupying a $4s$ orbital, is significantly involved in the copper-copper bonds in the metal copper. Sixteen years ago an analysis of the magnetic properties of the transition metal was made that indicated that the number of bonding electrons in the transition metals is much larger, of the order of magnitude of six. Iron, for example, can be described as having six valence electrons, which occupy hybrid d^3sp^2 orbitals. The six bonds, corresponding to these six valence electrons, resonate among the fourteen positions connecting an iron atom with its fourteen nearest neighbors. The bonds to the eight nearest neighbors have bond number approximately 5/8, and those to the six slightly more distant neighbors have bond number 1/6. In gamma iron, where each atom is surrounded by twelve equally distant neighbors, the bonds are half bonds. The concept that the structure of metals and intermetallic compounds can be described in terms of valence bonds that resonate among alternative positions, aided by an extra orbital on most or all of the atoms (the metallic orbital), has been found of value in the discussion of the properties of these substances. The resonating-bond theory of metals is supported especially strongly by the consideration of interatomic distances in metals and intermetallic compounds.

The iron atom has eight electrons outside of the argon shell of eighteen. Six of these electrons are assumed, in the resonating–valence-bond theory, to be valence electrons, and the remaining two are atomic electrons, occupying $3d$ orbitals, and contributing two Bohr magnetons to the magnetic moment of the atom. A theory of the ferromagnetism of iron has recently been developed, in which, as suggested by Zener (*Phys. Rev., 81,* 440 (1951)), the interaction producing the Weiss field in the ferromagnetic metal is an interaction of the spin moments of the atomic electrons and uncoupled spins of some of the valence electrons. It has been found possible to use spectroscopic energy values to predict the number of uncoupled valence electrons, and hence the saturation magnetic moment for iron: the calculation lead to 0.26 uncoupled valence electrons per atom, and saturation magnetic moment 2.26 Bohr magnetons, which might be subject to correction by 2 or 3 percent because of the contribution of orbital moment. The experimental value is 2.22. A calculated value of the Curie temperature in rough agreement with experiment is also obtained.

The valence theory of metals and intermetallic compounds is still in a rather unsatisfactory state. It is not yet possible to make predictions about the composition and properties of intermetallic compounds with even a small fraction of the assurance with which they can be made about organic compounds and ordinary inorganic compounds. We may, however, hope that there will be significant progress in the attack on this problem during the next few years.

Let us now return to the subject of the structural chemistry of organic substances, especially the complex substances that occur in living organisms, such as proteins. Recent work in this field has shown the value of the use of structural arguments that go beyond those of the classical structure theory of organic chemistry. The interatomic distances and bond angles in the polypeptide chains of proteins are precisely known, the bond distances to within about 0.02 Å and the bond angles to within about 2°. It is known that the amide groups must retain their planarity; the atoms are expected not to deviate from the planar configuration by more than perhaps 0.05 Å. There is rotational freedom about the single bonds connecting the alpha carbon atom with the adjacent amide carbon and nitrogen atoms, but there are restrictions on the configurations of the polypeptide chain that can be achieved by rotations about these bonds: atoms of different parts of the chain must not approach one another so closely as to introduce large steric repulsion, and in general the N-H and O atoms of different amide groups must be so located relative to one another as to permit the formation of hydrogen bonds, with N-H⋯ O distance equal to 2.79±0.10 Å and with the oxygen atom not far from the

N-H axis. These requirements are stringent ones. Their application to a proposed hydrogen-bonded structure of a poly-peptide chain cannot in general be made by the simple method of drawing a structural formula; instead, extensive numerical calculations must be carried out, or a model must be constructed. For the more complex structures, such as those that are now under consideration for the polypeptide chains of collagen and gelatin, the analytical treatment is so complex as to resist successful execution, and only the model method can be used. In order that the principles of modern structural chemistry may be applied with the power that their reliability justifies, molecular models must be constructed with great accuracy. For example, molecular models on the scale 2.5 cm=I Å have to be made with a precision better than 0.01 cm.

We may, I believe, anticipate that the chemist of the future who is interested in the structure of proteins, nucleic acids, polysaccharides, and other complex substances with high molecular weight will come to rely upon a new structural chemistry, involving precise geometrical relationships among the atoms in the molecules and the rigorous application of the new structural principles, and that great progress will be made, through this technique, in the attack, by chemical methods, on the problems of biology and medicine.

PAULING AND BEADLE

George W. Gray

❦❦❦

*In the mid-1930s, Linus Pauling began thinking about the chemistry of
living systems, focusing especially on the structures and activities of
hemoglobin and antibodies. After World War II he outlined a grand plan to
ally chemistry and biology in a joint attack on the molecules of life, and led
an effort at Caltech to bring in a biologist with standing equal to his own in
order to make it happen. The biologist he chose was the brilliant geneticist
George Beadle. The following piece, written by the eminent science writer
George Gray and published first in 1949 by **Scientific American**, describes
the outcome of their partnership and provides a good overview of the state of
molecular biology just a few years before the discovery of the structure of
DNA.*

More than four centuries have passed since Paracelsus of
Hohenheim gave scientific medicine its charter in his
celebrated hypothesis: *The human body is a conglomeration of
chymical matters; when these are deranged illness results, and naught but chymical
medicines may cure the same.*

It has taken human beings a long time to learn even a small part of
these "chymical matters." As recently as 1849 the molecular weight of
water was so uncertainly known that this principal ingredient of the body's
conglomeration was still being written as HO by many chemists. Indeed,
the idea that each atom has a definite combining power was yet to be
accepted. Now the situation has changed. Biochemistry is today the
principal battleground of science's attack on disease. The wealth of
physiologically useful chemicals whose identification came out of these
studies—such compounds as the vitamins, the hormones, and the
antibiotics, to name but three groups—provides powerful evidence in
support of the Paracelsian doctrine and has spurred research in hundreds of
universities, medical schools, and institutes.

A recent visit to the California Institute of Technology gave me the
opportunity to see at first hand a striking example of the present-day
partnership of chemistry and biology—a union which has been solemnized
at the institute in a large new joint project of its chemical and biological

divisions. The chemists and biologists here are not consciously seeking for new vitamins, new hormones, new antibiotics, or any other specific nutritional or therapeutic agent. Their quest is for more fundamental knowledge. They are conducting a systematic search into the ways in which the body's molecules behave. And because the living process is always associated with huge molecules comprising hundreds, thousands, and even tens of thousands of atoms in a single structure, the program at the institute is being focused primarily on these giant molecules. Their attractions and repulsions, their combinations and modifications, their breakdown into smaller units and the joining of these into new combinations—it is such goings-on that the Pasadena scientists are prying into with all the techniques that chemistry can bring to reinforce those of biology. Their inquiry is directed at the most fundamental of all biological processes: reproduction, nutrition, and growth, each studied at the molecular level.

Biochemistry has two avenues of approach. One may enter it from either the biological side or the chemical, and usually the main strength of a research program comes from one or the other of these two directions, seldom from both. A remarkable aspect of the dual project at Pasadena is its balance. This is not a case of a biological laboratory adding a chemical department to its facilities, nor yet that of a chemical laboratory taking an interest in biological problems. It is, rather, a joining of forces between two coordinate divisions, each of which is a leader in its field.

The Division of Chemistry at the California Institute was founded by Arthur A. Noyes, who had previously served as acting president of the Massachusetts Institute of Technology. He was a physical chemist; his emphasis was on the inorganic aspects of the science, and aspiring chemists from all over America came to California to study the fundamentals under the master.

Among these students was Linus Pauling, a recent graduate of the Oregon Agricultural College. Perhaps Noyes saw in him the man he wanted to train as his successor. At all events, the young Oregonian became a favorite pupil, spent three years of advanced study under Noyes, and was so imbued with the physical aspects of chemistry that he seriously considered specializing in atomic physics. A Guggenheim Fellowship enabled Pauling to spend a year in Munich with one of the world's leading theoretical physicists, Arnold Sommerfeld, and these studies were continued the following year with Niels Bohr at Copenhagen and Erwin Schrodinger at Zurich. But the problems that made the strongest appeal to him were in chemistry; so Pauling remained a chemist, meanwhile continuing his investigation of the forces that operate between atoms and molecules, a study which resulted in his great book, *The Nature of the Chemical Bond*. The California Institute of Technology made him a full professor in 1931, when he was only thirty years of age, and following Noyes' death in 1936, Pauling was appointed to succeed him as chairman of the division and director of the chemical laboratories.

"I was a physical chemist," explained Dr. Pauling,

> *with this dominating interest in the forces which cause atoms to join into molecules and molecules to react with one another. The forces are electrical, of course, and depend on the number of protons and electrons present and the order of their arrangement in the structures. This is essentially a physical subject; or, rather, it belongs to that borderland where chemistry and physics merge. In these investigations I naturally selected the simpler molecular structures to work with, such as the metals and inorganic compounds; but in the course of the research I also tested an organic substance whose molecule is large and complicated—the hemoglobin, which gives the blood cells their red color. I found that in arterial blood the hemoglobin was repelled by a magnet, but in venous blood it was attracted. This led to a study of the chemical bond between the hemoglobin and the oxygen which it picks up in the lungs. I wanted to consult someone who had specialized on hemoglobin and found the authority in A. E. Mirsky of the Rockefeller Institute for Medical Research. Mirsky came to the California Institute for a year, and we collaborated on a study which resulted in a joint paper.*

This paper attracted the attention of Karl Landsteiner, the discoverer of blood types, and Landsteiner asked Dr. Pauling if his theory of the chemical bond could throw light on a certain antibody reaction. Landsteiner's request introduced Pauling to the highly complicated specialty of immunology. The two men became close friends and frequent conferees on the subject. "From that time on," said Pauling, "I gave a great deal of thought to the chemical aspects of immunology, trying to understand, in terms of the chemical bond, how an antibody neutralizes a virus or other antigen." By 1939 he had arrived at a chemical picture of the reaction and reported his results to the American Chemical Society as "A Theory of the Structure and Process of Formation of Antibodies."

Thus under Pauling the chemistry division at the California Institute added to its program the investigation of hemoglobin, antibodies, and other molecular giants that originate only in living systems, while still continuing the basic work in the chemistry of inorganic and simpler organic substances.

Meanwhile a transition was also taking place in the institute's division of biology. This division had been organized in 1928 by Thomas Hunt Morgan, who had left the chair of experimental zoology at Columbia University to pioneer this new planting in California. Like Noyes in physical chemistry, Morgan was already world famous in genetics; and his coming to Pasadena brought several strong additions to the faculty, most of them geneticists, and attracted from all parts of the country students who wished to specialize in this science.

Genetics lends itself to mathematical treatment more easily than most biological sciences, and perhaps it is rightly called the most "physical" of the branches of biology. Certainly Morgan had a strong urge toward

Pauling teaching at Osaka University, March 1955

collaboration between biology on the one hand, and chemistry, physics, and mathematics on the other. After Morgan's retirement in 1941, the biological division was administered for several years by a temporary staff committee. Toward the end of 1945 a successor to Morgan was found in the person of Stanford University's professor of genetics, George W. Beadle.

Beadle's history had closely paralleled that of Pauling. Both men had been National Research Fellows; and as Pauling had come to the California Institute to study under Noyes, so Beadle had come to study under Morgan. It is also significant that at the time when Pauling was turning his attention more and more to the biological molecules, Beadle was becoming interested in chemistry as the handmaiden of genetics. During his ten years at Stanford he had devoted most of his research effort to experiments with the bread mold, *Neurospora*, and was able to demonstrate in this lowly fungus that the processes of nutrition are directed by the genes. Perhaps it is not undue praise to say that Beadle's work with the mold did more than any other research to establish the chemical nature of genic action.

With chemical research in charge of a biologically minded chemist, and with biological research placed under the direction of this chemically minded geneticist, the California Institute now offered an unusual opportunity. The divisions of biology and chemistry immediately prepared a prospectus outlining "a joint program of research on the fundamental problems of biology and medicine." The program would occupy fifteen years and would involve considerable enlargement of staff. Application was made to philanthropic foundations for support. It was estimated that about five years would be required to bring the program to its full operating capacity. As interim grants to assist the work during the "retooling period," the Rockefeller Foundation appropriated $50,000 in 1946 and an equal amount in 1947, following these in 1948 by a long-term appropriation of $700,000 to be paid in annual installments of $100,000. Thus $800,000 has been committed by this one agency within the last three years. In addition, the project has attracted support from other sources. It is getting $60,000 a year from the National Foundation for Infantile Paralysis, and lesser grants from the Nutrition Foundation and the Hermann Frasch Foundation. The work occupies an important place in the budget of the institute, and by 1951 it is expected that this research will entail annual expenditures of $400,000.

Of the two essentials to successful research—people and equipment— the human element is of course the more important. What makes the situation at the California Institute challenging is the presence there of the two staffs of scientists with their already integrated teamwork of biology and chemistry. In 1946, when the joint program was projected, the staff in biology, including all workers from professors to research fellows and assistants, was made up of thirty-two persons; and the corresponding groups in chemistry totaled eighty-six. At present biology is employing the services of seventy-nine and chemistry ninety-seven, a grand total of one hundred seventy-six for the two divisions, or an increase of 49 per cent over the status of three years ago.

Among the recent staff additions are John G. Kirkwood in chemistry and Max Delbrück in biology. Kirkwood is in the distinguished line of physical chemists. He was Todd Professor of Chemistry at Cornell in 1948 when called to the newly established Arthur A. Noyes professorship of physical chemistry at the California Institute. Like Dr. Pauling, he has a predilection for the giant molecules, and recently developed a new type of electrophoresis apparatus with which to study their properties. Tests made at Pasadena within the last few months show that the Kirkwood apparatus will separate the proteins of blood plasma to a finer degree than any other device heretofore used.

Delbrück is a physicist turned biologist. His primary training was in Germany in theoretical physics, but he became interested in bacteriology and came to the U.S. as a Rockefeller Fellow in biology. He has made many contributions to our knowledge of bacteriophages, the invisible viruses which prey upon bacteria. The viruses occupy a borderland between the living and the nonliving, between biology and chemistry, and study of them constitutes an important part of the joint program. Delbrück joined the institute faculty in 1947, coming from Vanderbilt University.

Among the specialized researchers on the combined staffs is Laszlo Zechmeister, formerly of the University of Pécs, Hungary, who came to the Institute as professor of organic chemistry in 1940. Zechmeister is an authority in chromatography—an amazing technique for separating organic pigments out of mixtures—and his specialty is contributing directly to the joint research program. Another worker is Dan H. Campbell, an immunochemist, brought here in 1942 from the University of Chicago. Campbell has been collaborating with Pauling in an effort to synthesize antibodies by direct chemical means—a daring project which, if successful, may revolutionize the control of infectious disease.

The plant and equipment of the combined divisions are already impressive, and additions are planned. Besides the main chemical and biological laboratory buildings, which adjoin each other, there are three off-campus laboratories of plant physiology, greenhouses, a ten-acre farm devoted to the study of genetics in corn, a marine laboratory at Corona del Mar on the Pacific shore, and a large new underground animal house on the institute campus. Construction of a new $2-million building, which will be used for the joint chemistry-biology program and will increase the research quarters of the two divisions by 75 per cent, may begin this year.

"We are seeking to uncover the principles that govern fundamental processes of life," explained Beadle. "If we could do so, the solution of practical problems in medicine would follow inevitably." Therefore, the researchers are studying genes, antibodies, viruses, hormones, biological pigments, and related structures. How does each behave biologically, and how can this behavior be accounted for chemically? Chemical behavior is related directly to the molecular structure of the reacting substances: therefore one of the principal objectives of the program is chemical analysis. What are the building blocks that enter into the construction of genes and the other molecules? How are these building blocks put together, in what order of arrangement, and what are the resulting size and shape of the structures?

"Science is still far from completely analyzing these biological agents," said Beadle, "but the investigations tend to show that the molecular form known as protein is the key structure. Apparently most of the bodies that we are studying in our program are either simple proteins or conjugated proteins."

Simple proteins are simple only by contrast with the vaster architecture of the conjugated molecules. Actually, a "simple" protein consists of hundreds, sometimes thousands, of atoms. When placed beside familiar inorganic molecules, such as those of water, sulfuric acid, ammonia, and table salt, even the smallest protein molecule is like a whale among minnows. But a protein is simple in this respect: when reactive agents are applied to break down its molecule, the molecule does not separate into its hundreds or thousands of individual atoms, but divides into characteristic groups of atoms which the chemists know as amino acids. It is as though when a house was demolished, it broke up into basement, rooms, and attic, rather than into individual bricks and boards. Twenty-three different amino acids have been found in proteins, and the possible combinations that may be formed from these twenty-three building blocks run into millions. It is no wonder that proteins occur in the wide variety which makes one person's meat another person's poison. But a number of the most familiar and wholesome substances of the body's equipment are simple proteins: pepsin and many of the other digestive enzymes, insulin and many of the hormones, albumin, fibrinogen, and many other components of the blood plasma.

The conjugated proteins represent a further step in structure. After a simple protein molecule has been built by the joining together of molecules of different amino acids, it may hook on to a pigment and form a conjugated protein such as the hemoglobin of the blood. Or it may attach itself to a complicated chain of sugar molecules known as a polysaccharide and form a conjugated protein of another type, such as the mucin of saliva. Another possibility is the joining of a protein with a vitamin—the enzyme carboxylase is of this type. Finally, proteins may be linked with nucleic acids to form nucleoproteins—and here we reach the ultimate of giantism among molecules. For if a simple protein is pictured as a whale among the minnows, a nucleoprotein may be likened to a leviathan with a form so tremendous that it might swallow the whale. Nucleic acid alone is a large structure—some of its molecules contain 160,000 atoms—and when units of this size combine with units the size of proteins, the combination is truly enormous. Some of the viruses which Wendell M. Stanley isolated in his studies at the Rockefeller Institute were identified as nucleoproteins and had a molecular weight up to eight million times that of hydrogen. Such structures comprise nearly a million atoms.

It is believed that both viruses and genes are nucleoproteins, while the antibodies are thought to be simple proteins consisting of chains of amino-acid residues folded together in a certain way. These folded chains of interlinked amino-acid residues are called polypeptides. According to Pauling's theory, countless numbers of them are afloat in the bloodstream; and whenever they encounter certain bacteria, viruses, or other foreign bodies in the blood, the mutual attractions between the two cause the chain to approach and attach itself to the invader. The action of the chemical bond thus causes the polypeptide chain to fold up and overlay a surface area of the microbe, forming a shield or encrustation which blocks the latter's activity.

"The genes, we believe, exercise an overruling control on all these activities," said Beadle.

> They do this, we think, by serving as the master patterns for the many proteins which function in the processes of life. Thus, there is probably a gene which serves as the template for the body's manufacture of insulin, another which provides the mold for pepsin, and so for albumin, fibrinogen, the polypeptide chain that forms antibodies, and all the rest.
>
> There are several thousand genes distributed among the forty-eight chromosomes of the human body cell, a number sufficient to provide templates for the thousands of big molecules required for health. Diabetes, on this theory, is a consequence of a missing or defective gene, leaving its victim unable to manufacture insulin. Similarly, the bleeders or hemophiliacs lack the normal gene for manufacturing a substance which is an essential component of the blood-clotting equipment.
>
> Our experiments with the bread mold, Neurospora, have demonstrated this genic control of the biochemical processes in numerous instances. We found, for example, that after exposure to ultraviolet radiation, Neurospora lost its ability to make certain vitamins. The genes which controlled this manufacture had been destroyed, and thereafter Neurospora languished unless these vitamins were supplied in its food. Similarly, Sterling Emerson of our laboratory found that a minute change in its genes caused the Neurospora to accept as food a compound that before the change had acted as a poison. Indeed, after mutation, the

Neurospora *would not grow unless fed a sulfonamide which previously had blocked growth and caused death.*

As a step toward understanding the proteins, the chemists are working first on the amino acids, trying to map precisely the structure of these protein building blocks. Robert B. Corey spent a year and a half analyzing the configuration of glycine, the simplest of the amino acids. He bombarded it with x-rays, and measured the angles at which the rays bounced off the molecule. In this way he not only determined the position of each carbon atom, each oxygen, and each hydrogen in the glycine, but actually measured the distances between the atoms. After completing this job, Corey went on to alanine, which is larger and more complicated. The experience he had gained on glycine stood him in good stead, and he required only a year to work out the exact pattern of alanine. He has now taken up a still more complicated amino acid, threonine. Step by step the group plans to move from the amino acids to more complicated structures, with the hope that eventually they may be able to dissect some of the proteins, perhaps even nucleoproteins, into their integral parts.

The strongest impression that one brings back from a visit to the institute team is the magnitude of the task of analyzing these invisible molecules. Henry A. Rowland used to tell his students at Johns Hopkins University that the mercury atom must be at least as complicated as a grand piano. Following this analogy one might say that the biological molecule, such as a unit of insulin, for example, is probably as complicated as a symphony orchestra. The grand piano of mercury has now been completely mapped in terms of electrons, protons, and neutrons, and the physicists are even able by the bombardment technique to make mercury from other elements. But the full symphony of insulin remains a chemical enigma. No one yet has analyzed it, and of course no synthesis of insulin has been achieved. Fortunately medical workers are able to use biologically active molecules without knowing very much about them; but they crave the control of processes and results which fundamental knowledge would give. Along this road, the scientists believe, lies the unmasking of stubborn mysteries: the elucidation of cancer, of aging, of the divine spark itself—the search for fundamental knowledge thus becomes the most practical of all biochemical quests.

SICKLE-CELL ANEMIA
AND THE ORIGINS OF MOLECULAR BIOLOGY

Bruno Strasser

After working on the molecular structure of simple substances, Pauling had the idea as early as 1934 of explaining the properties of hemoglobin in terms of its molecular structure—even though it is a very complicated molecule of 10,000 atoms. Karl Landsteiner at the Rockefeller Institute asked Pauling how he would explain the properties of antibodies in terms of their molecular structure. Pauling discovered that he and Landsteiner thought about the serologic problem in very different ways.

In November 1949, an article appeared in *Science* which would eventually play a fundamental role in the establishment of molecular biology and molecular medicine. Linus Pauling and his collaborators published a paper with the unusual title "Sickle-cell Anemia, a Molecular Disease," showing that the hemoglobin molecules of patients suffering from this deadly hereditary affliction had a different electrical charge than those of healthy patients. The paper had a powerful impact on the biomedical community and the public at large. Indeed, it soon became a "citation classic."

Pauling's paper was important and novel in two different ways. On one hand, it showed for the very first time that the cause of a disease could be traced to an altered *molecular structure,* raising hopes that all diseases might eventually be explained in a similar fashion. On the other hand, since this disease was known to be heritable, the paper argued that genes *determined precisely* the structure of proteins. These two points have become so obvious today, that it might seem surprising that they have a history.

Linus Pauling, who spent more than forty years at the California Institute of Technology, exemplifies better than anyone else the emerging "molecular vision of life" of the middle third of our century. As early as 1956, for example, Pauling endorsed the view that "man is simply a collection of molecules," and "can be understood in terms of molecules"— a view that gave him "great pleasure and satisfaction." Indeed, after his pioneering studies on the nature of the chemical bond in the 1920s and

Linus Pauling lecturing on sickle-cell anemia, Tokyo, February 1955

1930s, which earned him a world-wide reputation, Pauling started to investigate molecules of biological interest—which at that time essentially meant proteins. As he put it in 1937, "the secret of life itself [is] how a protein molecule is able to form, from an amorphous substrate, new protein molecules which are made after its own image."

Pauling's attention was drawn to sickle-cell anemia, a hereditary disease found mainly among people of African descent, in 1945 by William B. Castle, a clinician from Harvard Medical School. Both were serving on the Medical Advisory Committee which assisted Vannevar Bush in the elaboration of his famous report, *Science, the Endless Frontier.* Pauling had been involved in hemoglobin studies in war-related research on blood substitutes, and had investigated the magnetic properties of hemoglobin since 1935. He was thus already familiar with hemoglobin when Castle told him that only venous—deoxygenated—blood of sickle-cell anemia patients showed, upon microscopic inspection, sickle-shaped red blood cells. This indicated that the hemoglobin molecule was probably involved in the sickling process, causing the cells to acquire their distorted shape. Pauling then thought that for these patients, "perhaps the Hb [hemoglobin] molecule changes shape." He had been searching avidly for nearly ten years for a medical problem to solve in order to demonstrate the power of his physico-chemical approach to biology and medicine. Like many other scientists, he was also eager to convert wartime support—from the Office of Scientific Research and Development (OSRD), for example—into peace-time money, along the lines of Bush's *Endless Frontier,* which called for a more obvious relevance of scientific research to American public needs. Thus, the sickle-cell anemia project represented for Pauling a timely convergence of political, financial and intellectual interests.

Pauling assigned the sickle-cell anemia project to Harvey A. Itano, a young M.D. hired in 1946, as a thesis topic for his Ph.D. Drawing on the knowledge and resources of several medical practitioners, Itano tried, without success, several different physical and chemical methods to distinguish normal from sickle-cell anemia hemoglobin. He then turned to electrophoresis, a then-new technique designed to separate molecules according to their electrical charge, which had already been used to analyze blood proteins. Caltech was one of the few institutes in the world to own an electrophoresis apparatus, an instrument not yet commercially available at that time. This proved to be a good choice, and Itano was able, in 1948, to find a slight electrophoretic difference between normal and sickle-cell anemia hemoglobins.

Not only was Pauling's group able to demonstrate that patients with sickle-cell anemia had a different hemoglobin than healthy persons, but he also showed that blood taken from persons suffering from "sicklemia," a milder form of the disease, contained a mixture of normal and pathological hemoglobin—in about equal amounts. They thus concluded that "sicklemia" reflected a heterozygous condition and sickle-cell anemia, a homozygous condition. They reached this conclusion apparently independently of James Neel at Ann Arbor, who, on genetic grounds, arrived at the same result, which he published a few months earlier.

By the time Pauling *et al.*'s paper appeared, it was well known that human hemoglobins (adult and fetal) differed electrophoretically, and several diseases had been correlated with altered electrophoretic patterns of blood proteins. So what was new about the *Science* paper? Beadle and Tatum had elaborated the "one gene-one enzyme" hypothesis in the 1940s, but it was not yet clear what it was that genes control, beyond the absence or presence of a particular enzyme. Pauling's sickle-cell anemia work demonstrated that genes could alter *qualitatively* the structure of proteins— in this case, with dramatic consequences for human health. It also proposed a causal link—not a mere correlation—"between the existence of 'defective' hemoglobin molecules and the pathological consequences of sickle-cell disease."

But the sickle-cell anemia success did much more. Under Pauling's energetic advertisement in numerous speeches and papers, the discovery became emblematic of how basic science could solve medical problems. In 1956, for example, he asserted, "I believe that chemistry can be applied effectively to medical problems, and that through this application we may look forward to significant progress in the field of medicine, as it is transformed from its present empirical form into the science of molecular medicine." Immediately after the 1949 paper, Pauling tried to establish a medical research institute at Caltech devoted to "molecular medicine." Public and private funding agencies remained skeptical of Pauling's approach, however, and he was unable to attract the necessary funds.

Based on their knowledge of the molecular nature of sickle-cell anemia, Pauling and Itano proposed several treatments to prevent sickling. After

Pauling was a more important figure in molecular biology than is sometimes realized. Not only did he make certain key discoveries (that sickle cell anemia is a molecular disease, for example), but he had the correct theoretical approach to these biological problems.

Francis Crick (from What Mad Pursuit)

two years of clinical trials performed by George Burch, a physician from New Orleans, the results turned out to be disappointing and were never published. Unfortunately, this would not be the last of such failures. Even today, our extremely detailed understanding of the molecular etiology of sickle-cell anemia has led to new diagnostic possibilities, but little in the way of significant improvements in therapy.

In the 1950s, Itano and others moved on to generalize their approach to other blood pathologies. But for Pauling, the main question was to pinpoint the origin of the electrophoretic difference—presumably a difference in the amino acid composition of the normal and pathological hemoglobins. With the chemist Walter A. Schroeder, he performed chromatographic analyses of normal and sickle-cell anemia hemoglobin and was surprised to find, in 1950, that there was no difference in amino acid content, which could explain the electrophoresis result—a conclusion soon confirmed by others. Pauling thus thought that the electrophoretic difference resulted "from a difference in folding of the polypeptide chain." With the immunologist Dan Campbell, he found a serological difference between the two forms of hemoglobin. Furthermore, when denatured, hemoglobin no longer showed the electrophoretic difference. The most likely conclusion from these pieces of evidence was that the *same* polypeptide was folded, under genetic control, in two *different* ways which affected the electrophoretic mobility. This conclusion fitted perfectly in the "molding model" of protein synthesis. In the following years, Pauling often used the example of sickle-cell anemia hemoglobin to support his views on protein synthesis. In 1954, for example, in his Harvey lecture, he said "the gene responsible for the sickle-cell abnormality is one that determines the nature of the folding of polypeptide chains, rather than their composition."

This conception of protein synthesis thus gained unsuspected support from the results of sickle-cell anemia research. However, by the end of the 1950s, this conception would be completely abandoned, and replaced by the model we have adopted today, whereby genes determine the amino-acid sequences of proteins, and do not serve to direct their three dimensional folding. In this reversal, sickle-cell anemia research was again involved. Thus the case of sickle-cell anemia conveniently highlights the terms of this debate, which settled in the mid-1950s and only reopened recently, to some extent, with the discovery of chaperones.

Around 1950, the debate focused around the following questions: what determines the three dimensional structure of a protein? Does it "automatically" follow from its amino acid composition and sequence, or is some other component, genetic or non-genetic, involved in giving it its final configuration?

The idea that some substance other than the protein itself, such as the antigen for antibodies, the substrate for enzymes, or even the gene itself, was directing protein folding was favored by many researchers until the mid-1950s. Pauling, in a lecture held in 1948, summarized this theory of protein synthesis:

The mechanism of obtaining [immunological specificity] is one of moulding a plastic material, the coiling chain, into a die or mould, the surface of the antigen molecule. I believe that the same process of moulding of plastic materials into a configuration complementary to that of another molecule which serves as a template, is responsible for all biological specificity. I believe that the genes serve as the templates on which are moulded the enzymes which are responsible for the chemical characters of the organism.

Some people, however, had remained skeptical of Pauling and Schroeder's results. Francis Crick, for example, recalled that Schroeder's "method was in fact too crude to detect such a single change in amino acid composition. I clearly realized this at the time. ... I was convinced (perhaps rashly) that there would be a change in amino acid composition."

Such "moulding models" of protein synthesis were not advocated by "outsider" scientists, nor were they only theoretical speculations. Similar views were held around the same time by influential figures like the microbiologists Jacques Monod (Nobel prize in 1965) and Sol Spiegelman, the biochemists John Northrop (Nobel prize 1946), John Synge (Nobel prize 1952), and Felix Haurowitz, and the geneticist George Beadle (Nobel prize in 1958). The strongest empirical support for these ideas came from the study of antibody formation and enzymatic induction in bacteria.

Indeed, in 1957 big news came from Cambridge, England. Vernon Ingram, who had taken up Crick's skepticism, was able to point to a single amino acid difference between normal and sickle-cell hemoglobin that explained the electrophoretic difference. His success was the result of a new method he had devised, combining paper chromatography with electrophoresis for the separation of peptides—"fingerprinting," as he called it. The importance of this result went far beyond the etiology of a particular disease. Indeed, for the first time it was demonstrated, as Ingram wrote in 1957, that "an alteration in a Mendelian gene causes an alteration in the amino acid sequence of the corresponding polypeptide chain." He had brought the understanding of the role of genes one step further than Pauling. Not since the proposed double helix structure for DNA in 1953 had the research interests of geneticists, biochemists, and structuralists merged so closely in a single project.

Pauling immediately and radically changed his views about the mechanism of protein synthesis:

It is likely that the principal function of the gene involved in the manufacture of a protein is to determine the sequence of amino acids in the polypeptide chain of the protein molecules. ... it is probable that the polypeptide chain folds into its stable configuration automatically, that the stable configuration is determined by the amino-acid sequence.

This idea was forcefully elaborated by Crick as the "Central Dogma" in his famous 1957 lecture "On Protein Synthesis." It allowed many researchers to concentrate on how DNA sequences determine protein sequences, the "coding problem," or, to use Crick's new terminology, how DNA "information" is passed into protein.

Consensus spread rapidly. Indeed, when concluding the Cold Spring Harbor Symposia on Quantitative Biology of 1960, Jacques Monod and François Jacob (Nobel prize 1965) wrote:

> *A few years ago, the question was often debated whether any further (non-genetic) structural information needed to be furnished, or might conceivably be used in some cases, at the stage of tertiary folding in protein synthesis. [This] issue was not discussed during the conference, evidently because it is considered as settled.*

Sickle-cell anemia was not the only research line involved in this *denouement*. Most importantly, the work of Christian Anfinsen during the late 1950s and 1960s showed that denatured ribonuclease could regain its secondary and tertiary structure spontaneously, earning him the Nobel Prize for chemistry in 1972. Monod's model for enzymatic induction, where the substrate determined the enzyme's folding, was facing increasing conflicting experimental evidence, and started to be abandoned in the late 1950s, to be eventually replaced by the operon model. Similarly, the "molding model" of antibody formation, which Pauling had done much to popularize, was challenged by Frank Macfarlane Burnet (Nobel prize 1960) with his clonal selection theory of 1957, in which each cell produces antibodies with only one specificity. Joshua Lederberg (Nobel prize 1958) rapidly drew the conclusions for protein specificity, namely that antibodies with different specificities must have different amino acid sequences. Finally, the wider recognition during the 1950s that genes were nucleic acids, and not proteins, made it increasingly difficult to devise a mechanism by which they would act as three-dimensional templates for protein folding.

Thus, very different research programs, in biochemistry, immunology, genetics, physical chemistry, and hematology all converged in the second half of the 1950s to redefine one of the foundations of molecular biology: the relationships between sequences, structures, and functions. This shows how much what we today call "molecular biology" was, and still is, a highly interdisciplinary field, lacking methodological unity and resisting any subsumption under a coherent disciplinary label. Finally, this redefinition led to the primacy of sequences in explaining biological and pathological processes as well. The "Central Dogma," the genetic code, and finally the present excitement for sequencing and genomics, show how much this idea has become central in our understanding of life.

Just how it was that sequences of DNA, the hereditary material, determine the amino acid sequences of proteins—the "coding problem"— became a major focus of molecular biologists and biochemists in the following years. They deciphered the genetic code by 1966, and it was finally clear, as Crick put it, how DNA "information" was passed into protein. The "sequencing culture" has grown by leaps and bounds ever since, as shown by its most recent and visible example, the Human Genome Project. The sickle-cell anemia project represented a turning point in Pauling's career. From the mid-1950s, after he had received the Nobel Prize in chemistry (1954), he became increasingly involved in political activities, leaving him less time in the laboratory. He shifted his remaining research toward medical problems such as the molecular basis of mental deficiencies and his controversial vitamin C crusade. His medical research resonated with his peace activism, as in his claim that nuclear bomb testing was the source of an increased mutation rate, causing innumerable "molecular diseases."

The legacy of sickle-cell anemia research in the middle of our century can hardly be underestimated. It rapidly became a favorite example, in news editorials and textbooks, of how a molecular approach could explain biological and pathological processes. However, the story has often been told without regard to the fact that Pauling did not succeed simply by applying physical chemistry to a medical problem, but rather by relying on skills from the clinic as well as the laboratory, from biologists, biochemists, and physicians. Pauling's grand vision of molecularizing biology and medicine has been realized to an extent he could never have foreseen, even if our therapeutic power does not yet match our ever more profound understanding of the molecular basis of health and disease.

How I Developed an Interest in the Question of the Nature of Life

Linus Pauling

*In the spring of 1992, Pauling had completed a first draft of some material which was to make up a book that he proposed to call **The Nature of Life—Including My Life.** The book was to conclude with a chapter on this question: Do mind and body form one basic reality, or are there two such realities? The following excerpt was intended to be the first chapter of that book.*

Even as a child, I wanted to understand the world about me. As a small boy walking along in the rain in Portland, Oregon, I looked through my umbrella at an arc light about a block away. I saw a white spot in the direction of the arc light and also some colors, a sequence of violet, indigo, blue, green, yellow, orange, red, and I knew it was called a spectrum, with the sequence of colors in a rainbow. There were eight of these spectra: four rather close in to the white spot, one to the right, one to the left, one above, and one below, and four others, somewhat farther out, in between these directions. I puzzled over this observation. It is my memory that I did not have an idea about the cause of these spectra, but that I thought that I probably would learn the explanation later on, in the course of my studies of various subjects in school.

I think that for a number of years I expected to learn more about nature and how various natural phenomena are explained by continuing my studies and finding out what understanding human beings had amassed to explain their observations of the universe. It was not until several years later, beginning when I was studying chemical engineering in Oregon Agricultural College in Corvallis and bursting upon me almost explosively in the fall of 1922 when I became a graduate student in the California Institute of Technology, that I realized that I myself might discover something new about the nature of the world, have some new ideas that contributed to better understanding of the universe. For seventy years the motive to obtain greater understanding has dominated my life.

Up to 1929 I accepted as fact the existence of human beings and other living organisms and the astonishing capabilities that these organisms have. So far as I can remember, I did not make any effort to develop a real understanding of the nature of life until 1929.

When I was eleven I began to collect insects and to read about the different families of insects, but I did not find entomology very satisfying intellectually. When I was twelve years old I read about minerals and collected a few. Minerals interested me more than rocks. At that time I occasionally walked by a big house on Hawthorne Avenue, less than a mile from my home. This big house, in the center of an acre or two of land, was surrounded by a newly built rock wall. The rocks were granite, and there were pieces of granite, two or three inches in diameter, lying on the ground, after the stonemason who built the wall had chipped them from the granite blocks. I picked up some of these granite chips and looked at them carefully. There were in the rock three kinds of crystal grains, white or transparent grains, pink grains, and black grains, the black grains being flat plates. These grains were for the most part around an eighth or a quarter of an inch in diameter. From my reading I knew that the white or transparent grains were quartz, silicon dioxide, the pink grains were a form of feldspar, and the black grains were mica.

I was curious about granite and other rocks, but it seemed to me that before I could understand rocks I needed to understand minerals. Surely if I had an understanding of the nature of quartz, feldspar, and mica, their structure and their properties, that understanding would be basic to an understanding of the nature of rocks. Accordingly for a year I read about minerals and attempted to develop some understanding of their nature.

One thing that I learned from reading books about mineralogy was that minerals have a definite chemical composition. For example, the mineral quartz was described as silicon dioxide, with one atom of silicon combined with two atoms of oxygen. I then became especially interested in chemistry, as the result of being shown some chemical reactions, in which one substance changed into another substance or more than one other substance, by my best friend, Lloyd Jeffress, who was just my age (thirteen at the time).

I soon learned the elements of chemistry. About fifty years earlier (around 1865), chemists in Germany, England, and France had decided that the atoms in substances generally can be described as forming bonds with one another. It was accepted that the hydrogen atom can form one bond, the oxygen atom can form two bonds, the carbon atom can form four bonds, and the silicon atom can form four bonds. For fifty years after 1865 chemists had made great progress in understanding the properties of substances by discussing the various ways in which atoms can be attached to one another by these chemical bonds. It had been found that most of the substances in living organisms are compounds of carbon. For this reason, compounds of carbon began to be called organic compounds, and this usage has continued. Some remarkable ideas had been formulated.

First, it was suggested that the four bonds formed by a carbon atom are directed in space toward the corners of a regular or nearly regular tetrahedron. This idea, the idea of a tetrahedral carbon atom, explained in a reasonable way some of the remarkable properties of certain organic compounds, and it was accepted by most chemists. Chemists were able to assign structural formulas to the molecules of many organic compounds, showing the atoms as circles or symbols connected by lines representing the chemical bonds. Chemists, especially organic chemists, make much use of these chemical formulas in planning and interpreting their experimental work, and as a result the science of chemistry progressed very rapidly.

In 1919 I developed a great interest in the question of the nature of the chemical bond. Gilbert Newton Lewis, a great chemist who was the dean of the college of chemistry in the University of California in Berkeley, had in 1916 published a paper in which he said that the chemical bond consists of two electrons that are held jointly by the two atoms that the bond connects. I read his paper and papers written a couple of years later by another great chemist, Irving Langmuir, and from that time on I strove to get a better understanding of the structures of the crystals of quartz, feldspar, and mica in granite and of other inorganic substances.

I continue to be astonished at how great a change has taken place in our understanding of the nature of the world during the last seventy years. In the early 1920s I taught students in Oregon Agricultural College and California Institute of Technology who were beginning their study of chemistry. I told them that hydrogen has valence 1 (can form one chemical bond) and that carbon has valence 4, and that we can think of these atoms as having hooks on them, equal in number to the valence, so that a chemical bond would be formed between hydrogen and carbon by using the hydrogen hook to hook onto a carbon hook. Although I knew that Gilbert Newton Lewis had suggested that the hooks might be considered to be electrons, I do not think that I often mentioned this possibility.

Even Lewis did not make much effort to understand the properties of substances in relation to the formation of chemical bonds. For example, as late as 1923 he discussed the structure of quartz. He said that a quartz crystal is an aggregate of silicon dioxide molecules. Each molecule has a silicon atom using two of its valences to form a double bond to an oxygen atom, and the other two of its valences to form a double bond to another oxygen atom. He did not have anything to say about how these molecules interact with one another to make quartz as hard a substance as it is. Apparently the idea that quartz is a framework of atoms in which each silicon atom is surrounded by four other silicon atoms to give a framework to the whole crystal such that to break the crystal it is necessary to break chemical bonds, thus explaining the hardness of quartz, had not occurred to him.

I can understand why I became excited, in 1922, when I learned that the techniques of x-ray diffraction by crystals could be used to determine the arrangement of the bonds in a crystal such as quartz and to give additional information, such as the length of the bonds and the angles between bonds. I was fortunate to be able to make use of this technique, under the instruction of Roscoe Gilkey Dickinson, who had just in 1920 received his Ph.D. from the California Institute of Technology for his work on x-ray crystallography. During my first year as a graduate student I was able, with Dickinson's guidance, to determine the crystal structures of two substances, the mineral molybdenite (molybdenum disulfide) and an intermetallic compound of magnesium and tin. Each of these structure determinations provided valuable information about the chemical bonds and led to suggestions about the relation between structure and properties of substances.

Thus x-ray crystallography provided a great opportunity to make discoveries about the nature of the world. Also, beginning in 1925, a remarkable change occurred in theoretical physics, through the discovery of quantum mechanics. I was fortunate to be able to participate not only in the experimental field of x-ray crystallography but also in the theoretical field of quantum mechanics, especially in its application to the question of the nature of the chemical bond.

Pauling in CIT Laboratories, 1940s

This work kept me and my students busy for about fifteen years. My book *The Nature of the Chemical Bond* was published in 1939, somewhat revised in 1940, and revised again in 1960. Meanwhile, about 1929, an event occurred that in the course of a few years caused me to begin to think of a greater problem, that of the nature of life.

It had been decided by the leaders of the California Institute of Technology that this Institute, very strong already in physics and chemistry, should extend its field into biology, and Thomas Hunt Morgan had been given appointment as the chairman of the biology division. Morgan and his students had discovered the gene and laid the foundation for modern genetics through their work on the fruit fly, drosophila. When Morgan came to Pasadena he brought with him the most outstanding among his younger collaborators, so that the California Institute of Technology soon became the world leader in genetics. I was interested in what these biologists were doing, and discussed their work with them, especially with Morgan, Alfred Sturtevant, Calvin Bridges, Sterling Emerson, and Albert Tyler. I formulated a theory of the phenomenon of crossing over of chromosomes and presented it in the biology seminar. (It has never been published.) I soon learned that each of these biologists was working on some aspect of a general phenomenon that can be called biological specificity. The genes, for example, were known to be remarkably specific (precisely determined) in their functioning. These flies, the drosophila, usually have two wings, but a mutation in one of the genes might cause a fly to have four wings. The color of the eye is determined by the gene. A mutation might cause a change in color, or even absence of pigment. Moreover, a fertilized fruit fly egg produces another fruit fly, not a house fly. Aside from genetics, there are many other examples of biological specificity. The enzymes that operate to cause biochemical reactions to go at very high speeds often are highly specific, so that they cause only one kind of molecule to undergo reaction. I formed the idea that if one could understand biological specificity, one might then have an understanding of the nature of life.

Hemoglobin is a large molecule containing about ten thousand atoms, present in the blood, and responsible for the red color. In 1935 I became interested in hemoglobin and carried out experimental studies involving the interaction of the molecules with a magnetic field. As a result, I was invited in 1936 to speak at Grand Rounds in the Rockefeller Institute for Medical Research, in order to explain the nature of the discovery about hemoglobin. One of the persons present in the audience was Dr. Karl Landsteiner. He had discovered the blood groups in 1901, making it possible for blood to be safely transferred from one person to another person with matching blood type, and he had received the Nobel Prize in 1929 for this discovery. He asked me to come to his laboratory to discuss experiments that he had been carrying out in the field of immunochemistry. It was known that immunology is characterized by biological specificity. Immunity against one disease, such as measles, does not confer on the person immunity against another disease, such as typhoid fever. I knew this fact, but I did not have any special interest in it, because it seemed to me to be far too complicated a matter for me to be able to understand. However, Landsteiner told me that he had made many experiments in which he coupled a simple chemical substance, such a benzoic acid, to a protein and injected it into a rabbit. The rabbit then developed antibodies that would combine with the simple chemical substance, and this combination was highly specific, such that the antibody against benzoic acid would not combine with other somewhat similar simple substances, such as toluic acid. He asked if I could account for details in his observations on the basis of my knowledge of molecular structure and chemical bonding. Two years later he came to Cornell University, when I was lecturing there, to talk to me again about this matter, and I soon had formulated a program of research in these fields that would, I hoped, in the course of time lead to an understanding of biological specificity and perhaps even of the nature of life.

At the time, sixty years ago, when I began working on the problem of the nature of life, there were two general ideas that had been formulated by other scientists interested in the problem, and who had accepted, at least tentatively, the idea that molecules are responsible for the existence of living organisms and for the phenomenon of biological specificity. One idea, an obvious one, was that for some reason a molecule has the power to oversee the manufacture of other molecules identical to itself. The other idea was that a molecule may oversee the manufacture of another molecule that is complementary to the key that opens it. For a number of years I strove to find an answer to the question as to which of these alternatives was the correct one, and by 1940 I had concluded that although the evidence was not completely convincing, it was likely that the complementariness theory was correct.

In 1991 a remarkable book was published by the Time Inc. Magazine Company. The book has the title *The Meaning of Life*. It contains scores of photographs, often beautiful, striking, and moving. It also contains scores of statements made by individuals all over the world. These statements, too, often are beautiful, striking, and moving. An example is the statement made by Molly Yard, who was the president of the National Organization of Women, beginning with the following paragraph:

> *If anybody thinks he or she knows why we're here, more power to him or her. I myself don't know the answer to the mystery of creation. I never accepted the fact that everybody's going to go to heaven. It seems to me like a fairy tale, invented because the people found it hard to contemplate death. It is great for some people and that's fine.*
>
> *I often think we're like perennials that bloom. They're wonderful, they die, they come back the next year. We're part of a generation; it blooms, it dies, it's replaced by the next generation—and I find that very, very strengthening…*

The statement by the Dalai Lama begins as follows:

> *While we exist as human beings, we are like tourists on holiday. If we play havoc and cause disturbance, our visit is meaningless. If during our short stay—a hundred years at most—we live peacefully, help others, and at the very least, refrain from harming or upsetting them, our visit is worth while. What is important is to see how we can best lead a meaningful everyday life, how we can bring about peace and harmony in our minds, how we can help contribute to society.*

These human beings and many others wrote similar statements, about why we, human beings, exist on earth. The question that interested me sixty years ago was why there were living organisms of any sort on earth, that is, what was a possible mechanism by means of which life could come

For about forty years I have been thinking of writing a book on the molecular basis of biological specificity, and I am trying to settle down to writing it. My tentative title now is *The Nature of Life, Including My Life*. I felt that biological specificity was the characteristic property of living organisms, and that it needed to be explained. I think that our immunochemical work did that job.

Linus Pauling to science historian Lily Kay, January, 1993

Pauling lecturing, Japan,
March 1955

about, with its extraordinary capability of reproducing itself, in its many forms, precisely. My statement in this book reads as follows:

During a period of about a decade, beginning in 1926, my principal research effort was an attack on the problem of the nature of life, which was, I think, successful, in that the experimental studies carried out by my students and me provided very strong evidence that the astonishing specificity characteristic of living organisms, such as an ability to have progeny resembling themselves, is the result of a special interaction between molecules that have mutually complementary structures.

In a world that is not in thermodynamic equilibrium, such as our earth, parts of which are heated by sunlight, it is possible for certain chemical reactions to be favored, for example by the action of enzymes or other catalysts. A molecule or group of molecules that can catalyze its or their own production is thereby able to prosper. This process, over a period of four billion years, has led to the existence of human beings. So we are here, in this wonderful world, with its millions of different kinds of molecules and crystals, the mountains, the plains and the oceans, and the millions of species of plants and animals. We have developed a degree of intelligence that permits us to understand the wonder of the world, and also that has given us the power to destroy the world and the human race. With Benjamin Franklin I say, "O that moral Science were in as fair a way of improvement, that men would cease to be wolves to one another, and that human beings would at length learn what they now improperly call humanity."

THE DISCOVERY OF THE ALPHA HELIX

Linus Pauling

❦❦❦

Controversy has swirled around the discovery of the structure of the alpha helix ever since Linus Pauling and Robert Corey first published the work in 1950. Criticisms from British crystallographers were immediate; they had been competing to solve the structure for years, but soon accepted Pauling's work. In 1951, the American chemist Maurice Huggins claimed to have discovered the structure and challenged Pauling publicly; it soon became clear that while Huggins had proposed a general helical form for protein prior to 1951, he had not described the alpha helix in particular. In the 1990s Herman Branson, who shared credit on the initial paper with Pauling and Corey, claimed that his role was bigger than acknowledged. In this 1982 essay, Pauling offers his own memories of a great discovery.

By 1932 I felt reasonably well satisfied with my understanding of inorganic compounds, including such complicated ones as the silicate minerals. The possibility of getting a better understanding also of organic compounds then presented itself. There was as yet not any large amount of experimental information about bond lengths and bond angles in molecules of organic compounds. The first organic compound to have its structure determined, hexamethylene tetramine, had been investigated by Dickinson, together with an undergraduate student named Albert Raymond, in 1922. The carbon-nitrogen bond length had been found to be 1.47 Å, and the bond angles at both carbon and nitrogen were about 109.5°, the tetrahedral angle.

By 1932 structure determinations had been made also of a few other crystals containing molecules of organic substances, but not a great many. In 1930, however, I had learned about a new method of determining the structure of molecules that had been invented by Dr. Herman Mark, in Germany. It was the electron diffraction method of studying gas molecules. The determination of the structure of a crystal of an organic compound, even with rather simple molecules, at that time was often difficult because the molecules tended to be packed together in the crystal in a complicated way. The method of electron diffraction of molecules had the advantage that a simple molecule always gave a simple electron diffraction pattern, so that one could be almost certain of success in determining the structure by this method. My student Lawrence Brockway began in 1930 to construct the first electron-diffraction apparatus for studying gas molecules that had been built anywhere but in Mark's laboratory in Germany. Herman Mark had been good enough to say that he was not planning to continue work along this line and that he would be glad to see it done in the California Institute of Technology. He also gave me the drawings showing how the instrument could be constructed.

Within a few years we and other investigators had amassed a large amount of information about bond lengths and bond angles in organic compounds. This information had great value in permitting new ideas in structural chemistry, such as the theory of resonance, to be checked against experiment and even to be refined. For example, it was observed that in organic compounds many bonds between carbon atoms or a carbon atom and a nitrogen or oxygen atom were intermediate in length between a single bond and a double bond. This fact was interpreted as showing that the bonds were covalent single bonds with a certain amount of double-bond character. The observations were generally in accord with the results of quantum mechanical calculations, and it became clear by 1935 that a far more extensive, precise, and detailed understanding of organic compounds had been developed than had been available to chemists in the earlier decades.

It was just at this time that I began to think about proteins. The first protein to attract my interest was hemoglobin. I had read that the equilibrium curve for hemoglobin, oxygen, and oxyhemoglobin was not represented by any simple theoretical expression of the sort that physical chemists had devised for chemical equilibria. I also knew that some eight years earlier it had been shown by Adair in Cambridge that the hemoglobin molecule contains four iron atoms—that is, four heme groups, each being a porphyrin with an iron atom linked to it, and that the molecule could combine with as many as four oxygen atoms. I formulated a theory, published in 1935, on the oxygen equilibrium of hemoglobin and its structural interpretation. The theory was that each iron atom can attach one oxygen molecule to itself, by forming a chemical bond with it. There is an interaction, however, between each heme group and the adjacent heme groups such that addition of the oxygen molecule to one iron atom changes the equilibrium constant for the combination of the other iron atoms with oxygen molecules. I had several ideas as to the nature of the heme-heme interaction, and somewhat later my student Robert C. C. St. George and I published a paper showing that the addition of a group such as the oxygen molecule to one of the other iron atoms deforms the molecule through a steric hindrance effect in such a way as to make it easier for oxygen molecules to attach themselves to other iron atoms in the molecule. While thinking about the oxygen equilibrium curve in 1935 it occurred to me that measurement of the magnetic properties of hemoglobin, carbon monoxyhemoglobin, and oxyhemoglobin should provide information about the nature of the bonds formed by the iron atoms with the surrounding groups (two distinct kinds of compounds of bipositive iron were known) and the electronic structure of the oxygen molecule in oxyhemoglobin. Charles Coryell and I carried out measurements of the magnetic properties of these compounds, showing that the iron atoms change their electronic structure when the oxygen molecule is attached, and also that the oxygen molecule changes from having two unpaired electron spins to having none. My first work on proteins accordingly dealt essentially with the physical chemistry and

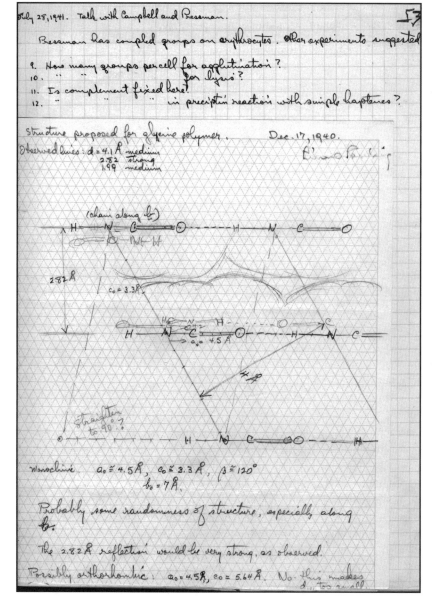

Pauling's research notes on immunology, 1940

structural chemistry of the heme group and the attached ligand, rather than with the apoprotein, the globin.

The measurement of the magnetic susceptibility of solutions of hemoglobin and related substances turned out to be a valuable technique, and we imme-diately began applying it to determine equilibrium constants, rates of reaction, and other properties. A leading protein chemist, Dr. Alfred Mirsky, was sent to Pasadena by the Rockefeller Institute of Medical Research to work with us during the year 1935-1936. He had been especially interested in the phenomenon of the denaturation of proteins by heat or chemical substances, such as hydrogen ion, hydroxide ion, urea, etc. After many discussions he and I formulated a general theory of the denaturation of proteins. The theory involved the statement that a native protein consists of polypeptide chains that are folded in a regular way, with the type of folding determined and stabilized by the weaker interactions, especially hydrogen bond formation. Denaturation, we said in our 1936 paper, is incomplete or complete folding of the polypeptide chains, producing molecules that could assume a large number of conformations, giving increased entropy and increased intermolecular interaction.

These considerations about the folding of the polypeptide chains in denatured protein molecules immediately raised the question, of course, as to the nature of the folding. It was a question to which I applied myself during the next fifteen years.

Shortly after x-ray diffraction had been discovered, several investigators had made x-ray diffraction photographs of protein fibers. These photographs for the most part showed only rather diffuse diffraction maxima, insufficient to permit structure determinations to be deduced from them. There were two principal types, one shown by keratin fibers such as hair, horn, porcupine quill, and fingernail, and the other shown by silk. William T. Astbury and his collaborators in the early 1930s had reported that the diffraction pattern of a hair changes when the hair is stretched. He called the normal pattern alpha keratin and the stretched-hair pattern, which is somewhat like that of silk, beta keratin. In the early summer of 1937, when I was free of my teaching duties, I decided to try to determine the alpha-keratin structure. My plan was to use my knowledge of structural chemistry to predict the dimensions and other properties of a polypeptide chain, and then to examine possible conformations of the chain, to find one that would agree with the x-ray diffraction data. The principal piece of information supplied by the rather fuzzy diffraction photographs of hair and other alpha-keratin proteins came from a rather diffuse arc on the meridian, above and below (that is, in the direction of the axis of the hair). The measured position of this reflection indicated that the structural unit in the direction along the axis of the hair would repeat in 5.10 Å. This fact required that there be at least two amino acid residues for this apparent repeat distance of the alpha-keratin structure.

Because of the large amount of theoretical and experimental progress that had been made, I felt that I could predict the dimensions of the peptide group with reliability. The alpha-carbon atom forms a single bond with a hydrogen atom, a single bond with the group R characteristic of the amino acid, a single bond to an adjacent main-chain carbon atom, and a single bond to the main-chain nitrogen atom. The single-bond lengths were known to within about 0.01 Å: 1.54 Å for C-C and 1.47 Å for C-N (as determined by Dickinson and Raymond as early as 1922, and verified in many compounds).

However, for the other bond between carbon and nitrogen we have to consider the theory of resonance. According to this theory there are two structures that can be written for a peptide group, in one of which the carbon-oxygen bond is a double bond, and in the other the carbon-oxygen bond is a single bond (one of the electron pairs in the double bond having shifted out onto the oxygen atom, giving it a negative charge) and the carbon-nitrogen main-chain bond is a double bond (with the nitrogen atom having a positive charge). Because of the separation of charges, the second structure is less stable than the first, and the estimate that could be made is that it should contribute about 40%, so that this bond has 40% double-bond character. The expected bond length is then 1.32 Å, rather than 1.47 Å. Moreover, because of the 40% double-bond character for this bond, these two atoms and the four adjacent atoms should all lie in the same plane, this quality of planarity being characteristic of compounds of molecules in which there are double bonds. In this way I reached the conclusion that these peptide groups in the molecule would have a well-defined rigid structure, and that there would be two degrees of freedom for the chain, rotation around the single bonds from carbon and nitrogen to the alpha carbon atom. Accordingly the conclusion, on the basis of the theory of resonance, that the peptide group should be planar greatly restricts the possible structures.

Despite this restriction, I was unable to find a way of folding the polypeptide chain to give a repeat in 5.10 Å along the fiber axis. After working for several weeks on this problem I stopped, having reached the conclusion that there probably was some aspect of structural chemistry characteristic of proteins and remaining to be discovered. This conclusion was, in fact, wrong, but it led to a large amount of experimental work.

Dr. Robert B. Corey was a chemist who, after getting his Ph.D. in chemistry in Cornell University and teaching analytical chemistry there for five years, had joined a leading x-ray crystallographer, Ralph W. G. Wyckoff, in the Rockefeller Institute for Medical Research. He worked with him on crystallographic problems for nine years, and then came, in 1937, to spend a year as research fellow in the California Institute of Technology. He and Wyckoff had made some x-ray photographs of proteins and he was interested in the problem of determining the structure of proteins. I told him about my failure to find a way of folding the polypeptide chains in alpha-keratin, and my conclusion that there might be some structural feature that we had ignored. I had assumed that the polypeptide chain should be folded in such a way as to permit the NH group to form a hydrogen bond with the oxygen atom of the carbonyl group of an adjacent

We have been tremendously interested in your broadside of papers on protein structures. Your solution of the alpha-keratin chain carries conviction. It fits in so beautifully with many facts. I think we were led astray in our review of chains by a feature of the Patterson projection which originates from something else than the chain structure. A spiral pattern has always appealed to me much more strongly. The Astbury chain always seemed such a very artificial one for so universal and fundamental a structure. I do congratulate you most warmly on what I feel is a very real and vital advance towards the understanding of proteins.

W. L. Bragg to Pauling, June 1951

Pauling holding an alpha
helix model

peptide group, with the N–H ⋯ O distance 2.90 Å, as indicated by structure measurements on compounds other than the amino acids. At that time there had been no correct structure determination made for any amino acid or any peptide. The state of x-ray crystallography was such that a year's work, at least, would be needed to make such a structure determination, even for such a simple compound as glycine, and the efforts of several investigators in other institutions to do such a job had resulted in failure. I suggested to Dr. Corey that he, together with graduate students, attack the problem of determining the structure of some simple amino-acid crystals and simple peptides. He agreed, and within little more than a year he and two graduate students (Gustav Albrecht and Henri Levy) had succeeded in making completely satisfactory determinations of the structures of glycine, alanine, and diketopiperazine. This work was continued with vigor, with many students and post-doctoral fellows in chemistry in the California Institute of Technology involved in it, during the following years, interrupted to a considerable extent, however, by the Second World War.

In the spring of 1948 I was in Oxford, England, serving as George Eastman Professor for the year and as a fellow of Balliol College. I caught cold, and was required to stay in bed for about three days. After two days I had got tired of reading detective stories and science fiction, and I began thinking about the problem of the structure of proteins. By this time Dr. Corey and the other workers back in Pasadena had determined with high reliability and accuracy the structures of a dozen amino acids and simple peptides, by x-ray diffraction. No other structure determinations of substances of this sort had been reported by any other investigators. I realized, on thinking about the structures, that there had been no surprises whatever: every structure conformed to the dimensions—bond lengths and bond angles, and planarity of the peptide group—that I had already formulated in 1937. The N–H ⋯ O hydrogen bonds, present in many crystals, were all close to 2.90 Å in length. I thought that I would attack the alpha-keratin problem again.

As I lay there in bed, I had an idea about a new way of attacking the problem. Back in 1937 I had been so impressed by the fact that the amino-acid residues in any position in the polypeptide chain may be of any of twenty different kinds that the idea that with respect to folding they might be nearly equivalent had not occurred to me. I accordingly thought to myself, what would be the consequences of the assumption that all of the amino-acid residues are structurally equivalent, with respect to the folding of the polypeptide chain? I remembered a theorem that had turned up in a course in mathematics that

Pauling sketches out the alpha helix discovery

I had attended, with Professor Harry Bateman as the teacher, in Pasadena twenty-five years before. This theorem states that the most general operation that converts an asymmetric object into an equivalent asymmetric object (such as an L amino acid into another molecule of the same L amino acid) is a rotation-translation; that is, a rotation around an axis combined with a translation along the axis and that the repetition of this operation produces a helix. Accordingly the problem became that of taking the polypeptide chain, rotating around the two single bonds to the alpha carbon atoms, with the amounts of rotation being the same from one peptide group to the next, and on and on, keeping the peptide groups planar and with the proper dimensions and searching for the structure in which each NH group performs a 2.90 Å hydrogen bond with a carbonyl group.

I asked my wife to bring me a pencil and paper, and a ruler. By sketching a polypeptide chain on a piece of paper and folding it along parallel lines, I succeeded in finding two structures that satisfied the assumptions. One of these structures was the alpha helix, with 4.6 residues per turn, and the other was the gamma helix. The gamma helix has a hole down its center that is too small to be occupied by other molecules, but large enough to decrease the van der Waals stabilizing interactions, relative to the alpha helix. It seems to me to be a satisfactory structure in every respect than this one, but so far as I am aware it has not been observed in any of the protein structures that have been determined so far, and it has been generally forgotten.

I got my wife to bring me my slide rule, so that I could calculate the repeat distance along the fiber axis. The structure does not repeat until after eighteen residues in five turns, the calculated repeat distance being 27.0 Å, which corresponds to 5.4 Å per turn. This value did not agree with the experimental value, given by the meridianal arcs on the x-ray diffraction patterns, 5.10 Å. I tried to find some way of adjusting the bond lengths or bond angles so as to decrease the calculated distance from 5.4 Å to 5.1 Å, but I was unable to do so.

I was so pleased with the alpha helix that I felt sure that it was an acceptable way of folding polypeptide chains, and that it would show up in the structures of some proteins when it finally became possible to determine them experimentally. I was disturbed, however, by the discrepancy with the experimental value 5.10 Å, and I decided that I should not publish an account of the alpha helix until I understood the reason for the discrepancy. I had been invited to give three lectures on molecular structure and biological specificity in Cambridge University, and while I was there I talked with Perutz about his experimental electron density distribution functions for the hemoglobin crystal that he had been studying. It seemed to me that I could see in his diagrams evidence for the presence of the alpha helix, but I was troubled so much by the 5.1 Å value that I did not say anything to him about the alpha helix.

On my return to Pasadena in the fall of 1948 I talked with Professor Corey about the alpha helix and the gamma helix, and also with Dr. Herman Branson, who had come for a year as a visiting professor. I asked Dr. Branson to go over my calculations, and in particular to see if he could find any third helical structure. He reported that the calculations were all right, and that he could not find a third structure. More than a year went by, and then a long paper on ways of folding the polypeptide chain, including helical structures, was published by W. Lawrence Bragg, John Kendrew, and Max Perutz, in *Proceedings of the Royal Society of London*. They described about twenty structures, and they reached the conclusion that none of them seemed to be satisfactory for alpha keratin. Moreover, none of them agreed with my assumptions, in particular the assumption of planarity of the peptide group. Lord Todd has told the story of his having told Bragg, when they were just beginning their work, that the main-chain carbon-nitrogen bond has some double bond character but that Bragg did not understand that that meant that the peptide group should be planar.

My efforts during a year and a half to understand the 5.1Å discrepancy had failed, but Dr. Corey and I decided that we should publish a description of the alpha helix and the gamma helix. It appeared in the *Journal of the American Chemical Society* in the fall of 1950. It was followed in 1951 by a more detailed paper, with Branson as co-author, and a number of other papers on the folding of the polypeptide chains. An important development had been the publication of x-ray photographs of fibers of synthetic polypeptides, in particular of poly-gamma-methyl-L-glutamate, by investigators at Courtaulds. These striking diffraction photographs showed clearly that the pseudo repeat distance along the fiber axis is 5.4 Å rather than 5.1 Å. There are strong reflections near the meridianal line, corresponding to 5.1 Å, but they are not true meridianal reflections. On the x-ray photographs of hair the reflections overlap to produce the arc that seems to be a meridianal reflection. It was this misinterpretation that had misled all of the investigators in this field. It was accordingly clear that the alpha helix is the way in which polypeptide chains are folded in the alpha-keratin proteins.

Moreover, we reached the conclusion, as did Crick, that in the alpha-keratin proteins the alpha helices are twisted together into ropes or cables. This idea essentially completed our understanding of the alpha-keratin diffraction patterns.

The apparent identity distance in the fiber x-ray diagrams of silk is somewhat smaller than corresponds to a completely extended polypeptide chain. We accordingly concluded that the polypeptide chains have a zigzag conformation in silk and the beta-keratin structure. We reported in detail three proposed sheet structures. The first one, which we called the rippled sheet, involves amino-acid residues of two different kinds, one of which cannot be an L-amino-acid residue, but can be a residue of glycine. It was known that *Bombyx mori* silk fibroin has glycine in 50% of its positions, with L-alanine or some other L-amino-acid residue (such as L-serine) in the alternate positions, so that the rippled sheet seemed to be a possibility for *Bombyx mori* silk fibroin. It turned out, however, that *Bombyx mori* silk fibroin has the structure of the antiparallel-chain pleated sheet. The third pleated sheet structure, the parallel-chain pleated sheet, is also an important one.

About 85% of the amino-acid residues in myoglobin and hemoglobin are in alpha-helix segments, with the others involved in the turns around the corners. In other globular proteins the alpha helix, the parallel-chain pleated sheet, and the antiparallel-chain pleated sheet all are important structural features. These three ways of folding polypeptide chains have turned out to constitute the most important secondary structures of all proteins. Dr. Corey, to some extent with my inspiration, designed molecular models of several different kinds that were of much use in the later effort to study other methods of folding polypeptide chains. I used these units to make about a hundred different possible structures for folding polypeptide chains. For example, if the hydrogen bonds are made alternately a little shorter and longer than 2.90 Å in a repeated sequence, an additional helical twist is imposed upon the alpha helix. Some of the models that I constructed related to ways of changing the direction of the axis of the alpha helix. I reported on all of this work at a protein conference in Pasadena in 1952, but then I became interested in other investigations and stopped working in this field.

It pleases me to think that our work in Pasadena in the Division of Chemistry and Chemical Engineering, first in collecting experimental information about the structure of molecules, then in developing structural principles, and then in applying these principles to discover the alpha helix and the pleated sheets, has shown how important structural chemistry can be in the field of molecular biology.

Time has shown that, so far, Pauling was right and Delbrück was wrong, as indeed Delbrück acknowledged in his book, *Mind into Matter.* Everything we know about molecular biology appears to be explainable in a standard chemical way.

Francis Crick (from What Mad Pursuit)

THE TRIPLE HELIX

Thomas Hager

❧❧❧

Not every race that Pauling ran ended in triumph. Like all great scientists, he was also capable of grand failures—although his were relatively few. The following piece takes a careful look at Pauling's mistakes in method and approach in the race for the structure of DNA. Many factors played a role in this episode: politics, international rivalry, hubris, and technological limitations. Above all, the piece demonstrates that during the early 1950s, the attention of Pauling and many other scientists was diverted away from DNA because very few researchers (Watson and Crick excepted) thought that the genetic material was DNA at all. Instead, most attention was focused on proteins.

In 1950, Linus Pauling astonished the scientific world by mapping a series of highly specific protein structures at the level of individual atoms. The achievement made news around the world. Proteins were staggeringly complex and difficult to study; cracking their detailed structures at the atomic level was a goal many had thought impossible at the time. But Pauling, using a combination of model-building, intuitive understanding, and a deep knowledge of structural chemistry, did it—a major reason he was awarded the Nobel Prize in Chemistry four years later.

In 1951, Pauling started reading in some depth and talking to others about the structure of deoxyribonucleic acid—everyone called it DNA—the most common form of nucleic acid in chromosomes. DNA did not appear like much of a problem compared to proteins. It was composed of just four subunits, called nucleotides, all of which appeared to be present in all DNA from all animals in approximately equal amounts, compared to protein's twenty-some amino acids, which varied widely in occurrence in various molecules. Each nucleotide consisted of sugar, a phosphate group, and one of four carbon-and–nitrogen ring structures called bases: adenine, guanine, thymine, and cytosine. The key to DNA would be figuring how each base joined with a sugar and a phosphate to make a nucleotide; then how the nucleotides joined to form chains. Compared to protein structures, Pauling thought, that should not be too hard to work out.

It was not a top-priority problem in any case. Many researchers wanted to find "the secret of life," the means by which living organisms passed their traits on to offspring, and everyone knew in 1951 that the genetic material was in the nucleus of cells, in chromosomes. DNA was by weight an important component of chromosomes, but so was protein, and it seemed likely to most researchers at the time that the protein portion carried the genetic instructions. Protein had the variety of forms and functions, the subunit variability, the sheer sophistication to account for heredity. DNA by comparison seemed dumb, more likely a structural component that helped form or unfold the chromosomes.

The only evidence to the contrary was a little-appreciated paper published in 1944 by Rockefeller Institute researcher Oswald Avery, who had found that DNA, apparently by itself, could transfer new genetic traits between *Pneumococcus* bacteria. But for years no one paid much attention to Avery's work. Pauling heard of it but thought it unimportant. "I knew the contention that DNA was the hereditary material," Pauling said. "But I didn't accept it. I was so pleased with proteins, you know, that I thought that proteins probably are the hereditary material rather than nucleic acids—but that of course nucleic acids played a part. In whatever I wrote about nucleic acids, I mentioned nucleoproteins, and I was thinking more of the protein than of the nucleic acids."

Through most of 1950 and 1951, Pauling put DNA on the back burner, focusing instead on refining his protein structures. There was another problem as well: DNA was notoriously hard to work with. The best clue to its structure would come from x-ray crystallography, the technique Pauling had used to solve proteins. But while any strand of hair could provide a decent x-ray photo of a protein, DNA had to be extracted from cell nuclei and separated from its attendant protein, a difficult process. The techniques of the day for isolating DNA in general degraded the molecule somewhat, and the final product was the sodium salt of DNA, called sodium thymonucleate. There was some doubt as to how the isolation process altered the molecule's structure, and even purified sodium thymonucleate was difficult to use for x-ray diffraction. Pauling was willing to reanalyze existing data, but the only usable x-ray photos of DNA in the literature, taken by William Astbury in England, were not very useful. While x-ray patterns from globular proteins generally provided too much data to analyze successfully, Astbury's DNA photos provided too little. Pauling could get some rough ideas of dimensions and the size of repeating units from these pictures, but they were too muddy to get much more. Astbury had been unable to get a good, clear picture.

But in the summer of 1951, Pauling heard about someone who had. A correspondent wrote Pauling that a fellow named Maurice Wilkins at King's College in England had x-rayed DNA with some success, but had

During a period of about a decade, beginning in 1936, my principal research effort was an attack on the problem of the nature of life, which was, I think, successful, in that the experimental studies carried out by my students and me provided very strong evidence that the astonishing specificity characteristic of living organisms, such as an ability to have progeny resembling themselves, is the result of a special interaction between molecules that have mutually complementary structures.

Linus Pauling

never done much with the results. Thinking that the data might be available, Pauling wrote Wilkins and asked for a look at his photographs.

Wilkins, who did indeed have the world's best x-ray photos of DNA, was not sure what to do when he read Pauling's letter.

A thin, bespectacled physicist and a man of many talents—he got his start separating uranium isotopes for the Manhattan Project—Wilkins was not in fact well trained in the interpretation of x-ray photos. He had a good technique for x-raying DNA, but he needed assistance on the project. He hired it in the form of a talented young crystallographer, Rosalind Franklin. Unfortunately, the relationship between Wilkins and Franklin got off to a rocky start. Wilkins thought Franklin had been hired to assist him and turned over to her his photos, his x-ray setup, and one of his graduate students. Franklin, however, was under the impression that she had been hired to work independently. By the time Pauling's letter arrived, the two had had a falling-out, leaving the question of how to proceed with DNA somewhat up in the air and making it more difficult to answer Pauling's request. Franklin had by then taken a proprietary interest in solving DNA's structure from the steadily better photos she was taking. It appears that Wilkins understood that, given good photos, Pauling had a good chance of beating everyone to the solution. His fears were increased by his suspicion that DNA might be a helix, a form familiar to Pauling from his protein work. Wilkins held on to Pauling's letter for a week while he mulled over alternatives. Then he wrote back that he was sorry but he wanted to look more closely at his data before releasing the pictures.

Undeterred, Pauling wrote Wilkins's superior, J. T. Randall, with the same request. Randall was sorry, too, replying, "Wilkins and others are busily engaged in working out the interpretation of the deoxyribonucleic acid x-ray photographs, and it would not be fair to them, or to the efforts of our laboratory as a whole, to hand these over to you."

That was in August 1951. Pauling put DNA aside until November, when he saw an article on its structure by fellow named Edward Ronwin in the *Journal of the American Chemical Society* (*JACS*). Pauling thought that Ronwin's work was wrong—it showed phosphorus atoms connected to five oxygens; Pauling believed the number should have been four. Pauling wrote a letter to the *JACS* about it. He was, as it turned out, right.

More important, it started him thinking again about how DNA might be built. Ronwin had put his phosphates down the middle of the molecule, with the flat bases sticking out to the sides. This was certainly possible—Astbury's x-ray photos did not rule out such an arrangement—and it would solve a major problem. The four bases of DNA came in two different sizes: two double-ring purines and two smaller pyrimidines with single rings. Say that it was a helix, as Astbury's photos indicated it might be. Trying to arrange the different-sized bases on the inside of a long helical molecule would create all sorts of fitting and stacking problems. Facing the bases out would make the molecule easier to solve, just as facing the amino-acid side chains away from the center of the protein spiral had made the alpha helix much easier to work with.

If the bases faced out, Pauling hypothesized, then the core of the helix would be packed with phosphates. Phosphates up the middle, bases facing out. It fit the available x-ray data. After Ronwin's paper, the problem of the structure of DNA began reducing itself in Pauling's mind to a question of packing phosphates together.

Then came an enormous distraction.

In the fall of 1951 Pauling received an invitation to a special meeting of the Royal

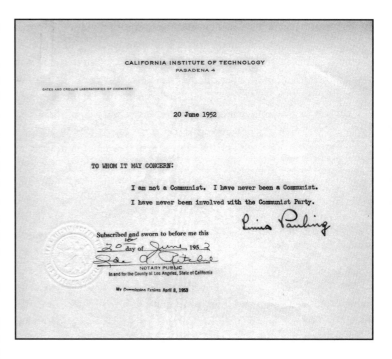

Statement by Pauling during passport imbroglio, 1952

Society designed specifically to address the many questions British researchers had raised about his many protein structures. The date was set for May 1, 1952.

Pauling was eager to go. In preparation, through the end of 1951 and on into the first months of 1952, he tested, refined, and rethought his proposed structures. He applied for a passport. And in February 1952, he was refused. The reason, he was told in a letter from the State Department, was that "the Department is of the opinion that your proposed travel would not be in the best interest of the United States."

Pauling's peace work for the past few years, his loud denouncements of U.S. nuclear policy and activism against atomic weapons, had engendered what was becoming a depressingly typical response: he was being denied the right to spread his ideas outside of the United States. He was denied the right to travel.

Through the remainder of the spring, he did everything he could to reinstate his passport. He hired a lawyer, provided reams of data on his political activities, appealed the decision, and garnered support from scientists around the world. All to no avail. The May meeting came and went; Pauling, without a passport, did not attend.

His case became a worldwide example of U.S. Cold War repression at its worst. On May 5, Secretary of State Dean Acheson read a telexed copy of a letter published that morning in the *Times* (London) by Sir Robert Robinson, Britain's leading organic chemist, winner of the Nobel Prize and a man known generally for his reserve. Sir Robert took the State Department to task for its "deplorable" actions in the Pauling case. "It would be insincere to pretend that we have no inkling of the reason for the drastic action taken by the American authorities," he wrote, "but that does not lessen our surprise and our consternation." In a cover note, a U.S. embassy attaché in London stressed that "this one case is resulting in a definite and important prejudice to the American national interest."

The French reaction was no better. Two days after the Royal Society meeting, in a slap directed at the U.S. government, the French elected Pauling "Honorary President" of a biochemistry symposium scheduled for Paris that summer. French scientists were united in their criticism of the Pauling case; the U.S. science attaché in Paris was informed by one physiologist that the Americans must be "losing their minds." The Pauling case was splashed across the front page of the left-wing *L'Humanité*, along with the story of French scientists denied visas to visit the United States. "The accumulating number of such cases is causing strong feelings and is resulting in considerable mistrust as to our motives," the attaché wrote his superiors in Washington, D.C.

The European outcry was heard in the offices of the New York *Times*, which ran a pair of news stories in early May along with an editorial, "Dr. Pauling's Predicament," calling for an investigation of passport policy. The State Department was quickly peppered with pro-Pauling protest letters. Under pressure, the State Department caved. Pauling applied for a new passport to attend the French meeting. And in mid-July, it was granted.

His arrival at the Paris International Biochemical Congress caused a sensation. News of his political troubles and defiance of the government had made him a hero in France, and a hastily arranged talk on protein structures drew an overflow crowd. Afterward, he was swarmed by researchers eager to shake the honorary president's hand and express their admiration for his principles. He and his wife Ava Helen received a stream of friends and well-wishers in their rooms at the Trianon.

A week or so after the Congress, Pauling attended the International Phage Colloquium at the centuries-old Abbey of Royaumont outside Paris, where he heard the American microbiologist Alfred Hershey describe an ingenious experiment that had everyone talking. In an attempt to settle the question of whether DNA or protein was the genetic material, Hershey and a coworker, Martha Chase, had found a way to tag the DNA and protein of a bacterial virus with separate radioactive labels. By tracking the labels, they were able to show persuasively that the protein did nothing. DNA alone directed replication.

This was a clear indication that DNA was the genetic material. As word of the Hershey-Chase experiment spread, phage researchers, geneticists, and biochemists interested in replication began to switch their focus from protein to DNA. Pauling, too, quickly realized that he had been on the wrong track. It was not that proteins were unimportant; they were still critical in the functioning of the body. But the secret of life was DNA.

It was an unnerving realization, but Pauling took it in stride. He was confident that he could solve DNA. The only problem would be if someone beat him to it, but he could not take the possibility very seriously.

I feel it to be my duty to testify that Professor Pauling is one of the most prominent and inventive scientists in this country. I have the highest esteem for his character and for his reliability as a man and as a citizen. To make it impossible for him by governmental action to travel abroad would—according to my conviction—be seriously detrimental to the interest and reputation of this country.

Albert Einstein to U.S. Secretary of State, May 1952

Reduplication of the Gene

Several times in the period around 1948 I stated that the gene probably consists of two complementary parts, each of which can then produce a replica of the other. For example, in the 21st Sir Jesse Boot Foundation Lecture delivered on Friday 28 May 1948 and published in 1948, I said

> The detailed mechanism by means of which a gene or a virus molecule produces replicas of itself is not yet known. In general the use of a gene or virus as a template would lead to the formation of a molecule not with identical structure but with complementary structure. It might happen, of course, that a molecule could be at the same time identical with and complementary to the template on which it is moulded. However, this case seems to me to be too unlikely to be valid in general, except in the following way. If the structure that serves as a template (the gene or virus molecule) consists of, say, two parts, which are themselves complementary in structure, then each of these parts can serve as the mould for the production of duplicates of itself. In some cases the two complementary parts might be very close together in space, and in other cases more distant from one another—they might constitute individual molecules, able to move about within the cell.

The preceding sentences are,

> I believe that the same process of moulding of plastic materials into a configuration complementary to that of another molecule, which serves as a template, is responsible for all biological specificity. I believe that the genes serve as the templates on which are moulded the enzymes that are responsible for the chemical characters of the organisms, and that they also serve as templates for the production of replicas of themselves.

Mention of mutually complementary structures in living organisms is given in the following paragraph.

Linus Pauling

Undated note by Linus Pauling

He knew that Wilkins and Franklin were at work on it—one of Pauling's colleagues had visited Franklin's laboratory while over for the Royal Society meeting in May and had seen some excellent x-ray photos she was getting of DNA—but there was no indication that the King's College group knew enough chemistry to be a serious threat. If Sir William Lawrence Bragg—Nobelist, head of the formidable Cavendish Laboratory at Cambridge, titan of x-ray crystallography and Pauling's arch-rival for years—were involved, that would be a different matter, but there was little indication from the Cavendish that anyone was looking at DNA. The only exception Pauling might have known about was an American in Cambridge on a postdoctoral fellowship, twenty-two-years-old James Watson, who had written a Caltech colleague of Pauling's a few months earlier, mentioning something about looking for a DNA model. It did not sound very serious. The gentlemen at the Cavendish had, in any case, not yet beaten Pauling in any significant race.

At the Royaumont meeting, Pauling talked with a group about solving DNA the way he had solved the protein alpha helix: use precise x-ray

Oauling's 1933 notes for the structure of nucleic acid

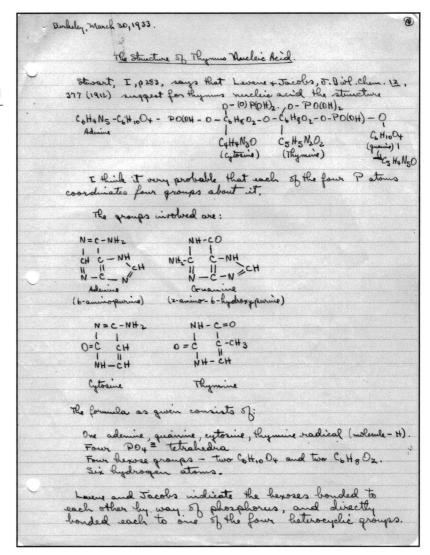

work to confirm the structure of the building blocks, then make a model of the most chemically probable long-chain structure that they would form. The same approach could be applied to DNA

James Watson was among the group gathered around Pauling at Royaumont, and he listened closely. He already knew that Pauling's approach was the way to solve DNA. He had already tried to use it, with a Cavendish labmate, a grad student named Francis Crick.

Watson and Crick made quite a pair: Crick, in his mid-thirties, old for a graduate student—his scientific progress delayed by wartime work—but self-confident and outgoing, talkative to a fault, with fashionable long sideburns and a love of three-piece suits; Watson, young, thin, and shy, with his American tennis shoes and crew cut. Erwin Chargaff painted an unkind contemporary picture of them: "One thirty-five years old, with the looks of a fading racing tout…an incessant falsetto, with occasional nuggets gleaming in the turbid stream of prattle. The other, quite underdeveloped...a grin, more sly than sheepish...a gawky young figure." Crick and Watson, he said, looked like "a variety act."

But they impressed each other. Crick soon understood why Watson "was regarded, in most circles, as too bright to be really sound." Watson wrote Delbrück a few weeks after meeting Crick that he was "no doubt the brightest person I have ever worked with and the nearest approach to Pauling I've ever seen." This was high praise, given both men's high regard for the wizard of Pasadena. "There was no one like Linus in all the world," Watson later wrote. "Even if he were to say nonsense, his mesmerized students would never know because of his unquenchable self-confidence."

The story of Crick and Watson's first attempt to solve the structure of DNA in the fall of 1951 has been told many times, most entertainingly in Watson's book *The Double Helix*. Suffice to say that it was brief and unsuccessful. Using Pauling's approach, within a few weeks they came up with a model of three helixes wound around each other, phosphates at the core. It seemed to fit the density data, the x-ray data were compatible with anything from two to four strands per molecule, and it solved a theoretical problem. If DNA was the genetic material, then it had to say something specific to the body; it had to have a language that could be translated somehow into the making of proteins. It was already known that the sugars and phosphates were simple repeating units, unvarying along the DNA strands. The bases were the variables. The bases varied, but the x-ray pattern indicated a repeating crystalline structure; ergo, the core—the part of the structure giving rise to the repeating patterns—must contain the repeating subunits, the sugars or phosphates, with the bases sticking out where they would not get in the way. DNA was, in other words, like the alpha helix. Watson and Crick were thinking very much like Pauling.

The problem was explaining how one could pack phosphates into the middle when at normal pH they would be generally expected to carry a negative charge. All those negative charges at the core would repel each other, blowing the structure apart. The triple helix they had devised was so pretty, though, and fit so much of the data that Crick and Watson figured there had to be a place for positive ions in the middle to cancel out the negative charges. They grabbed a copy of *The Nature of the Chemical Bond*, searched for inorganic ions that would fit their needs, and found that magnesium or calcium might fit. There was no good evidence for the presence of these positive ions, but there was no good evidence against them, either. They were trying to think like Pauling, after all, and Pauling would certainly have assumed that the structure came first and the minor details fell into place later.

The two young men, euphoric about cracking this important problem, invited Wilkins and Franklin to come to the Cavendish to see their triumph.

And Franklin tore it apart. The problem was not only the assumption that the molecule was helical—Franklin was not convinced that the x-ray data proved that it was—but their idea that positive ions cemented that center together. Magnesium or any other ions, she pointed out, would undoubtedly be surrounded by water molecules in a cell nucleus and rendered neutral. They could not hold the phosphates together. And water was important. Crick and Watson, she pointed out, had gotten some data wrong. According to Franklin, DNA was a thirsty molecule, drinking up ten times more water than their model allowed. The molecule's ability to soak up water indicated to Franklin that the phosphates were on the outside of the molecule where they would be encased in a shell of water. The wrong water content also meant that Crick and Watson's density calculations were off.

She was, as it turned out, right. The two men tried to convince Wilkins and Franklin to collaborate with them on another attempt but were turned down. When news of the fiasco reached the laboratory's director, Bragg, he quickly sent Crick back to proteins and Watson to a crystallographic study of tobacco mosaic virus.

But the pair, Watson in particular, did not stop thinking about nucleic acids. Pauling remembered Watson as "something of a monomaniac" where DNA was concerned. Rather than give up on the problem, Watson and Crick took it underground, talking it over quietly in their office or over drinks at a local pub. They might have gotten one model wrong, but they were certain their approach was right. Perhaps all they needed was a little more chemistry. For Christmas 1951, Crick gave Watson a copy of *The Nature of the Chemical Bond*. "Somewhere in Pauling's masterpiece," Watson remembered, "I hoped the real secret would lie."

For his part, Pauling, after the meeting in France, arrived in England eager to make up for the time lost because of his passport problems. Through August 1952 he toured the English protein centers, talking with his critics and answering their questions, convincing the British on some points, modifying his own thinking on others.

While visiting the Cavendish, Pauling was introduced to a number of the younger researchers and was especially interested in meeting Crick. Crick had been spending most of his time since being directed away from DNA on a problem Bragg had set his team working on after reading Pauling's protein papers, that of finding a mathematical formula for predicting how helixes would diffract x-rays. In the spring of 1952, Crick and two coworkers published a paper that provided the necessary mathematical treatment. It was Crick's first significant scientific success and proved immensely useful. He had proudly sent Pauling an advance copy.

Proteins were still in the forefront of Pauling's mind. During his month in England, Pauling thought so little about DNA that he did not even make an effort to visit King's College to see Wilkins and Franklin's increasingly valuable x-ray photographs. The reason was twofold, he later remembered: he was preoccupied with proteins, and he still assumed that Wilkins did not want to share his data.

It was a historic mistake. Franklin had new pictures now, crisp, focused patterns from DNA in its pure, extended, wet form, clearly showing both twofold symmetry—thus ruling out three-stranded structures—and the crosslike reflection characteristic of a helix. If Pauling had seen these—and there was no reason to think she would not have shown him; she had, after all, shown one of Pauling's coworkers just a few weeks earlier—if he had talked to Franklin, who was not shy about presenting her strong ideas about water content and its effect on the form of the molecule, if he had heard the ideas that had capsized the Crick-Watson model, Pauling would undoubtedly have changed the nature of his later approach. At the very least, a visit with Franklin would have impressed upon him that Astbury's earlier photos, the ones he was using, showed a mixture of two forms of the molecule.

Historians have speculated that the denial of Pauling's passport for the May Royal Society meeting was critical in preventing him from discovering the structure of DNA, that if he had attended the meeting he would have seen Franklin's work and had a better shot at following the right path. The idea nicely illustrates the scientific view that bureaucrats should not interfere in open communication between researchers. But the real problem was not the passport policy. Instead, three unrelated factors combined to set Pauling wrong. The first was his focus on proteins to the exclusion of almost everything else. The second was inadequate data. The x-ray photos he was using, Astbury's, were taken of a mixture of two forms of DNA and were almost worthless. The third was pride. He simply did not feel that he needed to pursue DNA full tilt. He was likely aware after his visit that Crick and Watson had made a stab at the structure and failed; he knew for certain that Wilkins was after it. But he did not consider them to be real competitors. How could they be? The protein triumph had proven that he was the only person in the world capable of solving large biological molecules.

"I always thought that sooner or later I would find the structure of DNA," Pauling said. "It was just a matter of time."

After missing his chance to see Franklin's data, Pauling returned to Caltech in September and threw himself into more protein work. "The field of protein structure is in a very exciting stage now," he wrote. "I have a hard time to keep from spending all of my time on this problem, with the neglect of other things." He worked out a way that his alpha helix could itself be twisted, like a piece of yarn wound around a finger, into a sort of coiled coil (a form that Crick had also surmised). Then he went further, proposing ways in which these coiled coils could wind about each other to form cables of various numbers of strands. He published his new ideas in October.

In the fall of 1952 Pauling's son Peter arrived at Cambridge to work as a graduate student. Twenty-one years old, breezy, fun loving—"slightly wild," according to Crick—Peter quickly fell in with Crick and Watson and their new office mate, Jerry Donohue, a Caltech expatriate who arrived that fall on a Guggenheim after working for years with Pauling.

The group formed one end of an important and unofficial communication center between Cambridge and Pasadena. Peter and Donohue were both in correspondence with Pauling; his replies provided Crick and Watson with at least a small idea of what Pauling was up to.

On November 25, 1952, three months after returning from England, Pauling attended a Caltech biology seminar given by Robley Williams, a Berkeley professor who had done some amazing work with an electron microscope. Through a complicated technique he was able to get images of incredibly small biological structures. Pauling was spellbound. One of William's photos showed long, tangled strands of sodium ribonucleate, the salt of a form of nucleic acid, shaded so that three-dimensional details could be seen. What caught Pauling's attention was the cylindrical shape of the strands: They were not flat ribbons; they were long, skinny tubes. He guessed then, looking at these black-and-white slides in the darkened seminar room, that DNA was likely to be a helix. No other conformation would fit both Astbury's x-ray patterns of the molecule and the photos he was seeing. Even better, Williams was able to estimate the sizes of structures on his photos, and his work showed that each strand was about 15 angstroms across. The molecule Williams was showing was not DNA, but it was a molecular cousin—and it started Pauling thinking.

The next day, Pauling sat at his desk with a pencil, a sheaf of paper, and a slide rule. New data that summer from Alexander Todd's laboratory had confirmed the linkage points between the sugars and phosphates in DNA; other work showed where they connected to the bases. Pauling was already convinced from his earlier work that the various-sized bases had to be on the outside of the molecule; the phosphates, on the inside. Now he knew that the molecule was probably helical. These were his starting points for a preliminary look at DNA. He did not know how far he would get with this first attempt at a structure, especially because he still had no firm structural data on the precise sizes and bonding angles of the base-sugar-phosphate building blocks of DNA, but it was worth a look.

Pauling quickly made some calculations to determine DNA's molecular volume and the expected length of each repeating unit along its axis. Astbury's photos showed a strong reflection at 3.4 angstroms—according to Pauling's calculations, about three times his estimated length of a single nucleotide unit along the fiber. Repeating groups of three different nucleotides seemed unlikely; a threefold chain structure would explain the repeat more easily. His density calculations indicated that three chains would need to pack together tightly to fit the observed volume, but that was all right. In crystallography, the tighter the packing, the better. After five lines of simple calculations on the first page of his attack on DNA, Pauling wrote, "Perhaps we have a triple-chain structure!"

He was immediately captivated by the idea; three chains wound around one another with the phosphates in the middle. Sketching and calculating, he quickly saw that there was no way for hydrogen bonds to form along the long fiber axis, holding the windings of the chain in place, as in the alpha helix. Without them, what held the molecule in shape? One place that hydrogen bonds could form, he saw, was across the middle of the molecule, from phosphate to phosphate. That was a surprise, but everything else seemed to be working out. After six pages of calculations, he wrote, "Note that each chain has...roughly three residues per turn. There are three chains closely intertwined, and held together by hydrogen bonds between PO_4s." The only problem was that there did not seem to be quite enough space in the center of the molecule, where the phosphates came into closest contact. He put down his pencil for the night.

Three days later, he came back to the problem. Accordingly to Astbury's figures, DNA was a relatively dense molecule, which implied tight packing at the core. But trying to jam three chains' worth of phosphates into Astbury's space restrictions was like trying to fit the stepsisters' feet into Cinderella's glass slipper. No matter how he twisted and turned the phosphates, they wouldn't fit. "Why are the PO_4 in a column so close together?" he wrote in frustration. If Astbury's estimates on distances could be relaxed a bit, everything would fit, but Pauling could not do that without deviating too far from Astbury's x-ray data. Pauling next tried deforming the phosphates' tetrahedra to make them fit, shortening some sides and lengthening others. It looked better, but still not right. He stopped again.

Next, he had an assistant go back through the literature in the chemistry library and pick up everything he could find on the x-ray crystallography of nucleic acids. There was not much to go on besides Astbury's work and that of Sven Furberg, a Norwegian crystallographer who had studied under Bernal and had found that the bases in DNA were oriented at right angles to the sugars. There was not one detailed structure of any purine or pyrimidine, much less a nucleotide.

On December 2 he made another assault, filling nine pages with drawings and calculations. And, he thought, he came up with something that looked plausible. "I have put the phosphates as close together as possible, and have distorted them as much as possible," he noted. Even though some phosphate oxygens were jammed uncomfortably close in the molecule's center, not only did it all just fit, but Pauling saw that the innermost oxygens packed together in the form of an almost perfect octahedron, one of the most basic shapes in crystallography. It was very tight, but things were lining up nicely. It had to be right. It had been less than a week since he first sat down with the problem.

The next day, Pauling excitedly wrote a colleague, "I think now we have found the complete molecular structure of the nucleic acids." During the next several weeks he ran downstairs every morning from his second-story office to Verner Schomaker's office, "very enthusiastic," Schomaker remembered, bouncing ideas off the younger man, thinking aloud as he checked and refined his model. He began working with his right-hand man, the careful and meticulous Robert Corey, to pinpoint the fine structure.

Pauling at the University of Glasgow, Scotland, 1948

Then came trouble. Corey's detailed calculation of atomic positions showed that the core oxygens were, in fact, too close to fit. In early December, Pauling went back to twisting and squeezing the phosphate tetrahedra. Someone brought up the questions of how his model allowed for the creation of a sodium salt of DNA, in which the positive sodium ions supposedly adhered to the negative phosphates. There was no room for sodium ion in his tightly packed core, was there? Pauling had to admit he could find no good way to fit the ions. But that would sort itself out later. The other results were positive. Running the proposed structure through Crick's mathematical formula indicated that his model helix would fit most of the x-ray data, although not all of it. Schomaker played with some models on his own and found a way to twist the phosphate tetrahedra so that they were not quite so jammed, but for the moment Pauling saw no reason to change his ideas. The core phosphates were too nearly close-packed not to be true.

And this was what the central problem had reduced itself to in his mind: a question of phosphate structural chemistry. The biological significance of DNA would be worked out later, he thought; if the structure was right, the biological importance would fall out of it naturally in some way. At this point it was his business to get the structure, not the function. So he ignored the larger context surrounding the molecule and focused single-mindedly on one thing: finding a way to fit those phosphates into the core so that the resulting helixes fit the available data.

His faith in this approach had been justified by his success with the alpha helix. He had built his protein spiral from strict chemical principles, published it in the face of contradictory data, and later found the facts he needed to answer his critics. He was confident now about his ability to jump ahead of the pack, to use his intuitive grasp of chemistry to tease out a structure that felt right. If you waited for every doubt to be answered first, you would never get credit for any discovery. And his DNA triple helix felt right.

A week before Christmas, he wrote Alex Todd at Cambridge, "We have, we believe, discovered the structure of nucleic acids. I have practically no doubt…The structure really is a beautiful one." Pauling knew that Todd had been working with purified nucleotides and asked him to send sample x-rays analysis.

Dr. Corey and I are much disturbed that there has been no precise structure determination reported as yet for any nucleotide. We have decided that it is necessary that some of the structure determinations be made in our laboratory. I know that the Cavendish people are working in this field, but it is such a big field that it cannot be expected that they will do the whole job.

He then wrote his son Peter and Jerry Donohue that he was hoping soon to complete a short paper on nucleic acids.

But the structure still was not quite right. Everything would seem to fall into place, then Corey would come up with another set of calculations showing that the phosphates were packed just a little too tightly, their atoms jostling each other a little too closely to be reasonable. Pauling would readjust and tinker, bend and squash, so close to the answer, yet unable to make it all fit perfectly.

He was becoming frustrated with it when another distraction cropped up: on December 23, professional FBI informer and darling of the congressional investigating committees Louis Budenz testified publicly, before a House special committee investigating charitable foundations, that Pauling, a member of the advisory board of the Guggenheim Foundation, was a concealed Communist. Budenz outdid himself, pouring out the names of twenty-three grantees of various organizations and three other officials, most of whom had no more to do with communism than did Pauling. His testimony would enrage a number of influential people associated with powerful foundations and eventually help spur a backlash against McCarthyism, but in the short term the timing of the announcement—two days before Christmas, at a time when the news media would be hungry for headlines but without the staff to do follow-up—did maximum damage to those named with little chance for response.

Pauling felt as if he had been sucker punched. His response was characteristically straightforward. "That statement is a lie," he told the press. "If Budenz is not prosecuted for perjury, we must conclude that our courts and Congressional committees are not interested in learning and disclosing the truth." When he discovered that Budenz was not liable for perjury because his testimony was protected by congressional privilege, Pauling tried another tack to get his accuser into court, calling Budenz a "professional liar" in the press in hopes that Budenz would sue him. Budenz did not take the bait.

Depressed about this unexpected political attack, Pauling took the unusual step of inviting some colleagues into his laboratory on Christmas Day to have a look at his work on DNA. He was tired of the niggling problems with his model and ready for some good news. He got it from his small audience, who expressed enthusiasm for his ideas. Much cheered, Pauling spent the last week of the year working with Corey on the finalization of a manuscript.

On the last day of December 1952, Pauling and Corey sent in their paper, "A Proposed Structure of the Nucleic Acids," to the *Proceedings of the National Academy of Sciences*. This was, they stressed, "the first precisely described structure for the nucleic acids that has been suggested by any investigator"—thus positioning the work as the nucleic acid equivalent to the alpha helix. He went through his reasoning for the core structure. Most of the paper concentrated on precisely stacking phosphate tetrahedra, but there was a little biology, too. In Pauling's model, the bases, the message-carrying portion of nucleic acids, were directed outward, like leaves along a stalk, with room enough to be put into any order, providing maximum variability in the molecule and thus maximum specificity in the message. Astbury had already noted that the 3.4-angstrom repeat in nucleic acid was about the same as the distance per amino acid along an extended polypeptide chain, raising the idea that new proteins might be struck directly off a nucleic acid mold. Pauling noted that his model allowed the same thing to happen, with the sides of four adjacent bases along his chains forming a space just right for fitting an amino acid.

There was, however, an uncharacteristic tentativeness in the piece. This was "a promising structure," Pauling wrote, but "an extraordinarily tight one"; it accounted only "moderately well" for the x-ray data and gave only "reasonably satisfactory agreement" with the theoretical values obtained by the Crick formula; the atomic positions, he wrote, were "probably capable of further refinement."

It was, in fact, a rush job. Pauling knew that DNA was important; he knew that Wilkins and Franklin were after it and that Bragg's group had already made at least one stab at it. He knew that it was a relatively simple structure compared to proteins. And he knew that whoever got out a roughly correct structure first—even if it was not quite right in all its details—would establish priority. That is what he was aiming for, not the last word on DNA but the first, the initial publication that would be cited by all following. It did not have to be precise. He wanted credit for the discovery.

The hurried haphazardness of the nucleic-acid paper can be understood by comparison to Pauling's protein work. Pauling's alpha helix was the result of more than a decade of off-and-on analysis and thousands of hours of meticulous crystallographic work. Before he published his model, his lab pinned down the structure of the amino-acid subunits to a fraction of a degree and a hundredth of an angstrom. There was an abundance of clean x-ray work available on the subject proteins, allowing Pauling to scrutinize and eliminate dozens of alternative structures. Two years passed between the time he came up with the rough idea for his helix and the time he published it. Much of that interval was spent with Corey, overseeing and refining the precise construction of a series of elaborate three-dimensional models.

None of that went into DNA.

Crick and Watson were downcast by the news from Peter in late December that Pauling had solved DNA. Alternating between bouts of despair and denial—trying to figure out how he could have beaten them and then deciding that he certainly could not have without seeing Wilkins and Franklin's x-ray work and then thinking, well, of course, he is Pauling, so anything is possible—they continued working on the problem themselves. If they could come up with something independently before Pauling's paper appeared, at least they might share credit.

The previous spring, a few months after they had been warned off DNA and a few months before Pauling's visit to the Cavendish, Crick and Watson had been introduced to Erwin Chargaff, the acerbic and opinionated Austrian-born biochemist who had been using chromatography to analyze the chemical compositions of nucleic acids. Chargaff was not impressed. "I never met two men who knew so little and aspired to so much," he said. "They told me they wanted to construct a helix, a polynucleotide to rival Pauling's alpha helix. They talked so much about 'pitch' that I remember I wrote it down afterwards, 'Two pitchmen in search of a helix.' " But this conversation was critical to Crick and Watson. Chargaff told them that there was a simple relationship between the occurrence of different bases in DNA, that adenine and thymine were present in roughly the same amounts and so were guanine and cytosine. One of each pair was a larger purine; the other, a smaller pyrimidine. Chargaff had told Pauling about the same relationship in 1947, and Pauling had paid little attention.

But it made all the difference to Crick and Watson. Franklin's criticisms had already pointed them toward putting the phosphates on the outside of the molecule; now they had the clue of a one-to-one relationship between the bases on the inside. They began thinking about helixes in which the purines and pyrimidines lined up somehow down the core of the molecule.

When Pauling's much-anticipated DNA manuscript arrived via Peter in early February 1953, both researchers were surprised to see something that looked like their own abortive three-chain effort, only more tightly put together. A few minutes' reading showed that there was no room at the core for the positive ions needed to hold together the negatively charged phosphates. Crick and Watson were dumbfounded. Pauling's structure depended on hydrogen bonds between the phosphate groups, but how could there be a hydrogen there when the phosphates in DNA lost their hydrogens at normal pH? "Without the hydrogen atoms, the chains would immediately fly apart," Watson said. They had already been through this with their own model, but they checked it again, and there it was in black and white in a respected text: the phosphates had to be ionized. The book they were looking at was Pauling's *General Chemistry*.

There was an immense feeling of relief. "If a student had made a similar mistake, he would be thought unfit to benefit from Caltech's chemistry faculty," Watson later said. He and Crick immediately were off to confirm their criticism with Cambridge's chemists. Before the day was out, Pauling's mistake was the talk of the college: Linus' chemistry was wrong.

Just as important for Watson, when he told Wilkins of Pauling's mistake and his idea that DNA was helical, he was given a reward: his first look at the more recent x-ray patterns Franklin had gotten from the molecule. She had found that DNA existed in two forms, a condensed dry form and an extended wet form the structure assumed when it drank up all that water. Astbury's photos, the ones Pauling had used, had been of a mixture.

The problem of the determination of sequence of amino-acid residues in the protein molecule through complementariness to the nucleic acid molecule is a very interesting one. Corey and I thought about it in connection with our proposed structure for nucleic acid (*Proc. Nat. Acad. Sci.* Feb., 1953) which stimulated Watson and Crick, who had a copy of the manuscript, to develop their structure, and I know that Watson and Crick have thought it over too. I feel that a decision has to be made through the consideration of the shapes of the molecules as to where the amino-acid residues fit in. The number of possibilities is, as you point out, about enough to explain the selection uniquely of the residues, in position of about 3.5 Angstrom from one another along the polynucleotide molecule.

Linus Pauling to George Gamow, December 1953

Franklin's recent shots, much clearer and of only the extended from, immediately confirmed to Watson that the molecule was a helix and gave him several vital parameters for its solution.

With obvious satisfaction, Crick wrote Pauling to thank him for providing an advance copy of his nucleic acid paper. "We were very struck by the ingenuity of the structure," he wrote. "The only doubt I have is that I do not see what holds it together."

Pauling's apparent misstep pleased Bragg so much that he agreed to let Crick and Watson go back full-time to DNA. There was a window of opportunity here, and he wanted the Cavendish to take advantage before Pauling had time to regroup.

Pauling, however, had already moved on to a new project, a theory of ferromagnetism that he worked on through the spring. He also began making plans for a major international protein conference in Caltech the next fall and was drawn back to DNA only when Peter wrote him in mid-February about the English hooting at his structure. Corey had by now finally finished checking Pauling's atomic coordinates, some of which appeared again to be unacceptably tight. "I am checking over the nucleic acid structure again, trying to refine the parameters a bit," Pauling wrote Peter back. "I heard a rumor that Jim Watson and Crick had formulated this structure already sometime back, but had not done anything about it. Probably the rumor is exaggerated." In late February he tried one of Schomaker's suggestions, of twisting the phosphate groups forty-five degrees, and found that it eased some of the strain.

Something was still wrong. When Pauling gave a seminar on his DNA structure at Caltech, the reception was cool; afterward, Delbrück told Schomaker that he thought Pauling's model was not convincing. He mentioned a letter he had gotten from Watson saying that Pauling's structure contained "some very bad mistakes" and in which Watson had added, "I have a pretty model, which is so pretty that I am surprised that no-one ever thought of it before." Pauling wanted to know more. He quickly wrote Watson, inviting him to his fall protein conference, mentioning that he had heard from Delbrück about his DNA work, and encouraging him to keep working on the problem. "Professor Corey and I do not feel that our structure has been proven to be right," he wrote, "although we incline to think that it is." In early March he drove with Ava Helen to the University of California at Riverside to examine a collection of organic phosphates there, finding candidates for structural analysis that would be similar to the phosphates groups in DNA, looking for models to tell him how much he could deform his tetrahedra. Crick's barb about what held the molecule together led him to gather chemical precedents for the existence of adjoining negative charges in the same molecule, and he began to reason to himself that perhaps the DNA core environment was a special one that allowed the phosphates to exist as he had proposed. It was still, to Pauling, a matter of phosphate chemistry. Meanwhile, Todd had sent him the requested samples of nucleotides, and Pauling started their x-ray analysis.

He was finally laying the groundwork for a reasonable structure. But it was too late.

Given the go-ahead to return to DNA, thanks to Pauling's paper, Crick and Watson each began feverishly devising models, focusing more on two-stranded models now that Chargraff had gotten them thinking of bases somehow pairing with each other. The "very pretty model" of which Watson had written Delbrück was one attempt, but it was wrong, as Jerry Donohue pointed out.

Donohue's input turned out to be critical. A *magna cum laude* graduate of Dartmouth who had worked and studied with Pauling at Caltech since the early 1940s, Donohue knew structural chemistry inside and out. Hydrogen bonding had been a specialty of his, and he saw that Crick and Watson, chemical novices that they were, had been playing with the wrong structures for guanine and thymine. He set them right, switching the hydrogen atoms essential for cross-bonding into their correct positions, destroying their earlier model and pushing them toward the correct solution.

With Donohue's corrections, Crick and Watson could now see hydrogen bonds forming naturally between specific pairs of purines and pyrimidines: adenine to thymine and guanine to cytosine. That was the last piece of the puzzle, and the result was dazzling. Matching a large with a small base down the middle not only smoothed the structure's outline but provided a simple explanation for Chargaff's findings. The resulting structure, a sort of ladder with pairs as the steps and the sugar-phosphate backbone as the runners, formed easily into a helix that matched the x-ray data.

More than beautiful, the structure had meaning. Each strand was a complementary mirror image of the other; if separated, each could act as a mold for forming a new double helix identical with the original. This immediately provided ideas about replication that Pauling's model, with its bases facing out and unrelated to each other, could not.

On March 12, Watson sent Delbrück a letter, illustrated with rough sketches, discussing their new model. He warned his mentor not to tell Pauling about it until they were more certain of their results, but Delbrück, never one to keep secrets, immediately showed the letter around. Pauling's mind raced as he read it. He saw immediately that the Cavendish structure was not only chemically reasonable but biologically intriguing. "The simplicity of the structural complementariness of the two pyrimidines and their corresponding purines was a surprise to me—a pleasant one, of course, because of the great illumination it threw on the problem of the mechanism of heredity," he said. In it he could see echoes of many of the things he had been thinking and writing about complementarity.

Pauling, while not yet ready to concede the race, was impressed. A few days after seeing Watson's letter, he wrote a colleague, "You must, of course, recognize that our proposed structure is nothing more than a proposed structure. There is a chance that it is right, but it will probably be two or three years before we can be reasonably sure…" A few days later, he received an advance copy of the Watson and Crick manuscript, which started by attacking his DNA model and ended by thanking Jerry Donohue for his help. Pauling looked it over and wrote his son, "I think that it is fine that there are now two proposed structures for nucleic acid, and I am looking forward to finding out what the decision will be as to which is incorrect. Without doubt the King's-College data will eliminate one or the other."

He still had not seen any of Franklin's or Wilkins's recent x-ray photos and withheld final judgement until he did. His chance would come soon: he was planning to go to Brussels in April for a Solvay Conference on proteins and intended to stop off in England on the way to see the Watson-Crick model and the photos from Wilkins's and Franklin's laboratories.

In early April, a few days after Crick and Watson submitted their DNA paper for publication, Pauling arrived in Cambridge. After spending the night with Peter, he walked into Crick's office and for the first time saw the three-dimensional model they had wired together out of diecut metal plates. Crick chattered nervously about the features of the double helix while Pauling scrutinized it. He then examined Franklin's photo of the extended form of the molecule. Watson and Crick waited. Then, "gracefully," Watson remembered, "he gave the opinion that we had the answer."

It was a joyful moment for the two young men and a deflating one for Pauling. He was amazed that this unlikely team, an adolescent postdoc and an elderly graduate student, had come up with so elegant a solution to so important a structure. If they were right, his own model was a monstrous mistake, built inside out with the wrong number of chains. But he recognized now that the Cavendish team was almost certainly right.

There was only one thing left for him to do: show the world how to handle defeat with style.

Pauling left Crick's office and met Bragg for lunch, during which Sir Lawrence vainly tried to restrain his ebullience. After so many years of coming in second, his team had finally beaten Pauling! Later, Pauling joined the Cricks at a pleasant dinner at their house at Portugal Place. Through it all he remained charming and funny and remarkably accepting of the new DNA structure, a true gentleman, both wise enough to recognize defeat and great enough to accept it with good humor. A day or two later both Bragg and Pauling went to the Solvay meeting—an occasional select gathering of the world's top researchers funded by a Belgian industrialist—where Bragg provided the first public announcement of the double helix. Pauling was generous in his support. "Although it is only two months since Professor Corey and I published our proposed structure for the nucleic acid, I think that we must admit that it is probably wrong," he told the group. "Although some refinement might be made, I feel that it is very likely that the Watson-Crick structure is essentially correct."

THE GENESIS OF THE MOLECULAR CLOCK

Gregory J. Morgan

❧❧❧

Linus Pauling's legacy can be judged partly by his foresight in the selection of research projects and collaborators. With a view to the future of evolutionary biology, he insisted that his postdoctoral fellow, Emile Zuckerkandl, examine the evolution of hemoglobin. This decision heralded one of the beginnings of contemporary molecular evolution, a field Zuckerkandl and Pauling helped to delimit as the study of the history of "one-dimensional" molecules, protein, RNA, and DNA. Over the last forty years, molecular evolution research has grown and flourished. However, one cannot understand Pauling's fruitful choice of this research agenda apart from considerations of the larger goals of Pauling's life. Exploring the evolution of molecules, Pauling hoped, would strengthen the argument against nuclear testing and increase our understanding of molecular disease.

INTRODUCTION

In the early 1960s, Emile Zuckerkandl and Linus Pauling proposed the simple but controversial idea of a "molecular evolutionary clock." The molecular clock hypothesis, as it came to be known, proposed that the rate of evolution in a given protein molecule is approximately constant over time. More specifically, it proposed that the time elapsed since the last common ancestor of two proteins would be roughly proportional to the number of amino acid differences between their sequences. The molecular clock, therefore, would not be a metronomic clock—that is, its "ticks and tocks" would not be uniform—but would instead be a clock based upon random mutation events. In practice, a molecular clock would allow biologists to date the branching points of evolutionary trees.

The molecular clock hypothesis, while rarely cited among Pauling's most important discoveries, has proven to be very influential. The UC Berkeley biologist Alan Wilson claimed that the molecular clock is the most significant result of research in molecular evolution. In his book *Patterns of Evolution*, Roger Lewin describes the molecular clock as "one of the simplest and most powerful concepts in the field of evolution." Francis Crick, co-discoverer of the structure of DNA, called the molecular clock a very important idea that turned out to be much truer than most thought when it was proposed.

ZUCKERKANDL AND PAULING'S COMPARATIVE HEMOGLOBIN RESEARCH

Pauling's research in molecular biology had its roots in the hemoglobin investigations he first undertook in the 1930s when he and Charles Coryell, a postdoctoral fellow, both motivated by purely chemical questions, examined the magnetic properties of hemoglobin. Hemoglobin research was conducted under Pauling's supervision for the next two decades. In 1949, using Tiselius moving band electrophoresis, Harvey Itano and Linus Pauling, with help from S. J. Singer and I. C. Wells, showed that molecules of sickle-cell hemoglobin moved differently than normal molecules of hemoglobin in an electric field. Accordingly, they coined the term "molecular disease" to describe sickle-cell anemia. (It was later shown that sickle-cell hemoglobin had one amino acid residue different than normal hemoglobin.)

Pauling began to think about evolution at the molecular level in a focused way during the 1ate 1950s. This interest had both scientific and political dimensions.

Pauling was aware of early evolutionary work with hemoglobin through reading Karl Landsteiner's landmark book *The Specificity of Serological Reactions* in 1936. In the second chapter of his book, Landsteiner discusses work that uses chemical differences to measure differences between species.

Portrait of Linus Pauling, 1958

For example, he considers the discovery that the shapes and angles of hemoglobin crystals are characteristic for each species, and the differences between crystals are more pronounced between species that are more distantly related to one another. In the fall of 1937, while Pauling was the George Fisher Baker Lecturer in Chemistry at Cornell University, Landsteiner and he spoke at length about serology. The meeting had a lasting effect on Pauling, affecting the trajectory of his subsequent research into both hemoglobin and immunology.

In the latter half of his life, Pauling became more interested in humanistic issues. His wife Ava Helen, who was perhaps more liberal and politically aware than he, influenced his political and ethical development. His ethical framework was made explicit—Pauling believed that the correct moral code should be based upon the minimization of human suffering. Accordingly, this ethical principle provided a motivational force that influenced two other elements in his life that led to his evolutionary work with hemoglobin—his spirited protest against the testing of nuclear weapons, and his interest in disease, especially molecular diseases such as sickle-cell anemia.

Between 1950 and 1963 Pauling became increasingly involved in the debate over the genetic effects of radioactive fallout. This in turn led him to think more deeply about mutation, molecular disease, and evolution, and provided motivation to conduct research on molecular evolution with Zuckerkandl. By 1955, Pauling was quoting the views of prominent geneticists such as Herman Muller, Kurt Stern, and Alfred Sturtevant in his ongoing debate with William Libby over the dangers of natural radiation and man-made radiation. In 1958 Pauling debated Edward Teller, the Hungarian physicist known as "the father of the H-bomb," on KQED, an educational television channel based in San Francisco. Teller brought up the question of genetic damage, arguing that very small amounts of radioactivity might be helpful rather than harmful. Countering this type of argument required that Pauling discuss evolution through mutation and natural selection.

After *Life* magazine refused to publish a reply to a defamatory protesting article by Teller and Latter, Pauling began writing his book *No More War!* In this popular book, Pauling included a six-page section called "Mutation and Evolution." To write his book and participate in the fallout debate, Pauling read, discussed, and became quite proficient in genetics and evolutionary theory. However, he needed a collaborator to pursue these questions further.

Emile Zuckerkandl was born into a prominent Viennese family in 1922. During the Second World War the Zuckerkandls fled Austria, first to Paris, and then to Algiers. After the war and a year's biological study at the Sorbonne in Paris, Zuckerkandl undertook graduate studies in physiology at the University of Illinois under the direction of C. Ladd Prosser. On completing his master's degree, Zuckerkandl returned to France, completed a doctoral degree at the Sorbonne, and secured a job at a marine laboratory in Roscoff, Brittany.

His early work on the molting cycle of crabs developed into an interest in the roles of copper oxidases and hemocyanin in the molting cycle. Although the position at the marine laboratory was pleasant, secure, and allowed Zuckerkandl to meet internationally respected biologists such as Ernst Mayr during the summers, Zuckerkandl and his wife, Jane, considered returning to America to escape the isolation of the remaining three seasons. Taking the advice of Professor Alfred Stern and others, Zuckerkandl wrote to Linus Pauling, who was planning a trip to France, and arranged a meeting with him in Paris in the summer of 1957. In a hotel in Paris, Zuckerkandl proposed a research project on hemocyanin and copper oxidases. Pauling was receptive. The famous chemist was impressed by the young researcher and recommended him for a post-doctoral fellowship in chemistry under his direction.

In September 1959, Emile and Jane Zuckerkandl arrived at Caltech. Zuckerkandl recounted his first meeting with Pauling: "He said, you know this subject of yours on hemocyanin and copper oxidases, I think the results are going to be difficult to interpret and I think you would do better to work on a protein about which more is known, ... why don't you work on hemoglobin?" Pauling suggested that Zuckerkandl analyze the hemoglobin of various primates using the newly invented electrophoretic-chromatographic technique of "finger-printing," recently popularized by Cambridge hemoglobin researcher Vernon Ingram. This technique combined two "one-dimensional" techniques of paper chromatography and paper electrophoresis to form unique two-dimensional patterns of hemoglobin cleaved into pieces. Using the technique on the hemoglobin of various species, Pauling hoped they could draw evolutionary conclusions. Pauling arranged for Zuckerkandl to work with his graduate student Richard T. Jones in Professor Walter Schroeder's laboratory, since at that time Pauling did not have a laboratory of his own.

For the first two or three months of Zuckerkandl's appointment, Jones taught Zuckerkandl how to finger-print proteins. After Zuckerkandl had perfected the technique, he widened the number of species in the analysis from primates to include cow, pig, shark, bony fish, lungfish and Echiurid "worm." Using this technique, Zuckerkandl, Pauling, and Jones drew qualitative conclusions from their comparative study, which they completed in the summer of 1960. Their study showed that the gorilla, chimpanzee, and human patterns were almost identical in appearance. The further the evolutionary distance from the primates, the more different was the hemoglobin "finger-print." While the qualitative differences were clear, measuring quantitative differences would require a more detailed description of the amino-acid sequences.

At this time, three rival laboratories were working on the complete amino acid sequences of two components of human hemoglobin (the alpha and beta chains): Walter Schroeder's laboratory at Caltech; Gerhard Braunitzer's laboratory at the Max Planck Institute in Munich; and Lyman Craig's laboratory at the Rockefeller Institute in New York City. Max Delbrück, returning to Caltech from a visit to Braunitzer's laboratory in Germany in the spring of 1960, brought back the sequence of the thirty terminal residues of the human beta chain, and Zuckerkandl was able to compare it with the preliminary results of Schroeder's group. Through this comparison, Zuckerkandl correctly inferred that the alpha and beta chains are homologous, that is, they have a common ancestor and arose as distinct chains through a duplication event. Once Schroeder returned from sabbatical in Denmark, he and Zuckerkandl discussed whether or not the similarity in sequence was evidence for common ancestry. Unfortunately, Schroeder disagreed with Zuckerkandl's inference and they did not publish the discovery. However, the idea that the hemoglobin chains were homologous legitimated further evolutionary analysis of the different chains *within* a single species as well as chains from different species.

In early 1961, Zuckerkandl began working with Schroeder in determining the amino acid composition of gorilla hemoglobin using an automatic amino-acid sequencer. The results of the compositional analysis, published in *Nature*, showed that the alpha chains of gorilla and human hemoglobin probably differed by only two residues and the beta chains by one. (It was later found that the gorilla and human alpha chain actually differed by only one residue.) Zuckerkandl and Pauling used these quantitative results in their next paper to calculate the time of divergence between gorilla and human using the evolutionary molecular clock.

In late November 1960, Pauling accepted an invitation to submit a paper to be published in a volume dedicated to Albert Szent-Györgyi, the Nobel Prize-winning discoverer of vitamin C. On June 22, 1961, Pauling wrote to inform Dr. Bernard Pullman, an editor of the volume, that he would write on "The Molecular Basis for Disease." Zuckerkandl recounts how Pauling came down from his office to Schroeder's lab, a floor below, to ask him to collaborate on the paper: "I said, I would with pleasure, and he said, 'you know it is for Szent-Györgyi, so we should say something outrageous!' " This set the tone for much of the future collaboration between Pauling and Zuckerkandl—Pauling would be invited to submit to a *Festschrift* volume without peer review, the article would be written by Zuckerkandl, and together they would publish the pioneering paper on molecular evolution. After Zuckerkandl traveled to Seattle and Berkeley to check some final details with geneticists there, the historic paper was finally completed and sent to the publishers on November 1, 1961. The Szent-Györgyi paper was written by Zuckerkandl, and many people did find parts of it outrageous, especially those traditional biologists and anthropologists who disputed the whole idea of the molecular clock.

The most novel feature of the historic article, titled, "Molecular Disease, Evolution, and Genic Heterogeneity," is the first application of the then-unnamed molecular evolutionary clock. The idea of using the number of amino acid substitutions to make temporal divergence estimates evolved as Zuckerkandl wrote the paper. In the article, Zuckerkandl and Pauling explicitly assume the homology of the globin genes: "in the course of time the hemoglobin chain genes duplicate, . . . the descendants of the duplicate genes 'mutate away' from each other, and the duplicates eventually become distributed through translocations over different parts of the genome." In a somewhat cautious manner, the authors then compared horse and human alpha chains to calibrate the clock:

> *It is possible to evaluate very roughly and tentatively the time that has elapsed since any of the hemoglobin chains present in a given species … diverged from a common chain ancestor. … From paleontological evidence it may be estimated that the common ancestor of man and horse lived … between 100 and 160 million years ago. … the presence of eighteen differences between human and horse alpha chains would indicate that*

each chain had nine evolutionary effective mutations in 100 to 160
millions [sic] of years. This yields a figure of 11 to 18 million years per
amino acid substitution in a chain of about 150 amino acids, with a
medium [sic] figure of 14.5 million years.

Using the figure of 14.5 million years per amino acid substitution per 150 residue polypeptide, Zuckerkandl and Pauling calculated the time of derivation from the common chain ancestor of the gorilla alpha and human alpha and gorilla beta and human beta chains, as 14.5 and 7.3 million years respectively. They note that the inferred divergence of gorilla and human of 11 million years, although a little lower than was thought, was consistent with the range estimated by paleontologists.

Pauling wove the idea of the molecular clock into numerous lectures he gave over the next five years. Often he would combine a lecture on molecular evolution with a lecture on science and peace. Pauling believed that, through the detailed determination of amino acid sequences of hemoglobin and other molecules, we would obtain much information about the course of the evolutionary process.

In September 1964, the Institute of Microbiology at Rutgers University held the seminal symposium, "Evolving Genes and Proteins," organized by Vernon Bryson and Henry Vogel. In many ways, this conference marks the beginning of the modern field of molecular evolution. Many eminent biologists were present to hear Zuckerkandl deliver a collaborative paper, "Evolutionary Divergence and Convergence in Proteins," that some consider to be most influential of Pauling's later career. This lengthy piece, written by Zuckerkandl, finally named the molecular evolutionary clock and derived the mathematical function that characterizes it.

Interestingly their derivation did not mention any selective processes. However, the remainder of the lengthy text gives ample evidence to suggest that natural selection leads to different probabilities of substitution at each site, and is consistent with Zuckerkandl's claim that natural selection is perfectly compatible with the clock. The 1965 article represented the pinnacle and culmination of the previous five fruitful years of collaboration between Linus Pauling and Emile Zuckerkandl.

EARLY REACTION TO THE MOLECULAR EVOLUTIONARY CLOCK

The biological and anthropological communities were at first unreceptive to the idea that evolution at the molecular level might proceed at a constant rate. One of the first confrontations between the champions of the new molecular approach and the heirs of the organismal orthodoxy occurred at a milestone conference entitled "Classification and Human Evolution" at Burg Wartenstein, Austria, in the summer of 1962. Zuckerkandl presented a paper whose title introduced the new controversial term "molecular anthropology." A "restricted committee" meeting consisting of B. Campbell, T. Dobzhansky, M. Goodman, G. A. Harrison, H. P. Klinger, E. Mayr, G. G. Simpson, and Zuckerkandl considered the utility of the molecular approach for anthropology and the study of evolution. Only Morris Goodman, who had used immunological properties of proteins to reconstruct phylogenies, shared Zuckerkandl's optimism about the utility of the molecular approach. Simpson and Mayr were skeptical of the clock hypothesis and the study of molecular evolution in general. Concerning the use of amino acid sequences as discontinuous characters, Simpson argued that they had no important advantage over morphological characters. For example, Simpson pointed out that the clock ignores variation in the rates of evolution and would be highly inaccurate when applied to short lapses of time. Furthermore, they were skeptical of the use of single characters, as they took a molecule to be, to accurately measure evolutionary rates and similarity between species. "Seemingly contradictory evidence (e.g., that of the hemoglobins as reported by Zuckerkandl in this book) indicates merely that in certain characters *Homo* and its allies [e.g., gorilla] retain ancestral resemblances and that these are not the characters involved in their radical divergence ...," Simpson wrote in 1963. Two years later he reiterated his well-received comments even more strongly:

> Zuckerkandl has shown that "From the point of view of hemoglobin structure, it appears that gorilla is just an abnormal human, or man an abnormal gorilla, and the two species form actually one continuous population." From any other point of view other than that properly specified, that is, of course, nonsense. What the comparison seems really to indicate is that in this case, at least, hemoglobin is a bad choice and has nothing to tell us about affinities, or indeed tells us a lie. ... Of course, as Zuckerkandl points out, we should not use just one kind of molecule but many, preferably proteins. However, if one can be misleading, so can many!

In a 1963 piece, Ernst Mayr echoed Simpson's criticism, "Man's shift into the niche of the bipedal, tool-making, speech-using hominid necessitated a drastic reconstruction of his morphology, but this morphology did not, in turn, require a revamping of his biochemical system." He wrote: "Different characters and character complexes thus diverged at different rates." Interestingly, Mayr and Simpson appear to be little concerned with defending any strong dependencies between evolution at the molecular and organismal levels.

A 1964 meeting at Rutgers proved to be a battle-ground between the molecularly and organismally inclined biologists, but nonetheless was marked by an unusually fruitful exchange among biochemists, molecular biologists, evolutionists, geneticists, taxonomists, exobiologists, and microbiologists. Zuckerkandl wrote to Pauling informing him that a long paper was needed, given the mostly negative reaction of people to what he now called "chemical paleogenetics." But the fast pace of advances in molecular biology, coupled with a growing appreciation for the value of the field, was helping to turn the tide.

CONCLUSION

The 1960s saw the development of the new field of molecular evolution. The series of largely theoretical papers that arose from the collaboration between Zuckerkandl and Pauling were founding documents of the new discipline. In these early years, there was no disciplinary journal. Instead, Zuckerkandl and Pauling published in *Festschrift* volumes. As an eminent scientist, Pauling was often invited to submit papers to these volumes. He then co-opted Zuckerkandl's co-authorship and they published papers principally written and conceived by Zuckerkandl. Without the constraints of peer review, this medium allowed them much freedom in articulating their position. These volumes and a number of seminal conferences disseminated their pioneering ideas such as the evolutionary molecular clock.

From the beginning, Zuckerkandl and Pauling's work sought to use the tools of molecular biology to enlighten studies of evolution. Pauling's initial motivation stemmed from his desire to show that radioactive fallout caused human suffering and did not, as Edward Teller suggested, improve the evolutionary process. With some foresight, he pushed Zuckerkandl into evolutionary hemoglobin research. Zuckerkandl and Pauling's focus of the primary structure (i.e., the amino acid sequence) of hemoglobin centered the emerging field of molecular evolution on a particular class of molecular phenomena.

In current biology, the molecular clock is often associated with the view that natural section is of little importance at the molecular level. Nonetheless when the clock was proposed in 1962 it was not intended to be a neutral clock. Instead, Zuckerkandl and Pauling were closer to their protagonists Mayr and Simpson in emphasizing the importance of selection. As a chemist and a biochemist/molecular biologist respectively, Pauling and Zuckerkandl viewed the protein molecule as a series of functionally constrained amino acid sites with the functional constraints enforced by natural selection. For Zuckerkandl and Pauling, then, promotion of the molecular clock hypothesis amounted to the commitment that molecular selection pressures remain approximately constant over evolutionary time.

ORTHOMOLECULAR MEDICINE DEFINED

Linus Pauling

*In 1967, Pauling wrote a paper, "Orthomolecular Psychiatry," which appeared in the April 19, 1968, issue of **Science**. It was in that paper that he first introduced the word "orthomolecular." Orthomolecular, he said in that article, meant, literally, "the right molecules in the right amounts." Pauling believed that this would be an important enough field of medicine to justify having its own name. He chose the word "orthomolecular" because it was broader in scope than the term "megavitamin," which was already being used in a different context.*

I believe that in general the treatment of disease by the use of substances such as ascorbic acid that are normally present in the human body and are required for life is to be preferred to treatment by the use of powerful synthetic substances or plant products, which may, and usually do, have undesirable side effects. Such substances as vitamin C and most of the other vitamins are remarkable for their low toxicity and absence of side effects when taken in amounts larger than those usually available in the diet. I have coined the term *orthomolecular medicine* for the preservation of good health and the treatment of disease by varying the concentrations in the human body of substances that are normally present in the body and are required for health. Dr. Bernard Rimland has emphasized my point by suggesting that conventional medicine, which uses drugs, be called toximolecular medicine.

Death by starvation, kwashiorkor, beriberi, scurvy, or any other deficiency disease can be averted by providing an adequate daily intake of carbohydrates, essential fats, proteins (including the essential amino acids), essential minerals, and thiamine, ascorbic acid, and other vitamins. To achieve the best of health, the rate of intake of essential foods should be such as to establish and maintain the optimum concentrations of essential molecules, such as those of ascorbic acid.

An example of orthomolecular medicine is the treatment of diabetes mellitus by the injection of insulin. Diabetes mellitus is a hereditary disease, usually caused by a recessive gene. The hereditary defect results in a deficient production by the pancreas of the hormone insulin. The primary action of insulin is to cause an increase in the rate of extraction of glucose from the blood into the cells, where it can be metabolized. In the absence of insulin the concentration of glucose in the blood of the patient becomes much greater than normal, resulting in manifestations of the disease.

Insulin extracted from cattle pancreas or pig pancreas differs only slightly in its molecular structure from human insulin, and it has essentially the same physiological activity. The injection of cattle insulin or pig insulin in a human is essentially the provision of the normal concentration of insulin in the body of the patient; it permits the metabolism of glucose to take place at the normal rate and thus serves to counteract the abnormality resulting from the genetic defect. Insulin therapy is accordingly an example of orthomolecular therapy. Its major disadvantage is that the insulin can only be introduced to the bloodstream by injection.

Another example of orthomolecular treatment of this disease, if it is not serious, is by adjusting the diet, regulating the intake of sugar, especially, in

Pauling's early (1966) thoughts on orthomolecular psychiatry

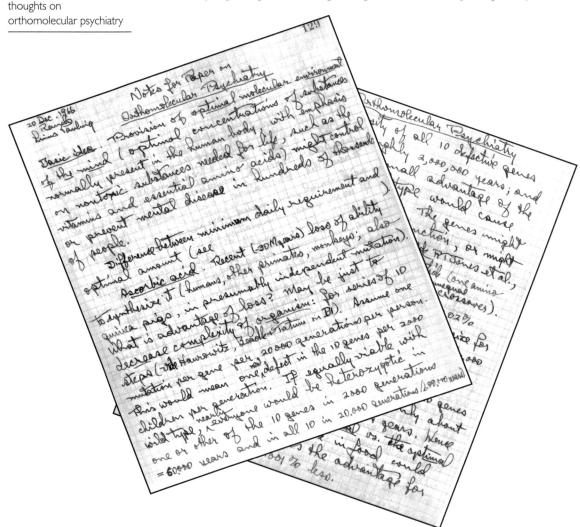

such a way as to keep the glucose concentration in the blood within the normal limits. A third example is increasing the intake of vitamin C to decrease the need for insulin. Dice and Daniel reported from the study of one diabetic subject that for each gram of L-ascorbic acid taken by mouth the amount of insulin required could be reduced by two units.

A fourth way to control diabetes, by using so-called oral insulin, a drug taken by mouth, does not constitute an example of orthomolecular medicine, because the oral insulin is a synthetic drug, foreign to the human body, which may have undesirable side effects.

Another disease that is treated by orthomolecular methods is phenylketonuria. It results from a genetic defect that leads to a decreased amount or effectiveness of an enzyme in the liver that in normal persons catalyzes the oxidation of one amino acid, phenylalanine, to another, tyrosine. Ordinary proteins contain several percent of phenylalanine, providing a much larger amount of this amino acid than a person needs. The concentration of phenylalanine in the blood and other body fluids of the patient becomes abnormally high, if he or she is on a normal diet, causing mental deficiency, severe eczema, and other manifestations. The disease can be controlled by a diet, beginning in infancy, that contains a smaller amount of phenylalanine than is present in ordinary foods. In this way the concentration of phenylalanine in the blood and other body fluids is kept approximately the normal level, and the manifestations of the disease do not appear.

A somewhat similar disease, which can also be controlled by orthomolecular methods, is galactosemia. It involves the failure of manufacture of the enzyme that carries out the metabolism of galactose, which is a part of milk sugar (lactose). The disease manifests itself in mental retardation, cataracts, cirrhosis of the liver and spleen, and nutritional failure. These manifestations are averted by placing the infant on a diet free of milk sugar, with the result that the concentration of galactose in the blood does not exceed the normal limit.

A conceivable sort of orthomolecular therapy of phenylketonuria or other hereditary diseases involving a defective gene would be to introduce the gene (molecules of deoxyribonucleic acid, or DNA), separated from the tissues of another person, into the cells of the person suffering from disease. For example, some molecules of the gene that directs the synthesis of the enzyme that catalyzes the oxidation of phenylalanine to tyrosine could be separated from liver cells of a normal human being and introduced into the liver cells of a person with phenylketonuria. This sort of change in the genetic character of an organism has been carried out for microorganisms but not yet of human beings, and it is not likely that it will become an important way of controlling genetic defects until many decades have passed.

Another possible method of orthomolecular therapy for phenylketonuria, resembling the use of insulin in controlling diabetes, would be the injection of the active enzyme. There are two reasons why this treatment has not been developed. First, although it is known that the enzyme is present in the liver of animals, including humans, it has not yet been isolated in purified form. Second, the natural mechanism of immunity, which involves the action of antibodies against proteins foreign to the species, would operate to destroy the enzyme prepared from the liver of animals of another species. This mechanism in general prevents the use of enzymes or other proteins from animals other than humans in the treatment of diseases of human beings.

There is still another possible type of orthomolecular therapy. The molecules of many enzymes consist of two parts: the pure protein part, called the apoenzyme, and a nonprotein part, called the coenzyme. The active enzyme, called the holoenzyme, is the apoenzyme with the coenzyme attached to it. Often the coenzyme is a vitamin in molecule or a closely related molecule. It is known, for example, that a number of different enzymes in the human body, catalyzing different chemical reactions, have thiamine diphosphate, a derivative of thiamine (vitamin B_1), as a coenzyme.

In some cases of genetic disease the enzyme is not absent but is present with diminished activity. One way in which the defective gene can operate is to produce an apoenzyme with abnormal structure, such that it does not combine readily with the coenzyme to form the active enzyme. Under ordinary physiological conditions, with the normal concentration of coenzyme, perhaps only 1 percent of the abnormal apoenzyme has combined with the coenzyme. According to the principles of chemical equilibrium, a larger amount of abnormal apoenzyme could be made to combine with the coenzyme by increasing the concentration of the coenzyme in the body fluids. If the concentration were to be increased one hundred times, most of the apoenzyme molecules might combine with the coenzyme, to give essentially the normal amount of active enzyme.

There is accordingly the possibility that the disease could be kept under control by the ingestion by the patient of a very large amount of the vitamin that serves as a coenzyme. This sort of orthomolecular therapy, involving only a substance normally present in the human body (the vitamin), is, in my opinion, the preferable therapy.

An example of a disease that sometimes is controlled in this way is the disease methylmalonicaciduria. Patients with this disease are deficient in the active enzyme that catalyzes the conversion of a simple substance, methylamolonic acid, to succinic acid. It is known that cyanocabolamin (vitamin B_{12}) serves as the coenzyme for this reaction. It is found that the provision of very large amounts of vitamin B_{12}, giving concentrations about a thousand times the normal concentration, causes the reaction to proceed at the normal rate for many patients.

The use of very large amounts of vitamins in the control of disease, called megavitamin therapy, is an important procedure in orthomolecular medicine. It is my opinion that in the course of time it will be found possible to control hundreds of diseases by megavitamin therapy. For example, Abram Hoffer and Humphry Osmond demonstrated that many patients with schizophrenia are benefited by megavitamin therapy. Their treatment includes the administration of nicotinic acid (niacin) or nicotinamide (niacinamide) in amounts of 3 grams (g) to 18 g per day, together with 3 g to 18 g per day of ascorbic acid, and good amounts of other vitamins.

It is usually thought that a drug that is claimed to be a cure for many different diseases cannot have any value against any one of them. Yet there is evidence that a large intake of Vitamin C helps to control a great many diseases: not only the common cold and the flu, but also other viral and bacterial diseases, such as hepatitis, and also quite unrelated diseases, including schizophrenia, cardiovascular disease, and cancer. There is a reason for this difference between vitamin C and ordinary drugs. On the one hand, most drugs are powerful substances that interact in a specific way with one kind of molecule or tissue or agent of disease in the body so as to help to control a particular disease. The substance may, however, interact in a harmful way with other parts of the body, thus producing the side effects that make drugs dangerous.

Pauling's 1967 notes on the use of large amounts of vitamin C to treat schizophrenia

Vitamin C, on the other hand, is a normal constituent of the body, required for life. It is involved in essentially all of the biochemical reactions that take place in the body and in all of the body's protective mechanisms. With the ordinary intake of vitamin C these reactions and mechanisms do not operate efficiently; the person ingesting only the 60-milligram (mg) Recommended Dietary Allowance (RDA) is in what might be called ordinary poor health—what the physicians and nutritionists call "ordinary good health." The optimum intake of vitamin C, together with other health measures, can provide really good health, with increased protection against all diseases. That increase in protection is secured by strengthening the immune system, a process in which vitamin C plays a crucial role. The optimum intake is necessarily large. When that lesson is learned and practiced, the protection provided by vitamin C may well be the most important of all methods of orthomolecular medicine. While less is known about the other vitamins, there is no doubt that, used in proper amounts, they also can be of great value.

It is especially important to try improved nutrition in the effort to control "incurable" diseases, as was pointed out by Cheraskin and Ringsdorf, who gave multiple sclerosis as one of their examples. A recommendation to try a drug when there is not strong evidence for its probable effectiveness should not be made, of course, because drugs are dangerous. It is fortunate that vitamins are so lacking in toxicity and harmful side effects that this caveat does not apply to them.

I remember a young physician who came to my home thirteen years ago and said, "Dr. Pauling, you saved my life. I was dying of chronic hepatitis, but I heard about high-dose vitamin C, and it has cured me."

Since then good studies of the value of vitamin C in the prevention and treatment of hepatitis have been made, but there are other diseases for which such studies have not yet been carried out. One of these is amyotrophic lateral sclerosis (ALS), brought to public attention as the disease of which the famous Yankee outfielder Lou Gehrig died. In August 1985 I received a letter from a physician who described himself in the following way:

> *I am a medical "miracle." I've suffered from ALS for over eight years, with loss of function pretty well localized, and no spreading. I take between 12 and 20 grams of ascorbic acid every day, avoid fats and greases, and take at least 200 mg of a full B complex every day.*

The acceptance of orthomolecular medicine would surely help somewhat to solve one of the great present-day problems, the high cost of health care. In 1965 the total public and private spending on health care in the United States was $40 billion; in twenty years it has increased tenfold, to $400 billion. The increasing cost of medical care, amplified by inflation, accounted for 76 percent of this increase and population growth for 11 percent. The cost of health care was 6 percent of the gross national product in 1965 and 11 percent in 1985. This increase reflects both the rapid rise in charges for medical services (after corrections for inflation) and the increasing availability of expensive high-technology methods of diagnosis and treatment. A recent discussion of high–tech cardiology mentioned some of the new technologies now in use: telemetry units for monitoring arrythmias, diagnostic cardiac catheterization, invasive electrophysiologic assessments, permanent artificial pacemakers, electrocardiography and Doppler studies of assessing cardiac function, nuclear imaging, open-heart surgery, and heart transplantation. The discussion went on to new technologies soon to be applied: magnetic resonance imaging, high-speed computerized tomography scanning of the heat; and implantable "cardioverters" that automatically correct potentially lethal arrhythmias. Additional technologies include implantable defibrillators in high-risk patients to restore the cardiac beat after arrest, artificial heart implantation, and laser angioscopy to visualize atherosclerotic coronary plaques directly and to guide the "recanalizing" of obstructive narrowing.

Among the problems associated with this development are the very high costs and the pressures from both patients and physicians to make sometimes inappropriate use of the techniques. Dr. George A. Beller, of the University of Virginia, listed ten forces that operate against cost containment in cardiology: First, physicians are motivated to provide the highest quality care possible, regardless of cost. Second, most physicians are still on a fee-for-service basis. Third, physicians are paid the highest premium for performing technologically sophisticated procedures. Fourth, physicians are likely to try to convince hospital administrators to acquire the latest innovations. Fifth, the administrators are under pressure to increase the hospital's share of patients in the face of competition and therefore view it desirable to acquire these technologies. Sixth, patients are attracted to hospitals offering the latest equipment, services, and modern technologies. Seventh, suppliers of high-tech goods and services have an interest in continued growth. Eighth, some physicians feel pressure to order tests that they know are probably unnecessary because a consultant has written them as suggestions in the patient's chart. If the patient does not do well, failure to follow the consultant's advice could be considered negligent in court. The fear of a malpractice suit is certainly an inhibiting factor in cost containment. Ninth, it is often difficult to distinguish tests that are undertaken for clinical research from tests that are necessary for clinical management. Tenth, the need for an ultimate diagnosis has been a prevailing factor in cardiologic practice.

Beller also pointed out that another force is our society's special sympathy for those who are suffering. He quoted Gregory Pence of the University of Alabama as saying,

> *Medical costs are uncontrollable because we lack moral agreement about how to deny medical services. Deciding how to say "no," and to say it with honesty and integrity, is perhaps the most profound, most difficult moral question our society will face in the coming years.*

These are difficult problems. I believe that orthomolecular medicine can contribute to their solution. Vitamins are much less expensive than drugs. The amount of suffering caused to the patient by the treatment should be taken into consideration—a high intake of vitamins improves the state of well–being of the patient and helps to control the unpleasant side effects of some conventional therapies. Finally, if the aim of medical care is not merely to cure sickness but to promote health, then it should be foremost in the physician's mind that improved nutrition can help the patient significantly in reaching the goal of a good and satisfying life.

"There Will Always Be Something Interesting"

Interview with Neil A. Campbell, October 22, 1980

❧❧❧

Linus Pauling was eighty years old when he granted the following interview to reporter Neil A. Campbell. Campbell caught his subject in a talkative and autumnal mood, thoughtfully noting those things that seemed, in retrospect, most important to him. When read in contrast to the young Pauling's enthusiastic belief in scientific progress expressed in "The Dawn of Man," it is especially interesting to note his comments to Campbell, late in the interview, about the potential effects of a full understanding of life at the molecular level: "We could expect that this would be the end of religious dogma and the bias that is associated with it," Pauling says. "But I don't think that that's the way the world works."

CAMPBELL: *Dr. Pauling, I think many students would begin by asking you why the modern biology curriculum includes so much chemistry?*

PAULING: Well, biology is moving in the direction of chemistry. The whole field of molecular biology, which one might say is modern biology, has developed since I was a student. Much of the understanding of biology that exists now is based on the structure of molecules and the properties of molecules in relation to their structure. If you have that basis, then biology isn't just a collection of disconnected facts. And, of course, chemistry itself has changed in the last sixty years from being largely a collection of disconnected facts to being a science with a good theoretical or structural basis. Just as we can understand some of the properties of living organisms in terms of the molecules that make up those organisms, we can understand the properties of molecules in terms of the atoms that make them up, and the way their atoms are connected in the molecule.

CAMPBELL: *You began your own career as a chemist. What attracted you to biology?*

PAULING: Well, I wanted to understand the world. And back in 1919, let's say, when I began thinking about problems and devoting more and more of my time to trying to understand the world, I was forced to study molecules with relatively simple structure. So in 1922, when I started my graduate work, I began using the technique of x-ray diffraction to determine structures for crystals of simple inorganic compounds—minerals. By 1930, I had become interested in applying the same techniques to organic compounds—relatively simple ones with five or ten atoms in the molecule. By 1935, I was ready to progress to the larger organic molecules that are characteristic of living organisms. It was hemoglobin, the oxygen-carrying protein of blood, that I first worked on. The hemoglobin molecule has about ten thousand atoms. My work with proteins and amino acids led to my interest in the molecular aspects of medical problems: sickle-cell anemia and other heredity disorders, and mental disease. Later, I became interested in vitamins; that's my present phase.

CAMPBELL: *You mentioned earlier that some very general theories have evolved in the field of chemistry. Some chemists and physicists seem to look down on biology, describing it as a "softer" science than their own. Is biology beginning to lose this image?*

PAULING: Oh yes. But, of course, the change began even before the development of ideas of molecular structure. Genetics was, I would say, the first part of biology to become a pretty good theoretical subject, based on the theory of the gene and patterns of inheritance of characteristics. This, of course, has become more refined in recent years, and has been extended by the discovery of the structure of DNA. Besides inheritance, many other biological phenomena can now be discussed in a quantitative way. There is still a very large empirical component to biology. I suppose this empirical component will exist into the distant future, because living organisms are so extremely complicated.

CAMPBELL: *So complicated, in fact, that a standard procedure for biochemists is to grind up cells to isolate specific subcellular organelles or molecules in order to study them under conditions that are more simple than those existing in the intact cell or organism. To what extent can we understand a living organism by investigating its isolated pieces, in contrast to trying to study processes in whole cells or organisms?*

PAULING: Well, I think you have to do both. Life is too complicated to permit a complete understanding through the study of whole organisms. Only by simplifying the problem—breaking it down into a multitude of individual problems—can you get the answers. In 1935, Dr. Charles Coryell and I made our discovery about how oxygen molecules are attached to the iron atoms of hemoglobin, not by getting a cow and putting it into our magnetic apparatus, but by getting some blood from the cow and studying this blood. We made some measurements on the blood, but we also separated the red cells from the blood and broke them so that we could make measurements on their contents. We got the same answer about oxygen binding from measuring the hemoglobin

Pauling at Oregon State University, 1986

solution, essentially the red cell contents, as we had obtained by making similar measurements on the whole blood taken from the cow.

Of course, the situation arises that the study of different parts of an organism leads to the question: "Do these parts interact?" Can we learn more about a living organism by putting two parts together to see to what extent the properties of the combination are different from those of the two separated parts? This approach permits further progress in understanding the organism. And yet I, myself, have confidence that all of the properties of living organisms could ultimately be discovered by this process of attempting to reduce the organism in our minds to a combination of the different parts; essentially the molecules that make up the organism.

CAMPBELL: *Your last point raises another question: If living organisms are made of lifeless molecules, then where is the dividing line between a molecular aggregation and life?*

PAULING: Perhaps I shouldn't let your question go by without challenging the expression "lifeless molecules." This is just a matter of words. I can ask, "If I crystallize a virus to obtain a crystal consisting of the molecules that make up the virus, are those molecules lifeless or not?

CAMPBELL: *It's a pretty arbitrary line, isn't it?*

PAULING: That's right! It's quite arbitrary. The properties of living organisms are those of aggregates of molecules. There may well be some point at which one tries to draw a dividing line. But it's very difficult to draw such a line between molecules that are lifeless and molecules that are not lifeless.

CAMPBELL: *Earlier you were talking about some of your work with hemoglobin. You were involved in the demonstration that sickle-cell anemia has a molecular basis.*

PAULING: Yes. Not only the demonstration, but formulating the idea!

CAMPBELL: *Right! And then you continued to work on the chemical aspects of various health problems. In recent years, you have promoted the idea of orthomolecular medicine. What, exactly, does orthomolecular medicine mean?*

PAULING: Orthomolecular medicine is the use of substances that are normally present in the human body. Concentrations of these substances can be varied to achieve the best of health, the greatest prevention of disease, and the treatment of disease. Orthomolecular medicine may be contrasted with toximolecular medicine, conventional medicine using toxic substances—drugs. Many of the orthomolecular substances are remarkably free from toxicity such that they show beneficial effect over a ten-thousand-fold range of concentrations in the human body. Well, if you take even ten times the amount of aspirin that many patients—persons with arthritis—take, you'd be dead. And hundreds of people die every year from aspirin poisoning. And all of the other drugs are highly toxic. Essentially every drug in the armamentarium of the toximolecular physician has great toxicity—lethality. You have to be quite careful that the patient sticks to the dosage that the physician has prescribed.

CAMPBELL: *Medicine is just one example of the extent to which science and the technology it breeds affect our lives. What kind of job is our educational system doing in preparing people to live in such a technological society?*

PAULING: Well, I think it's doing a poor job. It's too bad that so many people are ignorant about science. Newspaper reporters are especially bad. The newspaper will publish an article about a man who discovered a way so that you only need to put water in your gasoline tank…and you'll get energy out of it by burning the hydrogen. The press makes no mention of the fact that you have to first get the energy before you get the hydrogen from the water. If you have a source of energy, instead of synthesizing gasoline you can prepare hydrogen, and then burn the hydrogen in the internal combustion engine. Since this is nonpolluting, the idea may have some value. But the way the article will be written gives uninformed readers the impression that this hydrogen fuel is an alternative to solar energy, or geothermal energy, or energy obtained by burning coal or oil. No mention is made of the fact that you aren't producing any energy—you're using energy and getting some of it back.

About three years ago, I published an article on scientific education in which I said that science should be taught the way mathematics is taught. Science education should begin in kindergarten. In the first grade you would learn a little more, in the second grade, a little more, and so on. And all students should get this basic science training.

CAMPBELL: *Now I'd like to ask you about some of the most basic features of the chemistry of life. In a world with ninety-two elements, why are some of them— carbon—so prevalent in the architecture of biological molecules?*

PAULING: Well, it is possible with these elements, especially because carbon is included among them, to form very large molecules that are stable. This results from the stability of the carbon-to-carbon bond. You must have complexity in order to achieve the versatility characteristic of living organisms. You can achieve this complexity with carbon forming the molecular backbone, or with silicon forming the backbone. I think there might well be, as many science fiction writers have pointed out, planets with living organisms based upon silicon. One science fiction story imagined a process, analogous to respiration, that turned out bricks made of silicon dioxide as waste products.

CAMPBELL: *You mentioned the structural complexity of molecules constructed from carbon atoms. You were a pioneer in the study of life's most complex molecules, the proteins. Today, a great deal is known about the structure and function of proteins and other giant molecules found in living organisms. Are you at all surprised about how fast and far molecular biology has traveled in the past few decades?*

PAULING: It's gone along faster than I expected. In fact, I began trying to find the structure of proteins in 1937, and didn't succeed. So I began working with my collaborators to determine the three-dimensional structures of amino acids and simple peptides. In 1937, no one had yet determined such structures for any amino acid or simple peptide. By 1948, there were a dozen or more that had been determined, all of them in our laboratory in Pasadena. At that time, I realized that nothing new in the field of structural chemistry had been turned up during our studies. I had decided in 1937 that there probably was something strange about amino acids that I didn't know, because I couldn't explain the x-ray diffraction photographs of alpha keratin, the protein of hair. Nobody else could explain them either. We couldn't find the structure. Well, I was wrong in thinking that there was some new structural feature involved. And then in 1948, of course, I found the alpha helix and the pleated-sheet structures in proteins. I could just as well have found these structures in 1937. I'm surprised that nobody else had done this job in the eleven years that intervened—in a sense, surprised that I hadn't done it in '37, when my ideas were all the right ones. I just hadn't worked hard enough. Of course, you don't know how hard a problem is until it has been solved. You don't know that you will succeed if you work harder or longer on the problem. So I can understand, sometimes, that progress is slow. But then, of course, there does come a time when a lot of people accept some new idea and see ways in which it can be exploited. And because of the larger number of workers in the field, progress is rapid. That is what happened with the study of protein structure. There are, perhaps, a hundred protein molecules whose structures have been determined in detail now, giving much insight into the properties of proteins.

CAMPBELL: *Dr. Pauling, you have an impressive track record for asking key questions that stimulate new directions for research. The thing that has always impressed me most about our career has been the breadth of problems you've worked on, anticipating the way that biology was moving, or perhaps contributing to changes in direction. As you look ahead, can you foresee any new questions about the chemistry of life that may redirect your interests still another time?*

PAULING: I suppose if I knew the answer I'd change my interests now!

I remember…about 1930, I guess. Ernest Lawrence and I and our wives were going to dinner in San Francisco. We were walking along the street, uphill toward the restaurant. Our wives were in front of us talking, and Ernest said to me that he'd like to know whether Millkan—Robert A. Millkan, who pioneered the study of cosmic rays—had a great ability to see what fields were important and then to do some work in such a field, or whether the fact that he worked in a field made that field important.

In my own case, I tried to fit knowledge that I acquired into my system of the world—my understanding of the world. And much of the new information that I learned—discoveries that have been made—seemed to me to be compatible with my existing understanding of the world. When something comes along that I don't understand, that I can't fit in, that bothers me: I think about it, mull over it, and perhaps ultimately do some work with it. And that's perhaps the reason that I've been able to make discoveries in molecular biology, for example, in the early days when the subject didn't exist. Often I'm not very interested in something new that's been discovered, because even though it's new, it doesn't surprise me and interest me. For example, I was, for about ten years, a member of the scientific advisory board at Massachusetts General Hospital. One day when the board was sitting there, a professor, Henry K. Beecher, gave a talk on anesthesia. This was about 1952. He said that the inert gas xenon had been used as a general anesthetic in two operations on humans. It's a good anesthetic agent, perhaps the best, but the amount of xenon used for an operation costs $800. I said to my son, who was still a medical student there, "How can xenon, which is chemically inert, be an anesthetic agent?" I thought about that, and it was in '59 that I published my paper on a theory of general anesthesia. So, the fact that I couldn't understand why xenon would act as a general anesthetic agent led me to these ideas, and maybe was responsible for me deciding to do work on mental retardation and schizophrenia in 1953.

OLER (Publisher): *Dr. Pauling, if I understood you correctly earlier, you said that you were confident that the day will come when we will have a fairly complete understanding of life at the molecular level?*

PAULING: Yes, I think so.

OLER: *What are the cultural implications of that level of understanding?*

PAULING: Well, of course, if we were rational, we could expect that this would be the end of religious dogma and the bias that is associated with it. But I don't think that that's the way the world works. The French rationalists, of course, felt that they were going to free the world of the dominion of religious dogma. But they were too optimistic. So, we still have religious wars and much other irrationality. Still, I think that a more complete understanding of life will help.

OLER: *Do you see any adverse effects of that level of understanding in terms of limiting further inquiry?*

PAULING: No, I don't think so. Some scientists have thought that the time might come when living would be just a big bore. I don't think that will ever happen. I think there will always be something interesting remaining to be discovered.

III

LINUS PAULING

THE PEACE WORK

⋘

An Episode that Changed My Life

Linus Pauling

The atomic bombs that were exploded at the end of World War II profoundly altered our perception of the nature of the world. Pauling knew that if the human race were to survive, it must change its thinking about war. And this meant that in his role as a responsible citizen and educator he had to master international affairs. The following essay relates how he received a particular epiphany which would cause him to change his working habits for the rest of his life.

In 1945 there occurred an episode that changed my life. It consisted of a remark made to me by my wife after I had given a public lecture.

I studied chemical engineering in Oregon Agricultural College, and in 1922 began graduate work, which led to my Ph.D. in chemistry, with minors in physics and mathematics. My life had in fact been changed, very much for the better, when on June 17, 1923, Ava Helen Miller and I were married in Salem, Oregon.

Ava Helen Miller had studied chemistry, and it is clear that she had great interest in the family—her own family, consisting of her mother and her eleven brothers and sisters, several of whom were married, and her new family, which at first consisted of her and me, and later included our four children. She was interested in the work that I was doing, as an advanced student of chemistry, and then a teacher of chemistry and a scientific researcher in the California Institute of Technology. She strove to take as many burdens as possible from my shoulders, in order that I could devote myself to my scientific and educational work as effectively as possible.

During the Second World War, I continued my teaching, but also was engaged in many investigations of scientific and medical problems relating to the war effort, including work on explosives. I had been asked by Robert Oppenheimer to join him in the work on the atomic bomb at Los Alamos, but had decided not to do that, and instead to continue the work that I was doing in the California Institute of Technology and as a member of war research committees in Washington D.C. In August 1945 atomic bombs were exploded by the United States over Hiroshima and Nagasaki, Japan. Each of these bombs, involving only a few pounds of nuclear explosive, had explosive power equal to 15,000 or 20,000 tons of TNT. The nuclear explosive, plutonium or uranium 235, has twenty million times the explosive power of the same weight of TNT or dynamite. These two small bombs dest-royed the cities and killed about 250,000 people.

Linus and Ava Helen Pauling, 1939

Someone who knew that I was an effective lecturer about chemical subjects invited me to speak at a luncheon before the members of the Rotary Club in Hollywood, to tell them about the nature of this tremendously powerful new explosive, involving fission of the nuclei of the atoms. I did not have any classified information about the atomic bombs, and so I was free to speak. My presentation was essentially a scientific one, about the structure of atomic nuclei and the nature of the process of nuclear fission, and also about the Einstein relation between mass and energy, which explains why the splitting of atomic nuclei can result in the release of a tremendous amount of energy, far, far greater than can be released by any chemical reaction, as in the detonation of TNT. Later I gave a similar talk before another group, in which I discussed not only the nature of nuclear fission but also the change that had occurred in the nature of war, through the development of atomic bombs. I quoted Albert Einstein, who had said that the existence of these bombs, so powerful that a single bomb, lobbed over by a rocket, could destroy a whole city, required that we give up war as the means for settling disputes between the great nations, and instead develop a system of world law to settle these disputes. I also quoted statements by various politicians and students of international relations. After this lecture, when my wife and I had come home, she made the following statement to me: "I think that you should stop giving lectures about atomic bombs, war, and peace. When you talk about a scientific subject, you speak very effectively and convincingly. It is evident that you are a master of the subject that you are talking about. But when you talk about the nature of war and the need for peace, you are not convincing, because you give the audience the impression that you are not sure about what you are saying and that you are relying on other authorities."

These sentences changed my life. I thought, "What shall I do? I am convinced that scientists should speak to their fellow human beings not only about science, but also about atomic bombs, the nature of war, the need to change international relations, the need to achieve peace in the world. But my wife says that I should not give talks of this sort because I am not able to speak authoritatively. Either I should stop, or I should learn to speak authoritatively."

I had by this time begun to feel so strongly about these matters that I decided that I should devote half my time, over a period that has turned out to be nearly four decades, to learning about international relations, international law, treaties, histories, the peace movement, and other subjects relating to the whole question of how to abolish war from the world and to achieve the goal of a peaceful world, in which the resources of the world are used for the benefit of human beings, and not for preparation for death and destruction.

During the next years I gave hundreds of lectures about nuclear weapons, the need for world peace, and, from 1957 on for several years, the damage to the pool of human germ plasm and to the health of living people by the radioactive fallout from the atmospheric testing of atomic bombs. My life, ever since that day nearly forty years ago, no longer involved my whole-hearted efforts in teaching science and carrying on scientific research. Instead, half of my energy was devoted to that work, and the other half to working for world peace.

On 10 October 1963 I was notified that I had received the Nobel Peace Prize. Reporters asked me which of the two Nobel prizes I valued the more: the Nobel Peace Prize, or the prize in chemistry, which I had received in 1954. My reply was that the Nobel Prize in Chemistry pleased me immensely, but that it was given to me for enjoying myself—for carrying out researches in chemistry that I enjoyed carrying out. On the other hand, I felt that the Nobel Peace Prize was an indication to me that I had done my duty as a human being—my duty to my fellow human beings.

I think that my wife was pleased that I had taken her remark seriously enough to cause me to decide to devote myself, at least half of my efforts, to world peace and world problems generally. I was not alone in this effort; she was also very active in the peace movement, served as an officer of the Women's International League for Peace and Freedom and Women Strike for Peace, and gave a great many lectures about world peace, during the remainder of the nearly fifty-nine years of our marriage.

THE ULTIMATE DECISION

Linus Pauling

❧❧❧

Soon after the end of World War II, Pauling became an outspoken advocate of civilian control of nuclear weapons, world government, and international oversight of the development of new weaponry. By the early 1950s, under the strong influence of his wife, Ava Helen, he was spending about half of his time lecturing and writing about the dangers of nuclear war. The following piece captures much of Pauling's thinking about these issues at the time, highlighting the dangers of nuclear weapons and emphasizing his route to a more rational world by letting the citizens, informed by scientists, decide their fate rather than government leaders. Through years of tireless lecturing and writing, Pauling became by the mid-1950s a world leader in the peace movement.

Science has made great contributions to the modern world. It is hard to exaggerate the greatness of these contributions, the depth of understanding of the material world that has been obtained. We have seen significant improvement through science of the standard of living of people in all countries, but the improvement has not been nearly so great as it might be, because man, as he has learned to control nature, has not learned to control himself. In international affairs man has not progressed, but has retrograded, become more barbaric. We see nations using science, not to eliminate war, the scourge of the world, but instead to make it more horrible. Benjamin Franklin was prophetic when he said,

> The rapid progress true Science now makes occasions my regretting sometimes that I was born so soon. It is impossible to imagine the height to which may be carried, in a thousand years, the power of man over matter. O that moral science were in as fair a way of improvement, that men would cease to be wolves to one another, and that human beings would at length learn what they now improperly call humanity.

The world has finally come to the critical point in time—the point at which the ultimate irrevocable decision has to be made. This is the decision between, on the one hand, a glorious future for all humanity, and, on the other, death, devastation, and the complete destruction of civilization.

ORANGES ON THE MOON

I like to talk about atoms, and to think about them. We know a great deal about atoms and molecules now, and the physical scientists who have investigated this part of our world have done a good job. As I look at this crystal of uranyl nitrate hexahydrate that I hold in my hand I do not see the atoms that I know constitute the substance—to see them I need a complex instrument, which even includes some calculating machines. But I know that each uranium atom is 6.11 Å from other uranium atoms, with 1 Å equal to 1/254,000,000 of an inch, and I know how the uranium atom is surrounded by other atoms, of oxygen, nitrogen, hydrogen. To obtain this knowledge, the physical scientists have used very powerful instruments, capable of far greater magnification than the 200-inch telescope on Mt. Palomar; for the atoms in this crystal have the same apparent size to my eye as oranges on the surface of the moon—and no astronomer as yet has hopes of seeing oranges on the moon. And the nuclei in this crystal have the same apparent size as minute grains of dust, one-thousandth of an inch in diameter, on the surface of the moon. It is these tiny particles—our knowledge of and control over these tiny particles—that have made the world of today crucially different from the world of ten years ago.

A few pounds of uranium 235 or plutonium 239 and machinery for detonating it constitute an old-fashioned atomic bomb, of the Hiroshima-Nagasaki type. The reaction of these nuclei liberates in a millionth of a second as much energy as is liberated by the detonation of twenty million pounds of TNT. We know that at Hiroshima one of these old-fashioned bombs killed 80,000 people. A member of Congress stated that 1949-model bombs are six times as powerful as the earlier bombs. And now we, and presumably the Russians too, are working on hydrogen bombs. A hydrogen bomb consists of an old-fashioned atomic bomb surrounded by a ton, or perhaps ten tons or more, of hydrogen or other light elements, the nuclei of which can fuse together to form heavier nuclei, with the liberation of around five times as much energy, on a weight basis, as in a fission bomb. There may be present a hundred or a thousand or ten thousand times as much explosive material as in the old-fashioned atomic bomb (which serves simply as a detonator for the hydrogen bomb, by raising the temperature to several million degrees), and most scientists predict that hydrogen bombs a thousand times more powerful than an old-fashioned atomic bomb can be designed and constructed in a few months or years. There seems to be no theoretical limit on the size of these terrible weapons.

One hydrogen bomb would wipe New York out of existence, another Washington, another Chicago, another Los Angeles, another London, another Paris, another Moscow. What will there be left on earth then? Still hundreds of millions of people—if a billion people were to be killed by the detonation of two score hydrogen bombs in the first phase of an atomic war, there would still be a billion left. But the atmosphere over the whole earth would be filled with radioactive products of nuclear reactions. No human being, no animal, no plant over the surface of the earth would in future years be safe from the insidious action of these great quantities of radioactive materials. Even though, by centuries of effort, the physical destruction caused by these hydrogen bombs might conceivably be repaired, the biological effects never could be averted.

WE, THE PEOPLE, CAN DECIDE

Terrible as the situation is, we need not succumb to despondency; the decision about the future has not yet been made—and *we*, the *people*, can by the pressure of our opinions determine it. When, three years after John J. McCloy first brought the hydrogen bomb to public attention, interest in it became great, our leaders brought forth one plan: they said that the solution is for this country to "arm itself with the hydrogen super bomb to preserve the peace of the world." These were the words of Chairman Tom Connally of the Senate Foreign Relations Committee. They were subscribed to by Senator after Senator; and even a distinguished scientist, Harold Urey, expressed the firm belief that we would have to keep the rest of the world under control by force, by fear of the hydrogen bomb. President Truman announced that he had ordered production of the bomb "to see to it that our country is able to defend itself against any possible agressor." Twelve leading atomic scientists asked for a pledge against use of the bomb. Senator Brien McMahon proposed a new approach—a recovery program for the world, eliminating the causes of war. Senator Tydings suggested that President Truman propose an international disarmament conference to end the world's nightmare of fear. James Waburg called for outlawing all weapons. Professor Einstein asserted that the solution of the problem is formation of a supra-national judicial and executive body, and a declaration of the nations to collaborate loyally in the realization of such a restricted world government. It is now evident to everyone that our State Department is not omniscient, that our foreign policy is not perfect and incapable of amendment. We must instead find the solution—it has not been given to us—and we must all help.

FORCE MEANS FAILURE

Let me say a word about the scientists. Scientists have good imaginations about the atomic future, and only a few—Harold Urey, one or two others—have been so lacking in understanding of the nature of the physical world and the nature of human beings as to say that force is the solution. I cannot give you a blueprint for the future of the world. When I talk with my scientific colleagues I find that each of us has a slightly different plan—and none of us is sure that his plan will work. Only Harold Urey is sure that he knows the answer. He seems to think that the world is as simple as a deuterium atom, and that all we need to solve the world's problems is the hydrogen bomb. Harold, you are wrong. Force is not the solution. I do not know the solution; but I know that you are wrong. I know that *war must be averted* and that *the people of the world will not stand for rule by force.*

Can we, in the twentieth century, when democracy has spread over the surface of the globe as never before, accept the conclusion that great peoples will allow themselves to be ruled from outside by force? Can we believe that the people of the United States would submit passively to conquest by force, to rule through fear superimposed by any outside power? No—we know that, whatever the political future holds for the people of the United States, it must be a future determined by the will of the people of this country. In the same way, we can be sure that the people of Russia and of the other eastern countries would never submit passively to domination by the western powers, no matter whether they possessed the hydrogen bomb or not. A future of the world in which half of the people of the world are held in submission by the other half, through fear of this great super-weapon, could never be a safe future for anybody. The recent history of China shows how an effort to subjugate a great people, even supported by $6 billion worth of weapons, is necessarily doomed to ultimate failure. Just as the people of China are determining their own destiny, so will the people of each great region of this globe determine their destiny in the future—hydrogen bomb or no hydrogen bomb.

THE SOLUTION?

What, then, is the solution? We know what the solution is—we have seen it over and over again in the relations between people. How do people of different beliefs, different natures, different ideals, different races, get along together? How does a man get along with a neighbor whom he does not like? Not by preparing continually to fight him—that is not the civilized method. Instead, different people and different groups of people have learned to live together in peace, to respect one another's qualities, even the differences—they have learned this in every sphere except that of international relations. Now the time has come for nations to learn this lesson.

The question of an atomic war is not an ordinary political question. It is of equal concern to the left-winger, the right-winger, and the man in the middle of the road. The hydrogen bomb would not discriminate—it would kill them all. This problem of an atomic war must not be confused by minor problems, such as communism vs. capitalism, the trend toward socialism, the existence of dictatorships, the problem of race and class discrimination. It is a problem that overwhelms them—and if it can be solved, they too can be solved.

What is the solution? I do not know—but I say that *we must all work together to find it.* We cannot leave it to the President alone, to a few officials in the State Department. The *people* of the world, who are also facing a hydrogen-bomb death, must express themselves. The *scientists* must express themselves. Congress must call for extended public hearings on the hydrogen bomb and its impact on foreign policy. Senator McMahon's proposal that two-thirds of the money now spent on armaments should be used for increasing the welfare of human beings over the whole world should be considered. We have many brilliant men who have solved other problems—why does not Congress appropriate some millions of dollars to subsidize a great research program on the causes and methods of prevention of war, to be administered by the National Academy of Science? The United Nations *must* renew its efforts toward effective control of atomic energy. All of the proposals for real world government must be re-examined. And—most importantly of all—the United States and Russia must engage in two-power negotiations.

THE STAGE IS SET

I am sure that we may have hope. The stage is now set for a great act—the final abolition of war and the achievement of a permanent peace. Men of good will need only to work to this end to achieve it.

We shall not reach this end by presenting another Baruch plan. The world situation is such that the United States cannot remain safe to the last moment, retaining the decision to gave up atomic weapons until other nations have made their sacrifices. Russia, which needs power plants for industrial development to a far greater extent that we do, cannot be expected to give up nuclear power nor even to turn over control of nuclear power plants to an outside group dominated by the capitalistic West. These are difficult problems—but they can be solved, by attacking them in a true spirit of compromise and cooperation.

The solution of the world's problem—the problem of atomic war—is that we must—we *must*—bring law and order into the world as a whole. The leaders of all nations must abandon the policy of incitement of the East and West against one another, the policy of continued preparation for war, the policy of planning to rule the world by force. Our political leaders, impelled by the massed feelings of the people of the world, must learn that *peace* is the important goal—a peace that reflects the spirit of true humanity, the spirit of the brotherhood of man. It is not necessary that the social and economic system in Russia be identical with that in the United States in order that these two great nations be at peace with one another. It is only necessary that the people of the United States and the people of Russia have respect for one another, a deep desire to work for progress, a mutual recognition that war has finally ruled itself out as the arbiter of the destinies of humanity. Once the people of the world express these feelings, the East and the West can reach a reasonable and equitable decision about world affairs, and can march together side by side, toward a more and more glorious future.

AVA HELEN PAULING and LINUS PAULING
3500 Fairpoint St., Pasadena, California

AN APPEAL TO STOP THE SPREAD OF NUCLEAR WEAPONS

To the United Nations and to all nations in the world:

We, the men and women whose names are signed below, believe that stockpiles of nuclear weapons should not be allowed to spread to any more nations or groups of nations.

The Paulings' 1958 petition to the United Nations to stop above-ground nuclear testing

The world is now in great danger. A cataclysmic nuclear war might break out as the result of some terrible accident or of an explosive deterioration in international relations such that even the wisest national leaders would be unable to avert the catastrophe. Universal disarmament has now become the essential basis for life and liberty for all people.

The difficult problem of achieving universal disarmament would become far more difficult if more nations or groups of nations were to come into possession of nuclear weapons. We accordingly urge that the present nuclear powers not transfer nuclear weapons to other nations or groups of nations such as the North Atlantic Treaty Organization or the Warsaw Pact group, that all nations not now possessing these weapons voluntarily refrain from obtaining or developing them, and that the United Nations and all nations increase their efforts to achieve total and universal disarmament with a system of international controls and inspection such as to insure to the greatest possible extent the safety of all nations and all people.

Linus Pauling

Ava Helen Pauling

(Names of other initial signers are given on the opposite side)

	NAME OF SIGNER	ADDRESS
1		
2		
3		
4		
5		
6		
7		
8		
9		
10		

Please mail this sheet with signatures to us at the above address.

MEET THE PRESS

✦✦✦

On May 11, 1958, at the height of his efforts to stop the testing of nuclear weapons, Pauling appeared on Meet the Press, a nationally televised public affairs show. He thought that he was there to explain his views on the dangers of fallout. He seemed unaware that the show's host, Lawrence Spivak, and his panel of reporters, had built the show's ratings by routinely giving guests a tough grilling. The transcript that follows gives a picture of how Pauling and his cause were viewed by the mainstream press of the day. When the show was over, both Pauling and Ava Helen, who had watched the taping in the studio, were outraged.

ANNOUNCER: *Welcome once again to Meet the Press. Our guest is Dr. Linus Pauling, the noted scientist and Professor of Chemistry at California Institute of Technology. He has become one of the nation's most controversial figures as a result of his activity in the campaign to discontinue the testing of nuclear weapons. Earlier this year he presented to the United Nations a petition to outlaw further tests. His announcement said that this petition was signed by more than nine thousand scientists in forty-four countries. Dr. Pauling has been quoted as saying that extensive damage already has been done through human exposure to radiation.*

Among the many honors awarded to Dr. Pauling is the Nobel Prize which he won in 1954 for his discoveries of the forces holding protein and other molecules together. He was awarded a Presidential medal for his work for the government as a wartime consultant. His critics acknowledge his distinction in his particular field of science, but they have sharply questioned his qualifications as an expert in matters outside of this field or in matters of military security.

MR. SPIVAK: *Dr. Pauling, I have here a copy of the petition which you sent to the United Nations, and in it you call for "a just and effective international agreement to stop bomb tests." You say this would be a good first step. Do you think that the proposal of the West, made in August of 1957, is a "just and effective" method of stopping tests?*

DR. PAULING: Yes. I think that this would be thoroughly satisfactory if an agreement could be obtained about it. It was proposed that there be a stopping of all bomb tests by all nations, with a system of inspection, with some decrease according to specified plans in conventional armaments and, also, with a stopping of further stockpiling of nuclear weapons. This is just the same proposal as the Russians have made, except for the last one of these. The Russians have proposed that we stop the testing of all nuclear weapons with systems of inspection and with decrease in conventional armaments, too. I would be happy to see either one of these proposals made the basis of an international agreement.

MR. SPIVAK: *Do you understand that the Soviet Union has agreed to stop the manufacture and production of weapons?*

DR. PAULING: No, I believe that they have not—that the Russians have not agreed to stop further stockpiling and manufacture of nuclear weapons. I would like to see this done, but most of all I would like to see an international agreement made that would prevent nuclear weapons from being spread into the hands of further nations than the three that now possess them.

MR. SPIVAK: *If you think the suggestions made by the West were good ones, and the Soviets won't accept them, just what do we do?*

DR. PAULING: We try to arbitrate with them to find out what they will accept that we are also willing to accept, that the British will accept and the other nations. France is an important nation because if we don't watch out they will be a fourth H-bomb nation, and the world will be in just that much greater danger. We arbitrate to find out what sort of agreement can be made in the world today.

MR. SPIVAK: *How do you arbitrate with a nation that won't arbitrate? How do you make an agreement with a nation that has broken so many agreements? Isn't this the heart of our problem in dealing with the Soviets?*

DR. PAULING: The United States has broken many agreements, too, international agreements, treaties. Nations keep agreements, keep their treaties, so long as they continue to do them good. We are in the position now where an agreement could be made that would benefit every nation in the world. Every nation in the world, every person in the world is in great danger now, danger of destruction, annihilation by nuclear war. Now that we have weapons that are 20 millions times more destructive than the one-ton block busters of the Second World War, the whole world is in great danger. We are not safe. We are in danger now. I say, let's start making some agreements that will make the world a safer place, will make the United States safer.

MR. SPIVAK: *Everyone is in agreement on that. The problem is how to get an agreement with someone who won't make an agreement. Do you think that the security of the free world is dependent upon the nuclear power of the United States?*

DR. PAULING: I think we have to see to it that no one nation gets control over the world.

MR. SPIVAK: *That wasn't the question. Do you think at the present time the security of the free world is dependent upon the deterrent power of the United States?*

DR. PAULING: The security of the world is dependent now upon the deterrent power of nuclear weapons, and we have the greatest stockpile of nuclear weapons that is in existence.

MR. SPIVAK: *Are you suggesting that we just as well as the Soviet Union might conceivably start a surprise attack?*

DR. PAULING: Surely this is a possibility. All sorts of accidents can happen, psychological accidents and technical accidents.

MR. SPIVAK: *You think there is as great a possibility that we might start a war as they might start a war?*

DR. PAULING: That is right—by accident. You see, nobody is so insane now as to start a nuclear war. Practically everybody in the United States, practically everybody in Russia, practically everybody in Europe, would be killed. A few people in New Zealand and Australia might survive, and South Africa and South America or Argentina. Nobody is insane enough to start a nuclear war now. We know what a nuclear war would do. If you have read the testimony about the analysis of what a nuclear attack with twenty-five hundred megatons of dirty weapons on the United States would do—108 million people dead or seriously injured as a result of the first day of the attack—you know what this means. The only way that a nuclear war will start is through accident, and we have to solve our international problems now, not by war, but by some other method. We can do that by starting to make agreements. We had better start out.

MR. CONNIFF: *Dr. Pauling, it seems to me the American public is anxious to get to the facts, but here we have just witnessed you down-grading the whole community of scientists who have disagreed with your point of view. Wouldn't the American people be more inclined to believe scientists of the caliber of Dr. Teller and Dr. Libby, who have not been tainted—if that is the word I want—with a rather prolonged record of association with Communist fronts and causes, as you appear to have been in the past?*

DR. PAULING: First, Mr. Conniff, let me say that you are wrong in saying that the whole community of scientists is against me. They are with me. And on the other hand, you have Dr. Teller. I would like to see what the scientific community feels about my standing relative to Dr. Teller's. You have Dr. Teller, Dr. Libby—there you are. You have two or three scientists as spokesmen for the AEC on the one hand, and they make statements that are not honest, outright, forthright statements. They make dishonest, untrue, misleading statements. They mislead the American public.

MR. CONNIFF: *May I interrupt, sir? Wouldn't the American public, which, as I say, is anxious to get to the truth of these matters—doesn't the fact that you in the past have always rather mouthed the Communist point of view rather than what has been called the free world's point of view—doesn't that influence them? Wouldn't that influence them to put more credit in Dr. Libby and Dr. Teller?*

DR. PAULING: I deny that I have mouthed the Communist point of view. I challenge you to prove that I have. Senator Hennings said, to a man who was testifying, what you have said, that the communists are following Dr. Pauling's line—which has sometimes happened—that the Communists have followed Dr. Pauling's line. You know in the field of chemistry there has been a controversy. The Communists have been attacking me since 1950 because they don't like my ideas about chemistry, and I think they are getting straightened out.

MR. SPIVAK: *Dr. Pauling, a minute or so ago you said that the Communists have followed your line rather than you their line. Did I understand you correctly?*

DR. PAULING: I said that Senator Hennings had said that.

MR. SPIVAK: *Do you say that, too?*

DR. PAULING: It may be that they have followed my line.

MR. SPIVAK: *Senator Hennings might have been wrong, and you picked Senator Hennings because he said something you liked to hear him say. Do you think that the Communists have followed your line rather than you their line?*

Lawrence Spivak, center, with Linus Pauling

DR. PAULING: It may well be that they have. I follow my own line.

MR. SPIVAK: *You haven't followed their line at all?*

DR. PAULING: I haven't followed their line at all.

MR. SPIVAK: *Have you for example ever taken any part in anything toward the defense of American Communist spies?*

DR. PAULING: American Communist spies?

MR. SPIVAK: *That is right. Did you sign any petitions on the Rosenberg case? Or for Morton Sobell?*

DR. PAULING: Yes, I signed a petition on the Rosenberg case.

MR. SPIVAK: *Why, as a scientist and as someone who is interested in peace, do you get mixed up in movements of that kind?*

DR. PAULING: One of the reasons that I am interested in peace is that I am interested in individual human beings.

MR. SPIVAK: *Oh, no, I am not talking about peace, I am talking about this—*

DR. PAULING: I am interested in individual human beings. That is why I keep talking about the number of human beings who die of leukemia as a result of the bomb tests.

MR. SPIVAK: *Is that why you came to the aid of convicted spies who were executed?*

DR. PAULING: Convicted spies?

MR. SPIVAK: *Yes, the Rosenbergs.*

DR. PAULING: I am not sure that it is right to call them convicted spies.

MR. SPIVAK: *They were convicted as spies, and they were done away with as spies.*

DR. PAULING: Yes, but what for?

MR. SPIVAK: *They were executed as spies.*

DR. PAULING: Executed for what?

MR. SPIVAK: *So far as I know for treason, for giving away secrets of the United States.*

DR. PAULING: No, no, they weren't. They weren't even charged with treason.

MR. SPIVAK: *What were they executed for?*

DR. PAULING: They were charged with conspiracy and were executed for conspiracy.

MR. SPIVAK: *All, right, they were executed for conspiracy. I yield on your exactness in this. And you came to their aid? Because you are interested in human beings?*

DR. PAULING: That is right. I am interested in human beings; I am interested in the Constitution of the United States; I am interested in the individual.

MR. SPIVAK: *Why do you always seem to be interested in Communist human beings?*

Yes, most people don't know that that sort of thing happened. When that program ["Meet The Press"] came to an end, Spivak took off down the hall, running as fast as he could go, with my wife after him, waving her fists. I guess she had a hard time restraining herself during the program. But he managed to escape.

Linus Pauling, May 1984

DR. PAULING: I signed a petition for Gerald H. K. Smith, when he was denied the use of a hall in Los Angeles. I don't think he is a Communist.

MR. SPIVAK: *Would you have signed one for his freedom if he were arrested?*

DR. PAULING: Yes, I think so, if I thought that he was arrested on an unconstitutional charge or not given a proper trial.

MR. SPIVAK: *How do you explain this thing, for example: The House Un-American Activities Committee, which said, "His whole record indicates that Dr. Linus Pauling is primarily engrossed in placing his scientific attainments at the service of a host of organizations which have in common their complete subservience to the Communist Party of the United States of America and the Soviet Union," and they list some sixty organizations and petitions that you have signed in the interest of the Communist cause?*

DR. PAULING: Not one of which was on the Attorney General's list by the way, and this House Un-American Activities Committee never accused me of anything, never called me in. This is just an effort to keep the people from knowing what the truth is, to keep people like me from using their Constitutional rights of free speech. I think this is scurrilous behavior on the part of the Un-American Activities Committee.

MR. SPIVAK: *Did you sign a petition against our policy in Korea, too, in 1950, against our going into Korea?*

DR. PAULING: I don't know. I would have to see that.

MR. SPIVAK: *There was a Communist petition. Did you sign that too?*

DR. PAULING: I didn't sign any Communist petition.

MR. SPIVAK: *According to the information I have you signed such a petition.*

MR. BROOKS: *Would you like to answer that?*

DR. PAULING: I answered it.

MR. CONNIFF: *I would like to ask the question again, Dr. Pauling. When one is associated as many times as you have been with fronts and organizations that have been definitely plugging the Communist line whether it is your line or their line, it is the Communist line—*

DR. PAULING: I deny this.

MR. CONNIFF: *How can you expect the intelligent American to draw any other conclusion but that you are interested in the Communist cause?*

DR. PAULING: The intelligent Americans are the ones that I appeal to. Take the scientists, the American scientists. They are behind me 90 per cent; 95 per cent of them are behind me. They are intelligent Americans.

MR. WILSON: *In connection with these signatures of nine thousand that you got, scientists over the world joining you in your views on this whole subject, there are some people who say it takes a lot of money and organization to get that many signatures.*

DR. PAULING: Let me answer that. I paid for it myself. I got the money, my wife and I. It cost about $600. We got those signatures for three cents apiece. Every letter that I sent brought back ten, fifteen, twenty signatures.

MR. WILSON: *Then how does it happen that same day the Communist press all over the world blazoned this thing? All over—*

DR. PAULING: The newspaper services—I am afraid you know more about that than I do.

SCIENCE AND PEACE
NOBEL LECTURE, 1963

Linus Pauling

❦❦❦

*Pauling was very pleased, and very surprised, when he learned that he had won the Nobel Peace Prize for 1962. His efforts had been significant—especially his petitions rallying scientists around the world to the fight against nuclear testing—but he realized that others around the world, including his friends Bertrand Russell and the late Albert Einstein, as well as President John F. Kennedy, had also played vital roles in ending nuclear testing in the atmosphere. Pauling's Peace Prize was widely attacked in the U.S. press because it was seen as legitimizing his association with left-wing groups (**Life** magazine called it "A Weird Insult from Norway"). Pauling, however, was jubilant. His Nobel address on December 11, 1963, summarizes his thoughts after fifteen years of working for peace.*

I believe that there will never again be a great world war—a war in which the terrible weapons involving nuclear fission and nuclear fusion would be used. And I believe that it is the discoveries of scientists upon which the development of these terrible weapons was based that is now forcing us to move into a new period in the history of the world, a period of peace and reason, when world problems are not solved by war or by force, but are solved in accordance with world law, in a way that does justice to all nations and that benefits all people.

Let me again remind you, as I did yesterday in my address of acceptance of the Nobel Peace Prize for 1962, that Alfred Nobel wanted to invent "a substance or a machine with such terrible power of mass destruction that war would thereby be made impossible forever." Two-thirds of a century later scientists discovered the explosive substances that Nobel wanted to invent—the fissionable substances uranium and plutonium, with explosive energy ten million times that of Nobel's favorite explosive, nitroglycerine, and the fusionable substance lithium deuteride, with explosive energy ten million times that of nitroglycerine. The first of the terrible machines incorporating these substances, the uranium-235 and plutonium-239 fission bombs, were exploded in 1945, at Alamogordo, Hiroshima, and Nagasaki. Then in 1954, nine years later, the first of the fission-fusion-fission superbombs was exploded, the 20-megaton Bikini bomb, with energy of explosion one thousand times greater than that of a 1945 fission bomb.

This one bomb, the 1954 superbomb, contained less than one ton of nuclear explosive. The energy released in the explosion of this bomb was greater than that of all the explosives used in all of the wars that have taken place during the entire history of the world, including the First World War and the Second World War.

Thousands of these superbombs have now been fabricated; and today, eighteen years after the construction of the first atomic bomb, the nuclear powers have stockpiles of these weapons so great that if they were to be used in a war hundreds of millions of people would be killed, and our civilization itself might not survive the catastrophe.

Linus and Ava Helen Pauling at Nobel ceremonies, 1963

Thus the machines envisaged by Nobel have come into existence, and war has been made impossible forever.

The world has now begun its metamorphosis from its primitive period of history, when disputes between nations were settled by war, to its period of maturity, in which war will be abolished and world law will take its place. The first great stage of this metamorphosis took place only a few months ago—the formulation of the governments of the United States, Great Britain, and the Soviet Union, after years of discussion on the surface of the earth, in the oceans, and in space, and the ratification and signing of this treaty by nearly all of the nations in the world.

I believe that the historians of the future may well describe the making of this treaty as the most important action ever taken by the governments of nations, in that it is the first of a series of treaties that will lead to the new world, from which war has been abolished forever.

We see that science and peace are related. The world has been greatly changed, especially during the last century, by the discoveries of scientists. Our increased knowledge now provides the possibility of eliminating poverty and starvation, of decreasing significantly the suffering caused by disease, of using the resources of the world effectively for the benefit of humanity. But the greatest of all the changes has been in the nature of war—the several millionfold increase in the power of explosives, and corresponding changes in methods of delivery of bombs.

These changes have resulted from the discoveries of scientists, and during the last two decades scientists have taken a leading part in bringing them to the attention of their fellow human beings and in urging that vigorous action be taken to prevent the use of the new weapons and to abolish war from the world.

The first scientists to take actions of this sort were those involved in the development of the atomic bomb. In March 1945, before the first nuclear explosion had been carried out, Leo Szilard prepared a memorandum to President Franklin Delano Roosevelt in which he pointed out that a system of international control of nuclear weapons might give civilization a chance to survive. A committee of atomic scientists with James Franck as chairman on 11 June 1945 transmitted to the U.S. Secretary of War a report urging that nuclear bombs not be used in an unannounced attack against Japan, as this action would prejudice the possibility of reaching an international agreement on control of these weapons.

In 1946 Albert Einstein, Harold Urey, and seven other scientists formed an organization to educate the American People about the nature of nuclear weapons and nuclear war. This organization, the Emergency Committee of Atomic Scientists (usually called the Einstein Committee), carried out an effective educational campaign over a five-year period. The nature of the campaign is indicated by the following sentences from the 1946 statement by Einstein:

> Today the atomic bomb has altered profoundly the nature of the world as
> we know it, and the human race consequently finds itself in a new habitat
> to which it must adapt its thinking . . . Never before was it possible for one
> nation to make war on another without sending armies across borders.
> Now with rockets and atomic bombs no center of population on the earth's
> surface is secure from surprise destruction in a single attack . . . . Few men
> have ever seen the bomb. But all men if told a few facts can understand
> that this bomb and the danger of war is a very real thing, and not
> something far away. It directly concerns every person in the civilized world.
> We cannot leave it to generals, senators, and diplomats to work out a
> solution over a period of generations . . . . There is no defense in science
> against the weapon which can destroy civilization. Our defense is not in
> armaments, nor in science, nor in going underground. Our defense is in
> law and order . . . . Future thinking must prevent wars.

During the same period and later years many other organizations of scientists were active in the work of educating people about nuclear weapons and nuclear war; among them I may mention especially the Federation of American Scientists (in the United States), the Atomic Scientists' Association (Great Britain), and the World Federation of Scientific Workers (with membership covering many countries).

When I gave my Nobel address, the chairman of the Nobel Foundation said that I should refrain from mentioning Bertrand Russell. I think the Nobel Foundation had been pestered by so many people trying to get the Peace Prize for Russell that he had just got fed up and didn't want to hear Bertrand Russell's name. Of course, I left it in.

Linus Pauling, 1987

On 15 July 1955 a powerful statement, called the Mainau Declaration, was issued by fifty-two Nobel Laureates. This statement warned that a great war in the nuclear age would imperil the whole world, and ended with the sentences, "All nations must come to the decision to renounce force as final resort of policy. If they are not prepared to do so they will cease to exist."

A document of great consequence, the Russell-Einstein Appeal, was made public by Bertrand Russell on 9 July 1955. Russell, who for years remained one of the world's most active and effective workers for peace, had drafted this document some months earlier, and it had been signed by Einstein two days before his death, and also by nine other scientists. The Appeal began with the sentence,

> *In the tragic situation which confronts humanity, we feel that scientists should assemble in conference to appraise the perils that have arisen as a result of the development of weapons of mass destruction . . .*

and it ended with the exhortation,

> *There lies before us, if we choose, continual progress in happiness, knowledge, and wisdom. Shall we, instead, choose death, because we cannot forget our quarrels? We appeal, as human beings, to human beings: remember your humanity, and forget the rest. If you can do so, the way lies open to a new Paradise; if you cannot, there lies before you the risk of universal death.*

This Appeal led to the formation of the Pugwash Continuing Committee, with Bertrand Russell as chairman, and to the holding of a

Bertrand Russell (left) with Pauling

James B. Conant, President of Harvard University, refuses to sign Pauling's United Nations petition

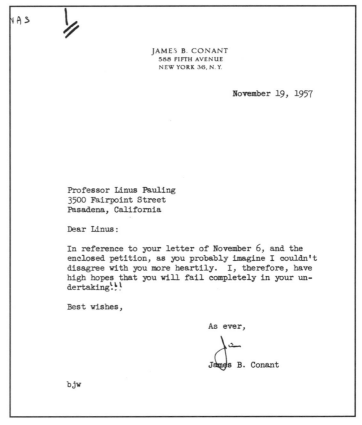

NAS

JAMES B. CONANT
588 FIFTH AVENUE
NEW YORK 36, N.Y.

November 19, 1957

Professor Linus Pauling
3500 Fairpoint Street
Pasadena, California

Dear Linus:

In reference to your letter of November 6, and the
enclosed petition, as you probably imagine I couldn't
disagree with you more heartily. I, therefore, have
high hopes that you will fail completely in your un-
dertaking!!!

Best wishes,

As ever,

James B. Conant

bjw

series of Pugwash Conferences (eleven during the years 1957 to 1963). Financial support for the first few conferences was provided by Mr. Cyrus Eaton, and the first conference was held in his birthplace, the village of Pugwash, Nova Scotia.

Among the participants in some of the Pugwash Conferences have been scientists with a close connection with the governments of their countries, as well as scientists without government connection. The Conferences have permitted the scientific and practical aspects of disarmament to be discussed informally in a thorough, penetrating, and productive way, and have led to some valuable proposals. It is my opinion that the Pugwash Conferences were significantly helpful in the formulation and ratification of the 1963 Bomb-test-ban Treaty.

Concern about the damage done to human beings and the human race by the radioactive substances produced in nuclear weapons tests was expressed with increasing vigor in the period following the first fission-fusion-fission bomb test at Bikini on 1 March 1954. Mention was made of radioactive fallout in the Russell-Einstein Appeal and also in the statement of the First Pugwash Conference. In his Declaration of Conscience issued in Oslo on 24 April 1957 Dr. Albert Schweitzer described the damage done by fallout and asked that the great nations cease their tests of nuclear weapons. Then on 15 May 1957, with the help of some scientists in

Washington University, St. Louis, I wrote the Scientists' Bomb-test Appeal, which within two weeks was signed by over two thousand American scientists and within a few months by 11,021 scientists, of forty-nine countries. On 15 January 1958, as I presented the Appeal to Dag Hammarskjöld as a petition to the United Nations, I said to him that in my opinion it represented the feelings of the great majority of the scientists of the world.

The Bomb-test Appeal consists of five paragraphs. The first two are the following:

> *We, the scientists whose names are signed below, urge that an international agreement to stop the testing of nuclear bombs be made now.*
>
> *Each nuclear bomb test spreads an added burden of radioactive elements over every part of the world. Each added amount of radiation causes damage to the health of human beings all over the world and causes damage to the pool of human germ plasm such as to lead to an increase in the number of seriously defective children that will be born in future generations.*

Let me now say a few words to amplify the last statement, about which there has been controversy. Each year, of the nearly one hundred million children born in the world, about four million have gross physical or mental defects, such as to cause great suffering to themselves and their parents and to constitute a major burden on society. Geneticists estimate that about 5 percent, 200,000 per year, of these children are grossly defective because of gene mutations caused by natural high-energy radiation—cosmic rays and natural radioactivity, from which our reproductive organs cannot be protected. This numerical estimate is rather uncertain, but geneticists agree that it is of the right order of magnitude.

Moreover, geneticists agree that any additional exposure of the human reproductive cells to high-energy radiation produces an increase in the number of mutations and an increase in the number of defective children born in future years, and that this increase is approximately proportional to the amount of the exposure.

The explosion of nuclear weapons in the atmosphere liberates radioactive fission products—cesium 137, strontium 90, iodine 131, and many others. In addition, the neutrons that result from the explosion combine with nitrogen nuclei in the atmosphere to form large amounts of a radioactive isotope of carbon, carbon 14, which then is incorporated into the organic molecules of every human being. These radioactive fission products are now damaging the pool of human germ plasma and increasing the number of defective children born.

Carbon 14 deserves our special concern. It was pointed out by the Soviet scientist O. I. Leipunsky in 1957 that this radioactive product of nuclear tests would cause more genetic damage to the human race than the radioactive fallout (cesium 137 and the other fission products), if the

My basic concept of Democracy is that no one man is wise enough to make the fundamental decisions determining the course of the Nation, but that the correct decisions are made by the people as a whole. The political opinions of the people can be represented by a distribution curve. If one end of the curve is suppressed, as by political pressure on a minority, the decisions made by averaging the remainder are wrong, by the Democratic criterion. I am convinced that the Constitutional provision of freedom of political belief is designed to preserve the basic Democratic procedure of obtaining the average of opinions of all citizens, and that when this principle is violated our Democracy is seriously endangered.

Loyalty statement by Linus Pauling, November 1950

human race survives over the eight-thousand-year mean life of carbon 14. Closely agreeing numerical estimates of the genetic effects of bomb-test carbon 14 were then made independently by me and by Drs. Totter, Zelle, and Hollister of the Unites States Atomic Energy Commission. Especially pertinent is the fact that the so-called "clean" bombs, involving mainly nuclear fusion, produce when they are tested more carbon 14 per megaton than the ordinary fission bombs or fission-fusion-fission bombs.

A recent study by Reidar Nydal, of the Norwegian Institute of Technology, in Trondheim, shows the extent to which the earth is being changed by the tests of nuclear weapons. Carbon 14 produced by cosmic rays is normally present in the atmosphere, oceans, and biosphere, in amount as to be responsible for between one and two percent of the genetic damage caused by natural high-energy radiation. Nydal has reported that the amount of carbon 14 in the atmosphere has been more than doubled because of the nuclear weapons tests of the last ten years, and that in a few years the carbon-14 content of human beings will be two or three times the normal value, with a consequent increase in the gene mutation rate and the number of defective children born.

Some people have pointed out that the number of grossly defective children born as a result of the bomb tests is small compared with the total number of defective children, and have suggested that the genetic damage done by the bomb tests should be ignored. I, however, have contended, as have Dr. Schweitzer and many others, that every single human being is important, and that we should be concerned about every additional child that is caused by our actions to be born to live a life of suffering and misery. President Kennedy in his broadcast to the American people on 26 July 1963 said,

> The loss of even one human life, or the malformation of even one baby— who may be born long after we are gone—should be of concern to us all. Our children and grandchildren are not merely statistics towards which we can be indifferent.

We should know how many defective children are being born because of the bomb tests. During the last six years I have made several attempts to estimate the numbers. My estimates have changed somewhat from year to year, as new information became available and as continued bomb testing increased the amount of radioactive pollution of the earth, but no radical revision of the estimates has been found necessary.

It is my estimate that about one hundred thousand viable children will be born with gross physical or mental defects caused by the cesium 137 and other fission products from the bomb tests carried out from 1952 to 1963, and 1,500,000 more, if the human race survives, with gross defects caused by the carbon 14 from these bomb tests. In addition, about ten times as many embryonic, neonatal, and childhood deaths are expected— about one million caused by the fission products and fifteen million by carbon 14. An even larger number of children may have minor defects caused by the bomb tests; these minor defects which are passed on from generation to generation rather than being rapidly weeded out by genetic death, may be responsible for more suffering in the aggregate than the major defects.

About 5 percent of the fission-product effect and 0.3 percent of the carbon-14 effect may appear in the first generation; that is, about ten thousand viable children with gross physical or mental defects and one hundred thousand embryonic, neonatal, and childhood deaths.

These estimates are in general agreement with those made by other scientists and by national and international committees. The estimates are all very uncertain, because of the deficiencies in our knowledge. The uncertainty is usually expressed by saying that the actual numbers may be only one-fifth as great or may be five times as great as the estimates, but the errors may be even larger than this.

Moreover, it is known that high-energy radiation can cause leukemia, bone cancer, and some other diseases. Scientists differ in their opinion about the carcenogenic activity of small doses of radiation, such as produced by fallout and carbon 14. It is my opinion that bomb-test strontium 90 can cause leukemia and bone cancer, iodine 131 can cause cancer of the thyroid, and cesium 137 and carbon 14 can cause these and other diseases. I make a rough estimate that because of this somatic effect of these radioactive substances that now pollute the earth about two million human beings now living will die five or ten or fifteen years earlier than if the nuclear tests had not been made. The 1962 estimate of the United States Federal Radiation Council was zero to one hundred thousand deaths from leukemia and bone cancer in the U. S. alone caused by the nuclear tests to the end of 1961.

The foregoing estimates are for 600 megatons of bombs. We may now ask: at what sacrifice is the atmospheric test of a single standard 20-megaton bomb carried out? Our answer, none the less horrifying because uncertain, is—with the sacrifice, if the human race survives, of about five hundred thousand children, of whom about fifty thousand are viable but have gross physical or mental defects; and perhaps also of about seventy thousand people now living, who may die prematurely of leukemia or some other disease caused by the test.

We may be thankful that most of the nations of the world have, by subscribing to the 1963 treaty, agreed not to engage in nuclear testing in the atmosphere. But what a tragedy it is that this treaty was not made two years earlier! Of the total of 600 megatons of tests so far, three quarters of the testing, 450 megatons, was done in 1961 and 1962. The failure to formulate a treaty in 1959 or 1960 or 1961 was attributed by the governments of the United States, Great Britain, and the Soviet Union to the existing differences of opinion about methods of inspection of underground tests. These differences were not resolved in 1963; but the treaty stopping atmospheric tests was made. What a tragedy for humanity

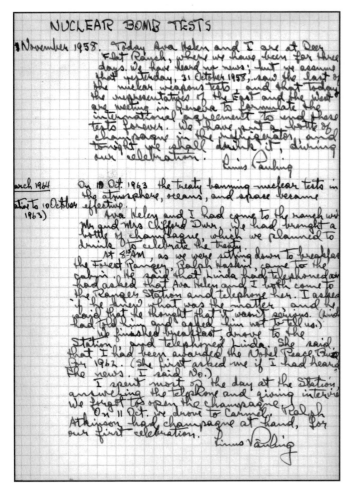

Linus Pauling celebrates the nuclear nonproliferation treaty ... and a Nobel Prize

that the governments did not accept this solution before taking the terrible step of resuming the nuclear tests in 1961!

I shall now quote and discuss the rest of the nuclear-test-ban petition of six years ago.

So long as these weapons are in the hands of only three powers an agreement for their control is feasible. If testing continues, and the possession of these weapons spreads to additional governments, the danger of outbreak of a cataclysmic nuclear war through the reckless action of some irresponsible national leader will be greatly increased.

An international agreement to stop the testing of nuclear bombs now could serve as a first step toward a more general disarmament and the ultimate effective abolition of nuclear weapons, averting the possibility of a nuclear war that would be a catastrophe to all humanity.

We have in common with our fellow men a deep concern for the welfare of all human beings. As scientists we have knowledge of the dangers involved and therefore a special responsibility to make those dangers known. We deem it imperative that immediate action be taken to effect an international agreement to stop the testing of all nuclear weapons.

How cogent is this argument? Would a great war, fought with use of the nuclear weapons that now exist, be a catastrophe to all humanity?

Consideration of the nature of nuclear weapons and the magnitude of the nuclear stockpiles gives us the answer: it is Yes.

A single 25-megaton bomb could largely destroy any city on earth, and kill most of its inhabitants. Thousands of these great bombs have been fabricated, together with the vehicles to deliver them.

Precise information about the existing stockpiles of nuclear weapons has not been released. The participants in the Sixth Pugwash Conference, in 1960, made use of the estimate 60,000 megatons. This is 10,000 times the amount of explosive used in the whole of the Second World War. It indicates that the world's stockpile of military explosives has on the average doubled every year since 1945. My estimate for 1963, which reflects the continued manufacture of nuclear weapons during the past three years, is 320,000 megatons.

This estimate is made credible by the following facts. On 12 November 1961 the U. S. Secretary of Defense stated that the U. S. Strategic Air Command then included 630 B-52s, 55 B-58s, and 1,000 B-47s, a total of 1,685 great bombers. These bombers carry about 50 megatons of bombs apiece—two 25-megaton bombs on each bomber. Accordingly, these 1,685 intercontinental bombers carry a load totaling 84,000 megatons. I do not believe that it can be contended that the bombs for these bombers do not exist. The Secretary of Defense also stated that the United States has over ten thousand other planes and rockets capable of carrying nuclear bombs in the megaton range. The total megatonnage of nuclear bombs tested by the Soviet Union is twice that of those tested by the United States and Great Britain, and it is not unlikely that the Soviet stockpile is also a tremendous one—perhaps one-third or one-half as large as the U. S. stockpile.

The significance of the estimated total of 320,000 megatons of nuclear bombs may be brought out by the following statement: if there were to take place tomorrow a 6-megaton war, equivalent to the Second World War in the power of the explosives used, and another such war the following day, and so on, day after day, for 146 years, this stockpile might be used in a single day, the day of the Third World War.

Many estimates have been made by scientists of the probable effects of hypothetical nuclear attacks. One estimate, reported in the 1957 Hearings before the Special Subcommittee on Radiation of the Joint Committee on Atomic Energy of the Congress of the United States, was for an attack on population and industrial centers and military installations in the United States with 250 bombs totaling 2,500 megatons. The estimate of casualties presented in the testimony, corrected for the increase in population since 1957, is that sixty days after the day on which the attack took place 98 million of the 190 million American people would be dead, and 28 million would be seriously injured but still alive; many of the remaining 70 million survivors would be suffering from minor injuries and radiation effects.

This is a small nuclear attack, made with use of about one percent of the existing weapons. A major nuclear war might well see a total of 30,000 megatons, one-tenth of the estimated stockpiles, delivered and exploded over the populated regions of the United States, the Soviet Union, and the other major European countries. The studies of Hugh Everett and George E. Pugh, of the Weapons Systems Evaluation Division, Institute of Defense Analysis, Washington, D. C., reported in the 1959 Hearings before the Special Subcommittee on Radiation, permit us to make an estimate of the casualties of such a war. This estimate is that sixty days after the day on which the war was waged 720 million of the 800 million people in these countries would be dead, 60 million would be alive but seriously injured, and there would be 20 million other survivors. The fate of the living is suggested by Everett and Pugh:

Finally, it must be pointed out that the total casualties at sixty days may not be indicative of the ultimate casualties. Such delayed effects as the disorganization of society, disruption of communication, extinction of livestock, genetic damage, and the slow development of radiation poisoning from the ingestion of radioactive materials may significantly increase the ultimate toll.

No dispute between nations can justify nuclear war. There is no defense against nuclear weapons that could not be overcome by increasing the scale of the attack. It would be contrary to the nature of war for nations to adhere to agreements to fight "limited" wars, using only "small" nuclear weapons—even little wars of today are perilous, because of the likelihood that a little war would grow into a world catastrophe.

The only sane policy for the world is that of abolishing war.

This is now the proclaimed goal of the nuclear powers and of all other nations.

We are all indebted to the governments of the United States, the Soviet Union, and Great Britain for their action of formulating a test-ban agreement that has been accepted by most of the nations of the world. As an American, I feel especially thankful to our great President, John F. Kennedy, whose tragic death occurred only nineteen days ago. It is my opinion that this great international agreement could not have been formulated and ratified except for the conviction, determination, and political skill of President Kennedy.

Draft of a cable that Pauling sent to the White House during the Cuban Missile Crisis

The great importance of the 1963 test-ban treaty lies in its significance as the first step toward disarmament. To indicate what other steps need to be taken I shall now quote some of the statements made by President Kennedy in his address to the United Nations General Assembly on the 26th of September, 1961:

The goal (of disarmament) is no longer a dream. It is a practical matter of life or death. The risks inherent in disarmament pale in comparison to the risks inherent in an unlimited arms race . . .

Our new disarmament program includes . . . :

First, signing the test-ban treaty by all nations . . . ;

Second, stopping production of fissionable materials and preventing their transfer to (other) nations . . .;

Third, prohibiting the transfer of control over nuclear weapons to other nations;

Fourth, keeping nuclear weapons from outer space;

Fifth, gradually destroying existing nuclear weapons;

And sixth, halting . . . the production of strategic nuclear delivery vehicles, and gradually destroying them.

The first of these goals has been approached, through the 1963 treaty, but not yet reached. Six weeks ago, by the vote 97 to 1, the Political Committee of the United Nations General Assembly approved a resolution asking that the eighteen-nation Disarmament Committee take supplementary action to achieve the discontinuance of all test explosions of nuclear weapons for all time. We must strive to achieve this goal.

The fourth action proposed by President Kennedy, that of keeping nuclear weapons from outer space, was taken two months ago, in the United Nations, through a pledge of abstention subscribed to by many nations.

Action on the third point, the prevention of the spread of nuclear weapons, could lead to a significant diminution in international tensions and in the chance of outbreak of a world war. The 1960 treaty making Antarctica a nuclear-free zone provides a precedent. Ten Latin-American nations have proposed that the whole of Latin America be made into a second zone free of nuclear weapons; and a similar proposal has been made for Africa. Approval of these proposals would be an important step toward permanent peace.

Even more important would be the extension of the principle of demilitarization to Central Europe, as proposed by Rapacki, Kennan, and others several years ago. Under this proposal the whole of Germany, Poland, and Czechoslovakia, and perhaps some other countries, would be largely demilitarized, and their boundaries and national integrity would be permanently assured by the United Nations. I am not able at the present time to discuss in a thorough way the complex problem of Berlin and Germany; but I am sure that if a solution other than nuclear destruction is ever achieved, it will be through demilitarization, not remilitarization.

President Kennedy, President Johnson, Chairman Khruschev, Prime Minister MacMillan, and other national leaders have proclaimed that, to prevent cataclysm, we must move toward the goal of general and complete disarmament, we must begin to destroy the terrible nuclear weapons that now exist, and the vehicles for delivering them. But instead of destroying the weapons and the delivery vehicles, the great nations continue to manufacture more and more of them, and the world remains in peril.

Why is no progress being made toward disarmament? I think that part of the answer is that there are still many people, some of them powerful people, who have not yet accepted that the time has now come to abolish war. And another part of the answer is that there exists a great nation that has not been accepted into the world community of nations—the Chinese Peoples Republic, the most populous nation in the world. I do not believe that the United States and the Soviet Union will carry out any major stage of the process of disarmament unless that potential great nuclear power, the Chinese Peoples Republic, is a signatory to the disarmament agreement; and the Chinese Peoples Republic will not be a signatory to such a treaty until she is accepted into the community of nations, under conditions worthy of her stature. To work for the recognition of China is to work for world peace.

We cannot expect the now-existing nuclear weapons to be destroyed for several years, perhaps for decades. Moreover, there is the possibility mentioned by Philip Noel Baker in his Nobel Lecture in 1959, that some nuclear weapons might be concealed or surreptitiously fabricated, and then used to terrorize and dominate the disarmed world; this possibility might slow down the program of destroying the stockpiles.

Is there no action that we can take immediately to decrease the present danger of outbreak of nuclear war, through some technological or psychological accident or as the result of a series of events such that even the wisest national leaders could not avert the catastrophe?

I believe that there is such an action, and I hope that it will be given consideration by the national governments. My proposal is that there be instituted with the maximum expedition compatible with caution a system of joint national-international control of the stockpiles of nuclear weapons, such that use could be made of the American nuclear armaments only with the approval both of the American government and of the United Nations, and that use could be made of the Soviet nuclear armament only with the approval both of the Soviet government and of the United Nations. A similar system of dual control would of course be instituted for the smaller nuclear powers, if they did not destroy their weapons.

Even a small step in the direction of this proposal, such as the acceptance of United Nations observers in the control stations of the nuclear powers, might decrease significantly the probability of nuclear war.

There is another action that could be taken immediately to decrease the present great hazard to civilization. This action would be to stop, through a firm treaty incorporating a reliable system of inspection, the present great programs of development of biological and chemical methods of waging war.

Four years ago the scientists participating in the Fifth Pugwash Conference concluded that at that time the destructive power of nuclear weapons was far larger than that of biological and chemical weapons, but that biological and chemical weapons have enormous lethal and incapacitating effects against man and could also effect tremendous harm by the destruction of plants and animals. Moreover, there is a vigorous effort being made to develop these weapons to the point where they would become a threat to the human race equal to or greater than that of nuclear weapons. The money expended for research and development of biological and chemical warfare by the United States alone has now reached $100 million per year, an increase of sixteenfold in a decade, and similar efforts are probably being exerted in the Soviet Union and other countries.

To illustrate the threat I may mention the plans to use nerve gases that, when they do not kill, produce temporary or permanent insanity, and the plans to use toxins, such as the botulism toxin, viruses, such as the virus of yellow fever, or bacterial spores, such as of anthrax, to kill tens of hundreds of millions of people.

The hazard is especially great in that, once the knowledge is obtained through a large-scale development program such as is now being carried out, it might well spread over the world, and might permit some small group of evil men, perhaps in one of the smaller countries, to launch a devastating attack.

This terrible prospect could be eliminated now by a general agreement to stop research and development of these weapons, to prohibit their use, and to renounce all official secrecy and security controls over micro-biological, toxicological, pharmacological, and chemical-biological research. Hundreds of millions of dollars per year are now being spent in the effort to make these malignant cells of knowledge. Now is the time to stop. When once the cancer has developed, and its metastases have spread over the world, it will be too late.

The replacement of war by law must include not only great wars but also small ones. The abolition of insurrectionary and guerrilla warfare, which often is characterized by extreme savagery and a great amount of human suffering, would be a boon to humanity.

There are, however, countries in which the people are subjected to continuing economic exploitation and to oppression by a dictatorial government, which retains its power through force of arms. The only hope for many of these people has been that of revolution, of overthrowing the dictatorial government and replacing it with a reform government, a democratic government that would work for the welfare of the people.

I believe that the time has come for the world as a whole to abolish this evil, through the formulation and acceptance of some appropriate articles of world law. With only limited knowledge of law, I shall not attempt to formulate a proposal that would achieve this end without permitting the possibility of the domination of the small nations by the world legislation under which there would be, perhaps once a decade, a referendum, supervised by the United Nations, on the will of the people with respect to their national government, held, separately from the national elections, in every country in the world.

It may take many years to achieve such an addition to the body of world law. In the meantime, much could be done through a change in the policies of the great nations. During recent years insurrections and civil wars in small countries have been instigated and aggravated by the great powers, which have moreover provided weapons and military advisors, increasing the savagery of the wars and the suffering of the people. In four countries during 1963 and several others during the preceding years democratically elected governments with policies in the direction of social and economic reform have been overthrown and replaced by military dictatorship, with the approval, if not at the instigation, of one or more of the great powers. These actions of the great powers are associated with policies of militarism and national economic interest that are now antiquated. I hope that the pressure of world opinion will soon cause them to be abandoned, and to be replaced by policies that are compatible with the principles of morality, justice, and world brotherhood.

In working to abolish war we are working also for human freedom, for the rights of individual human beings. War and nationalism, together with economic exploitation, have been the great enemies of the individual human being. I believe that, with war abolished from the world, there will be improvement in the social, political, and economic systems in all nations, to the benefit of the whole of humanity.

I am glad to take this opportunity to express my gratitude to the Norwegian Storting for its outstanding work for international arbitration and peace during the last seventy-five years. In this activity the Storting has been the leader among the parliaments of nations. I remember the action of the Storting in 1890 of urging that permanent treaties for arbitration of disputes between nations be made, and the statement that,

> *The Storting is convinced that this idea has the support of an overwhelming proportion of our people. Just as law and justice have long ago replaced the rule of the fist in disputes between man and man, so the idea of settling disputes among peoples and nations is making its way with irresistible strength. More and more, war appears to the general consciousness as a vestige of prehistoric barbarism and a curse to the human race.*

Now we are forced to eliminate from the world forever this vestige of prehistoric barbarism, this curse to the human race. We, you and I, are privileged to be alive during this extraordinary age, this unique epoch in the history of the world, the epoch of demarcation between the past millennia of war and suffering and the future, the great future of peace, justice, morality, and human well-being. We are privileged to have the opportunity of contributing to the achievement of the goal of the abolition of war and its replacement by world law. I am confident that we shall succeed in this great task; that the world community will thereby be freed not only from the suffering caused by war but also, through the better use of the earth's resources, the discoveries of scientists, and the efforts of mankind, from hunger, disease, illiteracy, and fear; and that we shall in the course of time be enabled to build a world characterized by economic, political, and social justice for all human beings, and a culture worthy of man's intelligence.

MAN—AN IRRATIONAL ANIMAL

Linus Pauling

❖❖❖

Following World War II, Pauling became convinced that the dangers of nuclear war presented scientists with unprecedented social and political responsibilities. He became convinced that the tensions between East and West, the Soviet Union and the United States, might lead to a world-wide cataclysm. As such, he began to speak on the idea of a one-world government based upon scientific reasoning. The following piece is a text of a talk originally delivered on September 5, 1949, at the Western Continental Congress for Peace in Mexico City.

During thirty years of scientific activity I have been deeply interested in the structure of the material universe in which we live. With increasing awe I have learned about the wonderfully complex way in which atoms are built out of electrons and atomic nuclei, molecules and crystals out of atoms, viruses and living cells out of molecules. There is beauty in the crystal of [gamma] bronze—an ordered arrangement of units consisting of thirty-one copper atoms for every eight tin atoms; and the same beautiful order appears over and over again in nature—until we reach man, and his social and political attitudes.

Here we see not order, but disorder. We see not reason but unreason. We see groups of men, who make up the nations of the world, devoting the material wealth of the world and the intellectual powers of man, the "rational" animal, not for the welfare of mankind, but for destruction.

How much longer are we going to behave in this irrational way? How many more devastating wars, how many more years of deprivation, will there be before the people of the world see the truth—that they do not need to destroy one another, and that their duty is to work for peace and for the happiness and welfare of mankind?

Many of the problems that face us at the present time are the result of the struggle that is going on between the East and the West—between Russia and the United States. The material welfare of the people of the

Pauling at home in Big Sur,
1987

world is significantly poorer because nearly 10 percent of the world's income is being used for war or preparation for war. We are experiencing a setback in the fight for human rights—the fight to make all men free and equal in the fundamental right of living with other men, because human rights and war are incompatible. War is the enemy of man.

The world looks to science for the ultimate solution of the problem of providing food for the ever-increasing world population, and of raising the standard of living of peoples over the entire globe. But scientific progress depends on freedom of thought and action of the scientist. Scientific knowledge is not a matter of geography, and the progress of science is hampered if there is not free intercourse among the scientists of the world—and yet, because of the political barrier between the East and the West, for several years American scientists and Russian scientists have not been able to discuss the problems of science with one another.

The fascists thought that science could be made national. Hitler forbade the study of Jewish science—of Einstein's theory of relativity; and the German nation suffered from this prohibition, because of its hindrance to scientific progress. Word has reached us in America that there is now a similar hindrance of the progress of biology in Russia, because of some political interference in the free activities of biological scientists, especially the geneticists. As Professor Shapley has stated,

> *The laws of natural science, in genetics, physics, astronomy, are above the dictates of social arbiters. Such a policy is wrong in the natural sciences. It has always failed to advance the human mind and the human kind whenever tried. I am sure that the great majority of the scientists of Eastern Europe agree, for they are too sincere workers who have made world-serving contributions.*

In our country too we have suffered from the war hysteria. Because of an unreasoning fear of Communism and of liberal political thought in general, many scientists have been forbidden to work in universities, even on problems of pure science that have no immediate bearing on the preparation for war. The time seems to be approaching when a scientist must express hatred for Russia in order to be allowed to carry on government-sponsored research. In a spirit of revulsion against loyalty probes, political control of thought, and political edicts on freedom of thought, able men have been led to abandon science as a career. The rights of free speech and free assembly and criticism have begun to suffer serious interference through political and social pressure.

There is one significant basis for hope now in existence—the United Nations, and especially its subsidiary organization, the United Nations Educational, Scientific, and Cultural Organization. Let me recall the preamble of UNESCO—"That since wars begin in the minds of men it is in the minds of men that the defenses of peace must be constructed"; and the conclusion of the preamble—that the signatory governments "create the United Nations Educational, Scientific, and Cultural Organization for the purpose of advancing through the educational, scientific and cultural relations of the peoples of the world, the objectives of international peace and of the common welfare of mankind for which the United Nations Organization was established and which its Charter claims." Here is our hope for peace—and yet it is a feeble hope, unless it can be nurtured. The budget of UNESCO is $7,800,000 this year—what a pittance this is in comparison with the scores of billions of dollars that are being spent on war and in preparation of war: $15 billion per year spent by the United States and similar amounts by Russian and other nations in preparing for war—and $7, 800,000 in the struggle for peace through UNESCO; six billion dollars wasted in China in a vain effort to support a corrupt, oppressive government, a billion dollars wasted in Greece—and only $7,800,000 for peace.

I regret that the USSR does not belong to UNESCO, and that, perhaps because of the pressure of the Cold War, she recently withdrew from the World Health Organization, and hope that this situation will soon change.

The atomic bomb and the possibility of a significant improvement in the standards of living throughout the world through the peace-time uses of atomic energy have great significance for the world of the future. Four years ago we were hopeful that a start towards a rational political world would be made through the institution of an effective system of international control of the atomic bomb and atomic energy. The influence of antiquated political concepts has, however, led to the, at least temporary, abandonment of this hope—the Atomic Energy Commission of the United Nations is no longer active.

The principal reason for the failure of the move toward international control of atomic energy seems to be opposition by all nations to the abandonment of national sovereignty in any degree. And yet we see national sovereignty being abandoned in the formation of groups of nations, such as those included in the Atlantic Pact, for the purpose of waging war. I believe that the sole justification for abandonment of national sovereignty is the assurance of peace through a worldwide supernational organization. The preparation for war on a greater scale is not a justification. The nations of the world need to transfer more of their sovereignty to the United Nations, and in the course of time to convert it into an effective world government.

We need to replace the spirit of Cold War aggression that we see determining relations between Russia and the United States and between other nations by the spirit of peace, the spirit of harmonious adjustment of international problems through arbitration, the spirit of world order, of a world of reason, based on an effective worldwide supernational government that maintains the peace but does not inflict one ideology or another on the member nations. We cannot place a simple trust in our national representatives—they have the duty of working for national supremity. It is *us, the people of the world,* who have the duty of working for peace, for the welfare and happiness of human beings everywhere. If another devastating world war comes, it will be because we have failed.

A World in which Every Human Being Can Live a Good Life

Linus Pauling

❧❧❧

There has been a great change in the world during the last several years. No longer does the threat of an all-destroying nuclear war between the United States and the Soviet Union determine our policies and action.

Our goal now should be a world such that every person born into it has the possibility of leading a good life, free of the fear of mutilation or death in war, free of the fear of poverty and starvation, free of the fear of incapacitation and early death caused by a miserable disease, and with every person having a good education, opportunity to work, good food, clothing, and leisure and income to enjoy the wonders of the world.

The immediate goals should inspire the following actions:

1. Decreasing the size of nuclear and conventional instruments of warfare from their present insane levels to more rational levels.

2. Immediately stopping research on new weapons, new delivery systems, and other aspects of militarism.

3. Stopping the spread of nuclear weapons to other nations through an effective nuclear-proliferation treaty.

4. Stopping the flow of all weapons and all other military machines to smaller and less technologically developed nations.

5. Striving to prevent and stop all wars.

6. Greatly decreasing the military budgets and increasing the expenditures of the world's wealth in ways that improve the quality of life and the well-being of all people.

7. Attacking the problems of overpopulation, malnourishment, starvation, and destruction of the environment and of the earth's nonrenewable resources.

Decisions can be made now that will determine the quality of life for human beings for hundreds of years. Now is the time for all nations and all people to cooperate in building a world free of war and militarism, a world based on rationality and ethics.

IV

LINUS PAULING

FACETS

❮❮❮

"…I think of myself as a multi-faceted crystal with many dimensions."

Linus Pauling

I must have been twelve or thirteen years old [in 1937], certainly old enough to be aware of these matters, when, one Sunday, I accompanied my parents to a fancy high-end Mexican restaurant in the foothills above Claremont. La Paloma had recently opened and acquired some fame for excellent food and entertainment. We drove out in our new 1932 Ford sedan, about a forty-five minute drive in those days, to the California hacienda-style building, a gracious and cool oasis in the sunshine. Our brunch proceeded without incident, with singers and dancers providing flamenco excitement. One of the singers was an extremely beautiful young woman, so beautiful that when she appeared on stage a hush fell over the busy dining room.

My mother was very beautiful as a young woman. There is no doubt that my father was very much in love with her and completely faithful. That did not mean, though, that he was impervious to the beauty of others. When the singer appeared, he could not stop staring, while my mother became more and more frosty. In the resultant glacial atmosphere we finished our meal in silence and the drive home was certainly longer than the drive out. I noticed that my father was always very careful thereafter to avoid any behavior that might trigger off my mother's jealousy. For him, she always came first.

Linus Pauling Jr., 2000

"This is [me] and my sweetheart. I am very anxious to have you meet him. He is such a lovely sweet man and Oh—I love him so. He looks rather happy, doesn't he? I don't look very well; I had been crying. I'm really most happy and proud to be near him. I love you, Linus. Your Ava Helen."
Oregon Agricultural College graduation, June 1922

I just saw a statement by Dr. Joyce Brothers about vacation, who said, you can never plan to go with your companion for longer than three days on vacation, because people can't stand being with one another for more than three days. She just doesn't know anything! 30 years ago, we were in our cabin here, and my wife said to me, "Do you know, we've been married for about thirty years now, and this is the first time you and I have been alone for a week without seeing another single human being?" Well, we were happy being by ourselves, without seeing another human being for a week, to say nothing about living together for 59 years; and rarely being away–years went by before we were ever away from one another a single night. Many years.

Linus Pauling, 1990

Linus and Ava Helen Pauling peeking through the window of the "City of Los Angeles" Union Pacific stream liner train. Spring 1938

Linus Pauling in 1986

I recall…Linus Pauling on a Sunday morning reading all of the "funny papers" published in the Los Angeles area. I suspect that he follows all of the comic strips published in America.

W .H. Latimer, 1951

A long about—when was it?—'37, I guess. Was it '37 when the Crellin Laboratory was being built? I guess so. There was a steam shovel digging a big hole because it had a basement and sub-basement, and in this big hole was the steam shovel. On the steam shovel was a sign, "Jesus Saves," that someone had painted, you know, but one morning when we looked down, there was the sign, "Jesus Saves, but Millikan Gets the Credit."

Linus Pauling, March 1964

LP: One interesting thing that you may not know is that I guess I introduced the proposition system into the United States.

Q: *Proposition system?*

LP: Yes, in doctor's examinations.

Q: *Oh, the Dutch theses?*

LP: The Dutch Stellingen. In 1935, I think it was, I'd been talking about these propositions. The doctor's examinations were pretty boring, for the faculty anyway. One of my students named Harker, David Harker, volunteered to prepare some propositions. So I said, "all right," and he brought in about four propositions. This was such a success that the division of chemistry and chemical engineering here required from then on that students prepare and submit a set of propositions. Then, when Harker went to Johns Hopkins, he got them to introduce the system there. Then other students went to Berkeley and various other places so that it's rather widespread. It even has spread to some physics departments. I wrote a paper about it. One of my papers is on the use of propositions in doctor's examinations.

Q: *Do you encourage the type that Goudsmit used in which he threw in one or two about Egyptian hieroglyphics?*

LP: Yes, what the Dutch called the 13th proposition, we encourage that, too. One of my students had a proposition that the Southern Pacific, instead of having trains over the Tehachapi, should run busses from Los Angeles to Bakersfield connecting with the train there; and a few years later they did. One student had a 13th proposition: 'It would be possible for the chemistry division to give two more graduate fellowships without any increase in the budget.' When he was asked, 'How could that be done?' he said, "Fire both of the janitors in the building and hire one good one.' He was complaining about the janitors. Well, I went down into the room in which our seminars used to be given, and opened the door. It was dark; I turned on the light, and there were the janitors sitting in the dark. Just sitting there.

Linus Pauling, March 1964

This is *The Nature of the Chemical Bond and the Structure of Molecules,* "written for Professor A.A. Noyes in heartfelt appreciation of his unfailing kindness," and so on, 1934. He was ill then, beginning to be ill and I think I wrote this just to cheer him up in a sense.

Linus Pauling, March 1964

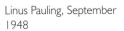

Linus Pauling, September 1948

At 10:00 a.m. on Monday, 12 July 1976 I had a phone call from Patricia Crown, who said that she was calling for Woody Allen. She asked if I would be willing to come to New York to appear in a scene in a movie that Woody Allen is making. It is a picture as yet untitled, designed for a general audience. The scene involves a movie theater, where a number of people of professorial type are in line before the box office to see "The Sorrow and the Pity." While they stand in line they are discussing me, perhaps in a derogatory way, and arguing with Woody Allen. Then he is to say "Why should we argue, when the person who knows more than anyone else about the matter is just coming around the corner?" She said I would then give them some information.

I said that I couldn't decide without seeing the script, and her reply was that the script had not been written for this part of the movie and would not be unless I agreed to come. I said that I liked Woody Allen, but felt that I should not do this job. The shooting will go on through the end of July and the first week in August.

Linus Pauling (notes to self), 1976

Professor Koshland, University of California, Berkeley (Biochemistry) told Ava Helen and me today that he happened to be seated beside a man on an airplane trip who, after they had talked a while, identified himself as an FBI man. Later he said to Professor Koshland "Do you know Dr. Linus Pauling?" Dr. Koshland said that he did, and awaited further comment. The FBI man said "Now there's really a great scientist. I owe a lot to him. Now I used to have all these bad colds...."

Linus Pauling (notes to self), 1976

Linus is a very persuasive man. I became his graduate student because of his persuasiveness. I had been a freshman at the California Institute of Technology but finished undergraduate work at the University of Chicago. After that, I was looking around for a graduate school and I decided to go to Chicago some more. One day that summer, the summer of 1953, I was with my friend Peter, Linus's middle son, swimming in the Pauling's pool in Sierra Madre, California. Linus came out, in necktie and vest, looked down at me in the water and said, "Well, Matt, what are you going to do next year?" I told him at length of my plans for graduate work at the University of Chicago. His response changed my life. He said, "That's a lot of baloney. You should come to Caltech and be my graduate student." So I did.

Matthew Meselson, 1980

Linus Pauling lecturing at Beacon Laboratories, Texas, April 1956

I remember when I was 11 years old that I asked myself what evidence I had that the rest of the world existed anywhere except in my consciousness. I could not think of any convincing evidence to the contrary. I was in danger of becoming a solipsist – I am not sure that I should say that I was in danger, but there was the possibility that I might have accepted this as a philosophy. As I continued to think about the problem, however, I recognized that the world as it presented itself to my senses seemed to be essentially symmetrical in its relation to me and to other young human beings, such as other students in the grammar school I was attending. This symmetry involves so many facets as to cause me to conclude that, despite the special relationship that my own consciousness had with me (in my interactions with the rest of the universe, as it presented itself to my senses), it was highly probable that I myself did not occupy a unique position in the universe.

The actions of individual human beings influence the history of the world. This fact is especially clearly recognized when we think about the influence that rulers and politicians have had on the history of the world – such people as Julius Caesar, Hitler, Abraham Lincoln. A writer such as William Shakespeare and a discoverer such as Christopher Columbus have clearly changed the world in such a way as to have influenced in a striking manner a tremendous number of people who have lived since their times. Actions taken by what might be called ordinary people have no doubt also had a large effect on the history of the world, even though we are not able to document such effects. On thinking about this whole question, I recognize that my questioner probably was correct in formulating the basis of his question to me; that is, in saying essentially that I had changed the lives of millions of people.

This thought gives me satisfaction, but I do not feel that I should claim special credit for my actions. I have acted in response to my education, my environment, and other factors, especially the influence on my thinking of ideas and convictions expressed by my wife. I have never had the feeling of being a martyr or of sacrificing myself, nor have I had the feeling of being ordained or selected in any way to assume a special position among the billions of people who have lived on earth.

There is one question, however, that raises itself in my mind from time to time, and to which I do not know the answer. This question deals with the theory of probability. My career has been unique. In a sense, the life of every human being is unique, but it seems clear to me that I have had the good fortune to lead a life that is significantly different in quality from that of most other human beings. Perhaps one person in a million, or one person in hundred thousand, or one person in ten million can be said to have led a life that differs as much from that of most other human beings as mine. Yet I myself – my consciousness, my ego – am associated with this unique life that I have led. The question that I ask myself is why this consciousness, which is I, should be associated with this life, rather than

Linus Pauling lecturing at Stanford Medical School, 1961

with one of the hundred thousand or million or ten million other lives that would have provided less satisfaction to me. If I were a solipsist, and able to determine the nature of the imagined universe about me, I might well have determined I in just the way that I have in fact experienced it. But I am not a solipsist – I believe that I am a human being, like other human beings. Accordingly the problem of my identity remains, to puzzle me.

Linus Pauling, 1981

P art of my job at Linus's assistant was to tell him what he was scheduled to lecture about. This was usually at his desk in the chairman's office on the first floor of Crellin, just where it is now. But sometimes, when he had just returned from a trip, I would meet him as he walked into the lecture hall at 11 A.M. in the Gates annex (the lecture hall now refurbished and renamed the Linus Pauling Lecture Hall) and asked me what it was he was supposed to talk about. He always proceeded to give a very well-organized and, of course, interesting lecture. Few of us can do that.

But on the occasions when I visited him in his office he would also tell me about his latest ideas—big ones such as the alpha helix structure, and little ones about the unexplained factlets of descriptive inorganic chemistry that fascinated him. Why is HF a weak acid? Why does sulfur form S_8 gas molecules? He told me his ideas about the answers, ideas that came to him, as he said, "with my feet higher than my head for convenience."

Norman Davidson, 1995

That was a memorable meeting in Amsterdam. I remember your plenary lecture, when you brought down the house by pushing three chalkboards to the front of the stage, continuing to talk while behind them! I also remember an incident in Amsterdam when you saved from possible injury or death a woman who was being dragged along the street alongside the wheel of a streetcar with which her clothes had become entangled.

David Shoemaker letter to Linus Pauling, 1982

I 'll tell you a story about [Norbert] Wiener at MIT who invented cybernetics. They moved and he couldn't remember his new house so he stopped a little kid on the street and said, "Do you know where Professor Wiener lives?" And the kid said, "Yes, that house, Papa."

Linus Pauling, April 1987

Linus Pauling at five years old, in a cowboy outfit, 1906

[In order for housewives to get food prices down] they must ask for less expensive packaging. When I go to the market I always carry my slide-rule to be sure the larger, bargain boxes of stuff are really bargains.

Linus Pauling, 1966

Pauling and his family sitting on the front porch of their Pasadena home, 1940

I read detective stories. I've soured on Agatha Christie. She lost me when she mentioned "the foul odor of carbon monoxide" which is an odorless gas.

Linus Pauling, 1987

During the Second World War, when the children were growing up, I think three of the children were still at home or—I don't know, perhaps the youngest one was still at home—she worked for a couple of years as a chemist on a war job making rubber out of plants that would grow in the Mojave.

She was interested in chemistry and knew a lot of chemistry but it was more an intellectual interest. She was planning to write a cookbook on the science of cooking, because she knew what happened when things were cooked. She knew what baking powder is and why you use it. She used to make her own baking powder, instead of just buying baking powder. Well, she never got that done. She was a very good cook, but she never wrote the book on the science of cooking.

… It probably wouldn't have had much of a sale, because the contents might well have been above the heads of most cooks.

Linus Pauling, 1990

B ut in particular since my wife died, eight years ago. I don't have
anything to do now, except make discoveries and write papers.

Linus Pauling, 1990

I remember once when he was at dinner with some board of directors,
and there were questions about virility. Pauling joked that he had not
made love since 1955. Then he looked at his watch and said, "But it's
only 20:55 now."

Richard Hicks, 1991

Linus and Ava Helen Pauling in Pasadena,
1925. Pauling wrote, "I had been working on
our model T Ford, putting in a new bearing."

Pauling with Linus Jr., 1925

L ate in the 1940s Linus Pauling was deep into solving the problem of protein structure. Like other leading chemists, he was captivated by the promise of finding "the key to whole subject of the molecular basis of biological reactions." But Pauling's approach was novel. A blend of new methods in organic chemistry and model-building, it departed radically from crystallographers' convention. Model-building (a hallmark that won him the title "atomic architect") became crucial in his quest. Though he had figured out the structure theoretically by 1949 it was the precise visualization of molecular arrangements and interactions through model-building which confirmed the periodic structure of the alpha-helix by 1951.

Pauling's bold approach hardly convinced everyone. It certainly did not impress Rockefeller officer W. F. Loomis during a site visit to Caltech in February 1951. Loomis was shown the various spiral structures Pauling claimed accounted for the chemical and physical data but they differed radically from structures postulated by all leading crystallographers. Loomis acknowledged that "He [Pauling] certainly is imaginative, daring, and brilliant, but he has gone off the deep end in some cases (such as the 'artificial antibody' story) and his many stimulating pictures, models, etc., may be largely figments of his own imagination rather than lasting and sound science. Like R.J. Williams, he has no further worlds to conquer in straight science, so why not shoot at the moon."

Lily E. Kay, 1993

Of course we know of the complementarity in the DNA molecules and how the complementarity allows for the duplication, and we know in the clarity of hindsight that Chargaff's numbers were an important clue in the elucidation of the structure of DNA. And 15 or 20 years ago I asked my father if he had any insight as to why he hadn't stumbled across the import...of Chargaff's numbers. And his response was an interesting one. Some of you may know that in 1948 we lived in Oxford, England, where my father was a visiting professor at Balliol College, the Eastman professor, as kind of sabbatical leave, and we crossed on the Queen Mary. And we returned home in August, I guess...in the Queen Mary and Chargaff was on the ship. And so the scientists got together and talked, and Daddy learned of Chargaff's numbers straight from the horse's mouth. Well, some of you know...that Chargaff had a reputation of being a difficult personality. And Daddy told me that he thought it may well be that if he had read Chargaff's papers, rather than hearing about the results directly from Chargaff, he would have paid more attention to them and the outcome might have been different. Never know, never know.

Crellin Pauling, 1994

When I arrived in 1949 to be a post-doctoral fellow, I began to see a fair amount of Linus and typically I'd walk into his office, he'd have his feet up on his desk and he would be dictating— dictating *College Chemistry*. And that interested me that he could just sit there and out would roll this material. So I asked him, I said, "Did you have to go over the text very much after you've dictated it, to change it?" "No," he said, "I just have to correct any mistakes that Bea Wulf makes"— his secretary.

Alexander Rich, 1994

Linus Pauling in 1954

Graduate students at Caltech were, as a group, in awe of Linus Pauling, who had a tendency to pad through Gates and Crellin (the building which comprised the site of the chemistry department) in his house slippers on Saturday morning. I felt this way one Saturday when he walked into my office, sat down and put his feet up on the adjoining desk, and said, "How are things going?" As it happened, they were going pretty well and I was just a bit relieved when he stood to go without asking me any penetrating questions. Then he noticed a key chain on my desk which had attached to it a small device consisting of an eyepiece with a lens containing a photograph which could only be viewed by looking directly into it against a strong light. The photograph was that of a beautiful girl, completely naked, standing on a large black rock in the middle of a rushing mountain stream. Pauling picked up the device and clapped it to his eye. "Hmmm," he said, "Basalt." And he walked out without another word. I was stunned, and had to look for myself for I had never noticed the rock. I think it was then that I first realized what a wonderful sense of humor Linus Pauling had, and what a showman he could be even on a small scale.

Ken Hedberg, 1995

Linus and Ava Helen
Pauling, 1924

My own experience with Linus stems from his invitation to come as a postdoctoral fellow in 1949, a few years after Norman Davidson arrived. I came from the East Coast, having just graduated from Harvard Medical School, and arrived suitably adorned with coat and tie. I walked into Linus' office, and there I saw this man with a flowery Hawaiian shirt and a big smile. I thought to myself, "Gee, this is different."

Alex Rich, 1995

Usually I eat two eggs in the morning, sometimes bacon, but I happen to be lazy enough not to cook more than one thing for a meal. The last two days I was eating oxtail soup with vegetables. I don't know what I'll have today. Perhaps some fish. In my book I say you shouldn't eat sweet desserts, but I also quote a professor who says that this doesn't mean that if your hostess has made this wonderful dessert you should turn it down. My wife used to say I always looked for that hostess.

Linus Pauling, 1987

From the beginning, Pauling's scientific qualities set him apart. In the early thirties, Noyes is reported to have said of his successor at Caltech, "Were all the rest of the chemistry department wiped away except [Pauling], it would still be one of the most important departments of chemistry in the world."

Judith Goodstein, 1996

In the early 1960s the physicist Richard Feynman took a trip to Las Vegas, primarily I think to conduct field research into the private lives of showgirls. But on this particular trip, very early one morning he found himself sharing a ride through the desert with a trio of local prostitutes—one reason why biographies of Feynman are popular. Small talk in the car turned to the subject of where he worked, and when Feynman told the group that he was a researcher at Caltech, he was surprised to hear one of the women reply, "Oh, isn't that the place where that scientist Pauling comes from?"

Feynman asked them how they knew about Pauling. The women answered that they had read about him in a recent issue of *TIME* magazine, in a cover story about U.S. science that they had combed through for pictures of the youngest and handsomest researchers. I guess that even at age sixty or so, Pauling stood out in the group.

Tom Hager, 1996

Linus and Ava Helen Pauling holding Linus Jr., Pasadena, 1927

I n 1948 Pauling formulated the "postulate of the essential electroneutrality of atoms: namely, that the electronic structure of substances is such as to cause each atom to have essentially zero resultant electrical charge. These resultant charges are possessed mainly by the most electropositive and electronegative atoms, and are distributed in such a way as to correspond to electrostatic stability." By that time I had left Caltech to teach at the University of Minnesota, but Eddie Hughes reported to me that the following exchange took place in Pauling's presentation of the electroneutrality principle:

Student: "Can you derive the principle?"
Pauling: "No. There is no derivation."
Student: "Then how did you arrive at this principle?"
Pauling: "I made it up."

William Lipscomb, 1996

Pauling, 1935

Pauling became Chairman of Chemistry and Chemical Engineering at Caltech in 1936. He looked so young that Ava Helen suggested that he grow a beard. One day Pauling was walking in Los Angeles when a distinguished elderly gentleman stopped him to ask, "Of what cult are you the Swami?" Linus and the man discovered a mutual interest in polyhedra.

It was on a transcontinental train that Linus and Ava Helen were riding when he decided to visit the train's barber for a haircut and to have the beard shaved off. Ever conscious of his image as seen by others, he returned to his seat by Ava Helen and pretended to make advances which sprained the eyebrows of several other passengers who were saying "Just wait 'til the guy with the beard comes back."

William Lipscomb, 1996

Pauling with a model of the alpha helix.

That fall, in 1953, it came time for me to have a research problem, so I went to see Linus in his office in the Crellin Lab, and he took a rock down off of a shelf near his desk and announced that this was a tellurium mineral – he had worked on tellurium minerals, years earlier – and that this would have an interesting crystal structure. The discussion went something like this:

LP: *Well, Matt, you know about tellurium, the group VI element below selenium in the periodic chart of the elements?*

ME: Uh, yes, Sulfur, selenium, tellurium …

LP: *I know that you know how bad hydrogen sulfide smells. Have you ever smelled hydrogen selenide?*

ME: No, I never have.

LP: *Well, it smells much worse than hydrogen sulfide.*

ME: I see.

LP: *Now, Matt, hydrogen telluride smells as much worse than hydrogen selenide as hydrogen selenide does compared to hydrogen sulfide.*

ME: Ahh …

LP: *In fact, Matt, some chemists were not careful when working with tellurium compounds, and they acquired a condition known as "tellurium breath." As a result, they have become isolated from society. Some have even committed suicide.*

ME: Oh.

LP: *But Matt, I'm sure that you would be careful. Why don't you think it over and let me know if you would like to work on the structure of some tellurium compounds?*

Matthew Meselson, 1996

I arrived at Oxford [in 1948] bearing a dozen fresh eggs and a large wheel of ripe Danish brie cheese, having heard that things were tough in England after the war. I learned that Linus Pauling had difficulty finding enough nutritious food, so I gave him my eggs. I was invited to the Pauling's for dinner one day, so I took the cheese along. After dinner, we sat by the fire, popped chestnuts, and consumed the cheese in its entirety. A few days later I visited Pauling in the apartment at Balliol College that he was using for his scholarly work. He had an electric space heater turned on its side, and on it was a pot of boiling water. In the pot was one of the eggs I had given him. In that room I saw history being made. With a pair of scissors he was cutting cardboard to make models of planar amide groups and taping them together to form a helix. Thus, in the early spring of 1948, was born the alpha-helix.

David Shoemaker, 1996

Linus Pauling in England, 1948

When I saw the alpha-helix and saw what a beautiful, elegant structure it was, I was thunderstruck and was furious with myself for not having built this, but on the other hand, I wondered, was it really right? So I cycled home for lunch and was so preoccupied with the turmoil in my mind that didn't respond to anything. Then I had an idea, so I started back to the lab. I realized that I had a horse hair in a drawer. I set it up on the X-ray camera and gave it a two hour exposure, then took the film to the dark room with my heart in my mouth, wondering what it showed, and when I developed it, there was the 1.5 angstrom reflection which I had predicted and which excluded all structures other than the alpha-helix. So on Monday morning I stormed into my professor's office, into Bragg's office and showed him this, and Bragg said, "Whatever made you think of that?" And I said, "Because I was so furious with myself for having missed that beautiful structure." To which Bragg replied coldly, "I wish I had made you angry earlier."

Max Perutz, BBC Interview, 1997

Most people seem to think that work such as mine, dealing with the properties of atoms and molecules, should be classed with physics; but I (as I have said before) feel that the study of chemical substances remains chemistry even though it reach the state in which it requires the use of considerable mathematics. The question is more than an academic one, for the answer really determines my classification as a physicist or chemist.

Linus Pasuling to A. A. Noyes, 1926

Pauling liked to begin his lectures on vitamin C by displaying a test tube half filled with a white powder. He said that it contained the amount of vitamin C synthesized daily by a goat, or about 13 grams. While holding another tube with just a smidgen of white powder at the bottom, he stated that this small amount represented the RDA for vitamin C established for humans by the Food and Nutrition Board of the National Academy of Sciences. After pausing, he then declares, "I think that goats know more than the Food and Nutrition Board about nutrition!"

Steve Lawson, 2000

My father would go to bed after watching the news, about 6:30 or 7:00, [and] read until 9:00. When he woke up at 3:00 or 4:00 in the morning he'd get up and cook his breakfast and get to work. I asked him, how did he go to sleep? And he said he'd take the cube root of some number between 8 and 27. The first digit is obviously 2.... I never asked him whether he had a snazzy way or some algorithm; I'd do it by trial and error, but it doesn't work for me.

Peter Pauling, BBC Interview, 1997

Linus and Ava Helen Pauling working on bomb test petition, 1957

DecEmber 8, 1941 was a memorable day on the normally quiet Caltech campus. That morning, the campus was bristling with military vehicles manned by the National Guard troops. The Caltech registrar, an officer in the National Guard, had called them in to "defend" the Caltech campus. Notices were posted for an emergency convocation at 10:00 a.m. in Culbertson Hall and students were drafted to guard doors not manned by the National Guard and armed with pick axe handles.

Classrooms were empty and groups were listening to the radio and discussing the evolving news coming from Pearl Harbor. At 10 a.m. we dutifully assembled in Culbertson Hall where our registrar, in full National Guard uniform complete with pistols, gave a most intemperate speech about the dastardly "Japs" that would have done credit to any American Legion hall that day.

Linus Pauling was standing in the back of the hall as he had come in late and interrupted the speech by bursting out with the question "By what authority have you called this impromptu convocation?" He then proceeded to remind the registrar that Caltech was known for being a place of thoughtful and factual reason but the registrar had turned it into a place of pure hysteria. The student body stood up and clapped for Linus. The registrar dismissed the meeting and retreated in some disarray. For many of us, Linus won his Nobel Peace Prize that day!

This campus furor was a surprise to many of us for the Nisei were second and third generation American citizens and were fellow classmates all through our grade school and high school experience. When the authorities immediately began rounding them up and carting them off to detention camps we were outraged. Linus and his wife Ava Helen had a Nisei gardener and they brought him and his family to live in their garage in an effort to keep him from being "detained." Later over the Paulings' vigorous objections the Nisei family was forcibly removed and sent off to a dentention camp.

Doug Strain, 2000

At about 12:28 A.M. on 5 November I woke, opened my eyes, and was astonished and frightened by a hallucination. Hovering over me was the head of a man, glaring at me, with a diabolical expression and flashing eyes. The face was a coppery red color, with highlights, as though oily. It seemed to be about a foot (25 cm) in diameter, and about five feet (125 cm) above me—not so far away as the ceiling. After about two seconds, or perhaps somewhat more, its aspect changed to that of another face, not menacing, and then to that of another, and another. I had ceased to be frightened in a few seconds, when I decided that I was experiencing a natural phenomenon.

After about two minutes (estimated) I looked at a clock (with red digits, visible at 12 feet distance); it was 12:30 A.M. The room was dimly lit by the clock and light from the edges of the drawn curtains (there were electric lights outside).

The faces were surrounded by darkness, extending uniformly to the periphery of my vision. They were not sharply outlined, but faded into the darkness. The solid angle subtended by the red glow may have been somewhat less than stated above.

Portrait of Linus Pauling ca. 1974

Without moving (except to move my head) I observed the phenomenon until 12:52 A.M. I found that the face moved as I rotated my head. It seemed to be in the center of my visual field at all times. It remained when I closed my eyes and when I put my hands over my eyes. At times it disappeared, but returned in a few seconds. It was always dimmer than it had seemed when I first wakened.

The eyes seemed to shine, but intermittently—that is, they seemed to flash.

Throughout this period of over twenty minutes the face or other vision changed, usually every two or three seconds.

For a while it seemed to be not a face but a red marine invertebrate, such as a [left blank in Pauling's manuscript]. A portion here or there would glow, as though fluorescent, or occasionally flash.

I decided that the red color was caused by the excitation of one of the receptors in the fovea. I had attended a cocktail party, and ingested perhaps 50ml of ethanol (as vodka) and eaten some pretzels, at 5 to 6 P.M. At 7:30 P.M I had eaten a large ice cream sundae, with hot chocolate sauce. At 9:30 P.M I went to bed, but had trouble sleeping. At 11:30 P.M I noticed that I was unusually warm, and thought that I was oxidizing the sugar of the ice cream at a high rate. I went to sleep, and then wakened, as described above. I had been dreaming, but could not remember the dream.

After seeing the marine invertebrates I again saw faces, perhaps through an effort of will. The color remained red, as though only the red receptors were being stimulated.

The vision that I first saw seemed real enough to frighten me. I remained somewhat apprehensive for perhaps thirty seconds. If the face had not changed its aspect quickly and if I had not had some understanding of physiology I might have attributed supernatural significance to the phenomenon.

I had taken about two grams of ascorbic acid at 9:30 P.M.

Linus Pauling, 12:53 A.M. Monday 5 November, 1974

Pauling at Painted Canyon, California, ca. 1933

I watch a moderate amount of television, mainly the news but, on occasion, if I can find an old Doris Day movie I watch it. My favorite is *Lover Come Back,* which has in it a character named Linus, who is described as the greatest chemist in the world. In the movie, an advertising man gets himself in a pickle because he's been advertising the unveiling of some great discovery. He doesn't have a great discovery so he goes to the greatest chemist in the world, Linus, who's not interested – he's only interested in pure science. Unfortunately for the advertising man, he's very ethical, but not after the guy pulls out thousand-dollar bill after thousand-dollar bill. Linus says he'll take over. In the laboratory, various things are bubbling. Outside, a great cloud of green smoke comes out. Inside, he is at the black board doing calculations. Finally, all the reporters come in to see the greatest chemist in the world's new invention and there are trays with red and green cookies. It turns out each one is the equivalent of a double martini.

Linus Pauling, 1987

Besides directing many people's research, Pauling used to deliver a freshmen's introductory course of lectures which he first published as a textbook of general chemistry in 1947. Its 1970 edition contains over 900 pages; it begins with an introduction to the atomic and molecular structure of matter, covers most important aspects of physical and inorganic chemistry, touches on the elements of organic and biochemistry, and ends with nuclear chemistry. The lectures were spectacular and often dramatic. Jack Dunitz described one to me: A large beaker filled with what looked like water stood on the bench. Pauling entered, picked up a cube of sodium metal from a bottle, tossed it from hand to hand (done safely if your hands are dry) and warned of its violently explosive reaction with water. He then threw it into the beaker. As students cowered in fear of an explosion, he said nonchalantly "but its reaction with alcohol is much milder."

Max Perutz, I wish I'd made you angry earlier, 1998

Pauling lecturing to high school students, 1965

Year after year I've found great pleasure in thinking of something new about the world....When Ernest Lawrence got married (the fellow who invented the cyclotron at Berkeley) I was an usher at the wedding, in 1931. I drove back in the car with some people and I said that I was feeling happy because I had in my pocket a crystal of sulvanite, Cu_3VS_4. And...I had just determined the structure...of this and it was a very striking structure; anomalous, it didn't fit in with my ideas about sulfide minerals. But I knew what the structure was, nobody else knows, nobody in the world knows what the structure is and they won't know until I tell them. This is an example of the feeling of pleasure I had on discovering something new in the world.

Linus Pauling, All Things Considered, *National Public Radio, February 28, 1991*

SELECTED BIBLIOGRAPHY

❖❖❖

Linus Pauling published over 1,100 articles and sixteen books over the course of his lifetime. The following represents a selection of those items which seem to the editors to be particularly significant.

SELECTED ARTICLES BY LINUS PAULING

"The Manufacture of Cement in Oregon," *The Student Engineer* (The Associated Engineers of Oregon Agricultural College, Corvallis, Oregon) 12 (June 1920): 3-5.

"The Crystal Structure of Molybdenite," *Journal of the American Chemical Society* 45 (1923): 1466-1471. [Roscoe G. Dickinson and Linus Pauling].

"The Inter-Ionic Attraction Theory of Ionized Solutes. IV. The Influence of Variation of Dielectric Constant on the Limiting Law for Small Concentrations. *Journal of the American Chemical Society* 47 (1925): 2129-2134. [P. Debye and Linus Pauling].

"The Entropy of Supercooled Liquids at the Absolute Zero," *Journal of The American Chemical Society* 47 (1925): 2148-2156. [Linus Pauling and Richard C. Tolman].

"The Prediction of the Relative Stabilities of Isosteric Isomeric Ions and Molecules," *Journal of the American Chemical Society* 48 (1926): 641-651. [Linus Pauling and Sterling B. Hendricks].

"Die Abschirmungskonstanten Der Relativistischen Oder Magnetischen Röntgenstrahlendubletts," [German: The Screening Constant of Relativistic Or Magnetic X-Ray Doublets] *Zeitschrift Für Physik* 40 (1926): 344-350.

"The Theoretical Prediction of the Physical Properties of Many-Electron Atoms and Ions. Mole Refraction, Diamagnetic Susceptibility, and Extension in Space," *Proceedings Of The Royal Society: A* (London) 114 (1927): 181-211.

"The Shared-Electron Chemical Bond," *Proceedings of the National Academy of Science* 14 (1928): 359-362.

"The Coordination Theory of the Structure of Ionic Crystals," in *Festschrift Zum 60. Geburtstage Arnold Sommerfelds*, Verlag Von S. Hirzel, Leipzig, (1928): 11-17.

"The Nature of the Chemical Bond. Application of Results Obtained from the Quantum Mechanics and from a Theory of Paramagnetic Susceptibility to the Structure of Molecules," *Journal of the American Chemical Society* 53 (1931): 1367-1400.

"The Nature of the Chemical Bond. II. The One-Electron Bond and The Three-Electron Bond," *Journal of the American Chemical Society* 53 (1931): 3225-3237.

"The Nature of the Chemical Bond. III. The Transition from One Extreme Bond Type to Another," *Journal of the American Chemical Society* 54 (1932): 988-1003.

"The Nature of the Chemical Bond. V. The Quantum-Mechanical Calculation of The Resonance Energy of Benzene And Naphthalene And The Hydrocarbon Free Radicals," *Journal of Chemical Physics* 1 (1933): 362–374. [Linus Pauling and G. W. Wheland].

"The Nature of the Chemical Bond. VI. The Calculation from Thermochemical Data of the Energy of Resonance of Molecules among Several Electronic Structures," *Journal of Chemical Physics* 1 (1933): 606–617. [Linus Pauling and J. Sherman]

"The Nature of the Chemical Bond. VII. The Calculation of Resonance Energy in Conjugated Systems," *Journal f Chemical Physics* 1 (1933): 679-686. [Linus Pauling and J. Sherman].

"Covalent Radii of Atoms and Interatomic Distances in Crystals Containing Electron- Pair Bonds," *Zeitschrift Für Kristallographie*. A 87 (1934): 205–238. [Linus Pauling and M. L. Huggins].

"The Structure of the Carboxyl Group. I. The Investigation of Formic Acid by the Diffraction of Electrons," *Proceedings of the National Academy tf Science* 20 (1934): 336-340. [Linus Pauling and L. O. Brockway].

"The Oxygen Equilibrium of Hemoglobin and Its Structural Interpretation," *Proceedings of the National Academy Of Science* 21 (1935): 186-191.

"The Structure and Entropy of Ice and of Other Crystals with Some Randomness of Atomic Arrangement," *Journal of the American Chemical Society* 57 (1935): 2680-2684.

"On The Structure of Native, Denatured, and Coagulated Proteins," *Proceedings of the National Academy Of Science* 22 (1936): 439-447. [A. E. Mirsky and Linus Pauling].

"The Structure of the Pentaborane B_5H_9," *Journal of the American Chemical Society* 58 (1936): 2403-2407. [S. H. Bauer and Linus Pauling].

"The Nature of the Interatomic Forces in Metals," *Physical Review* 54 (1938): 899-904.

"The Structure of Proteins," *Journal of the American Chemical Society* 61 (1939): 1860-1867. [Linus Pauling and Carl Niemann].

"A Theory of the Color of Dyes," *Proceedings of the National Academy of Science* 25 (1939): 577-582.

"A Theory of the Structure and Process of Formation of Antibodies," *Journal of the American Chemical Society* 62 (1940): 2643-2657.

"The Nature of the Intermolecular Forces Operative in Biological Processes," *Science* 92 (1940): 77-79. [Linus Pauling and Max Delbrück].

"Serological Reactions with Simple Substances containing two or More Haptenic Groups," *Proceedings of the National Academy of Science* 27 (1941): 125-128. [Linus Pauling, Dan H. Campbell, and David Pressman].

"The Manufacture of Antibodies *In Vitro*," *Journal of Experimental Medicine* 76 (1942): 211-220. [Linus Pauling and Dan H. Campbell].

"The Serological Properties of Simple Substances. I. Precipitation Reactions between Antibodies and Substances Containing two or More Haptenic Groups. *Journal of the American Chemical Society* 64 (1942): 2994-3003," [Linus Pauling, David Pressman, Dan H. Campbell, Carol Ikeda, and Miyoshi Ikawa].

"The Serological Properties of Simple Substances. II. The Effects of Changed Conditions and of Added Haptens on Precipitation Reactions of Polyhaptenic Simple Substances," *Journal of the American Chemical Society* 64 (1942): 3003-3009. [Linus Pauling, David Pressman, Dan H. Campbell, and Carol Ikeda].

"The Serological Properties of Simple Substances. III. The Composition of Precipitates of Antibodies and Polyhaptenic Simple Substances; the Valence of Antibodies," *Journal of the American Chemical Society* 64 (1942): 3010-3014.

"The Serological Properties of Simple Substances. IV. Hapten Inhibition of Precipitation of Antibodies and Polyhaptenic Simple Substances," *Journal of the American Chemical Society* 64 (1942): 3015-3020. [David Pressman, David H. Brown, and Linus Pauling].

"The Serological Properties of Simple Substances. V. The Precipitation of Polyhaptenic Simple Substances and Antiserum Homologous to the *P*-(*P*-Azophenylazo)-Phenylarsonic Acid Group and Its Inhibition by Haptens," *Journal of the American Chemical Society* 65 (1943): 728-732. [David Pressman, John T. Maynard, Allan L. Grossberg, and Linus Pauling].

"The Serological Properties of Simple Substances. VI. The Precipitation of a Mixture of Two Specific Antisera by a Dihaptenic Substance Containing the two Corresponding Haptenic Groups; Evidence for the Framework Theory of Serological Precipitation," *Journal of the American Chemical Society* 66 (1944): 330-336. [Linus Pauling, David Pressman, and Dan H. Campbell].

"The Serological Properties of Simple Substances. VII. A Quantitative Theory of the Inhibition by Haptens of the Precipitation of Heterogeneous Antisera with Antigens, and Comparison with Experimental Results for Polyhaptenic Simple Substances and for Azoproteins," *Journal of the American Chemical Society* 66 (1944): 784-792. [Linus Pauling, David Pressman, and Allan L. Grossberg].

"The Serological Properties of Simple Substances. VIII. The Reactions of Antiserum Homologous to the *P*-Azobenzoic Acid Group," *Journal of the American Chemical Society* 66 (1944): 1731-1738. [David Pressman, Stanley M. Swingle, Allan L. Grossberg, and Linus Pauling].

"The Serological Properties of Simple Substances. IX. Hapten Inhibition of Precipitation of Antisera Homologous to the *O*-, *M*-, And *P*-Azophenylarsonic Acid Groups," *Journal Of The American Chemical Society* 67 (1945): 1003-1012. [Linus Pauling and David Pressman].

"The Serological Properties of Simple Substances. X. A Hapten Inhibition Experiment Substantiating the Intrinsic Molecular Asymmetry of Antibodies," *Journal of the American Chemical Society* 67 (1945): 1219-1222. [David Pressman, John H. Bryden, and Linus Pauling].

"The Serological Properties of Simple Substances. XI. The Reactions of Antisera Homologous to Various Azophenylarsonic Acid Groups and the *P*-Azophenylmethylarsinic Acid Group with some Heterologous Haptens," *Journal of the American Chemical Society* 67 (1945): 1602-1606. [David Pressman, Arthur B. Pardee, and Linus Pauling].

"The Use of Punched Cards in Molecular Structure Determinations. I. Crystal Structure Calculations," *Journal of Chemical Physics* 14 (1946): 648-658. [P.A. Shaffer, Jr., Verner Schomaker, and Linus Pauling].

"The Use of Punched Cards in Molecular Structure Determinations. II. Electron Diffraction Calculations," *Journal of Chemical Physics* 14 (1946): 659-664. [P.A. Shaffer, Jr., Verner Schomaker, and Linus Pauling].

"An Instrument for Determining the Partial Pressure of Oxygen in a Gas," *Journal of the American Chemical Society* 68 (1946): 795-798. [Linus Pauling, Reuben E. Wood, and J. H. Sturdivant].

"Atomic Radii and Interatomic Distances in Metals," *Journal of the American Chemical Society* 69 (1947): 542-553.

"The Metallic State," *Nature* 161 (1948): 1019.

"Molecular Architecture and the Processes of Life," [21st Sir Jesse Boot Foundation Lecture, 28 May 1948], (Nottingham, England: Sir Jesse Boot Foundation, 1948), 1-13.

"The Resonating-Valence-Bond Theory of Metals," *Physica* 15 (1949): 23-28.

"Sickle Cell Anemia, a Molecular Disease," *Science* 109 (1949): 443. [Linus Pauling, Harvey A. Itano, S. J. Singer, and Ibert C. Wells].

"Two Hydrogen-Bonded Spiral Configurations of the Polypeptide Chain," *Journal of the American Chemical Society* 72 (1950): 21. [Linus Pauling and Robert B. Corey].

"The Ultimate Decision," *Southwest Retort* 2, 8 (May 1950): 14-17.

"The Structure of Proteins: Two Hydrogen-Bonded Helical Configurations of the Polypeptide Chain," *Proceedings of the National Academy of Science* 37 (1951): 205-210. [Linus Pauling, Robert B. Corey, and H. R. Branson].

"Atomic Coordinates and Structure Factors for Two Helical Configurations of Polypeptide Chains," *Proceedings of the National Academy of Science* 37 (1951): 3235-240. [Linus Pauling and Robert B. Corey].

"The Structure of Synthetic Polypeptides," *Proceedings of the National Academy of Science* 37 (1951): 241-250. [Linus Pauling and Robert B. Corey].

"The Pleated Sheet, a New Layer Configuration of Polypeptide Chains," *Proceedings of the National Academy of Science* 37 (1951): 251-256. [Linus Pauling and Robert B. Corey].

"The Structure of Feather Rachis Keratin," *Proceedings of the National Academy of Science* 37 (1951): 256-261. [Linus Pauling and Robert B. Corey].

"The Structure of Hair, Muscle, and Related Proteins," *Proceedings of the National Academy of Science* 37 (1951): 261-271. [Linus Pauling and Robert B. Corey].

"The Structure of Fibrous Proteins of the Collagen-Gelatin Group," *Proceedings of the National Academy of Science* 37 (1951): 272-281. [Linus Pauling and Robert B. Corey].

"The Polypeptide-Chain Configuration in Hemoglobin and Other Globular Proteins," *Proceedings of the National Academy of Science* 373 (1951): 282-285. [Linus Pauling and Robert B. Corey].

"Stable Configurations of Polypeptide Chains," *Proceedings of the Royal Society* (London) 141 (1953): 21-33. [Linus Pauling and Robert B. Corey]

"A Proposed Structure for the Nucleic Acids," *Proceedings of the National Academy of Science* 39 (1953): 84-97. [Linus Pauling and Robert B. Corey].

"A Theory of Ferromagnetism," *Proceedings of the National Academy of Science* 39 (1953): 551-560.

"An Investigation of the Structure of Silk Fibroin," *Biochimica Et Biophysica Acta* 16 (1955): 1-34. [Richard E. Marsh, Robert B. Corey, and Linus Pauling].

"The Structure of Tussah Silk Fibroin (With a Note on the Structure of –Poly-L- Alanine)," *Acta Crystallgrapica.* 8 (1955): 710-715. [Richard E. Marsh, Robert B. Corey, and Linus Pauling].

"Specific Hydrogen-Bond Formation between Pyrimidines and Purines in Deoxyribonucleic Acids," (in Linderstrom-Lang Festschrift). *Archives of Biochemistry and Biophysics* 65 (1956): 164-181. [Linus Pauling and Robert B. Corey].

"Genetic and Somatic Effects of Carbon-14," *Science* 128 (1958): 1183-1186.

"Fallout: Today's Seven-Year Plague," [Text of a Speech Delivered in the Fall of 1959 at Carnegie Hall, New York City, at a Meeting Sponsored by the National Committee For A Sane Nuclear Policy] *Mainstream* 13 (2), 1-20 (February 1960).

"A Molecular Theory of General Anesthesia," *Science* 134 (1961), 15-21.

"Molecular Disease, Evolution, and Genic Heterogeneity," In *Horizons In Biochemistry* (Szent-Györgyi Dedicatory Volume), Michael Kasha and Bernard Pullman, Eds., Academic Press, New York, 1962, Pp. 189-225. [Emile Zuckerkandl and Linus Pauling].

"The Electroneutrality Principale [Sic] and the Structure of Molecules," *Anales De La Real Sociedad Espaiola De Fisica Y Quimica* (Madrid) B 60 (2-3) (1964): 87-90.

"The Nature of the Iron-Oxygen Bond in Oxyhemoglobin," *Nature* 203 (1964): 182-183.

"Evolutionary Divergence and Convergence in Proteins," in *Evolving Genes And Proteins*, Vernon Bryson And Henry J. Vogel, Eds., Academic Press, New York, 1965, Pp. 97-166. [Emile Zuckerkandl and Linus Pauling].

"The Close-Packed-Spheron Model of Atomic Nuclei and Its Relation to the Shell Model," *Proceedings of the National Academy of Science* 54 (1965): 989-994.

"The Resonating-Valence-Bond Theory of Superconductivity: Crest Superconductors and Trough Superconductors," *Proceedings of the National Academy of Science* 60 (1968): 59-65.

"Orthomolecular Psychiatry: Varying the Concentrations of Substances Normally Present in the Human Body may Control Mental Disease," *Science* 160 (1968): 265-271.

"Evolution and the Need for Ascorbic Acid," *Proceedings of the National Academy of Science* 671 (1970): 1643- 1648.

"Fifty Years of Progress in Structural Chemistry and Molecular Biology," in *Daedalus* 99 (4) (Fall 1970): 988-1014.

"Orthomolecular Psychiatry," in *Orthomolecular Psychiatry: Treatment of Schizophrenia*, David Hawkins and Linus Pauling, eds., W. H. Freeman, San Francisco, 1973, pp. 1-17.

"Results of A Loading Test of Ascorbic Acid, Niacinamide, and Pyridoxine in Schizophrenic Subjects and Controls," in *Orthomolecular Psychiatry: Treatment of Schizophrenia*, David Hawkins and Linus Pauling, eds., W. H. Freeman, San Francisco, 1973, pp. 18-34. [Linus Pauling, Arthur B. Robinson, Susanna S. Oxley, Maida Bergeson, Andrew Harris, Paul Cary, John Blethen, and Ian T. Keavenyl]

"Quantitative Chromatographic Analysis in Orthomolecular Medicine," in *Orthomolecular Psychiatry: Treatment of Schizophrenia*, David Hawkins and Linus Pauling, eds., W.H. Freeman, San Francisco, 1973, pp. 35-53. [Arthur B. Robinson and Linus Pauling].

"Ascorbic Acid and the Glycosaminoglycans: An Orthomolecular Approach to Cancer and Other Diseases," *Oncology*, 27 (1973): 181-192. [Ewan Cameron and Linus Pauling].

"Valence-Bond Theory of Compounds of Transition Metals," *Proceedings of the National Academy of Science* 723 (1975): 4200-4202.

"Supplemental Ascorbate in the Supportive Treatment of Cancer: Prolongation of Survival Times in Terminal Human Cancer," *Proceedings of the National Academy of Science* 73 (1976): 3685- 3689. [Ewan Cameron and Linus Pauling].

"Ascorbic Acid and Cancer: A Review," *Cancer Research* 39 (1979): 663-681. [Ewan Cameron, Linus Pauling, and Brian Leibovitz].

"Apparent Icosahedral Symmetry is Due to Directed Multiple Twinning of Cubic Crystals," *Nature* 317 (1985): 512-514.

"The Future of Orthomolecular Medicine," in *The Roots of Molecular Medicine: A Tribute to Linus Pauling*, Richard P. Huemer, ed. New York: W. H. Freeman, 1986, pp. 249-253.

"The Nature of the Chemical Bond Fifty Years Later: The Relative Electronegativity of Atoms Seen in Perspective," in *Molecular Structure and Energetics, Vol. 1*, Joel F. Liebman and Arthur Greenberg, eds., Deerfield Beach, FL: VCH Publishers, 1986, pp. 1-15. [Linus Pauling and Zelek S. Herman].

"So-Called Icosahedral and Decagonal Quasicrystals are Twins of an 820-Atom Cubic Crystal," *Physical Review Letters* 58 (1987): 365-368.

"Evidence From X-Ray and Neutron Powder Diffraction Patterns that the So-Called Icosahedral And Decagonal Quasicrystals of Mnai$_6$ and Other Alloys are Twinned Cubic Crystals," *Proceedings of the National Academy of Science* 84 (1987): 3951-3953.

"The So-Called Icosahedral Quasicrystals of Manganese-Aluminum and Other Alloys," *Quimica Nova* 11 (1) (Jan. 1988): 7 6-9.

"Sigmaphase Packing of Icosahedral Clusters in 780-Atom Tetragonal Crystals of Cr$_5$Ni$_3$Si$_2$ and V$_{15}$Ni$_{10}$Si that by Twinning achieve 8-Fold Rotational Point-Group Symmetry," *Proceedings of the National Academy of Science* 85 (1988): 2025-2026.

"High-Resolution Transmission Electron-Micrograph Evidence that Rapidly Quenched Mnal$_6$ and Other Alloys are Icosatwins of a Cubic Crystal," *Comptes Rendus De L'Acadamie Des Sciences* Parts 306, Série II, No. 16 (1988): 1147-1151. [Linus Pauling, Zelek S. Herman, and Peter J. Pauling].

"Icosahedral Quasicrystals as Twins of Cubic Crystals Containing Large Icosahedral Clusters of Atoms: The 1012-Atom Primitive Cubic Structure of Al$_6$CuLi$_3$, The C- Phase A1$_{37}$Cu$_3$Li$_{21}$Mg$_3$, and Gamg$_2$zn$_3$," *Proceedings of the National Academy of Science* 85 (1988): 3666-3669.

"Unified Structure Theory of Icosahedral Quasicrystals: Evidence from Neutron Powder Diffraction Patterns that Alcrfemnsi, Alculimg, and Tinifesi Icosahedral Quasicrystals are Twins of Cubic Crystals Containing about 820 or 1012 Atoms in a Primitive Unit Cube," *Proceedings of the National Academy of Science* 85 (1988): 8376-8380.

"The Role of the Metallic Orbital and of Crest and Trough Superconduction in High-Temperature Superconductors: The First Two Years," (Proceedings of a conference held 11-13 April 1988 in Tuscaloosa, Alabama), Robert M. Metzger, ed., New York: Gordon and Breach Scientific Publishers, 1989, pp. 309-313.

"The Discovery of the Structure of the Clay Minerals," *CMS News* (A Publication of The Clay Minerals Society), (September 1990): p.25-27.

"Case Report: Lysine/Ascorbate-Related Amelioration of Angina Pectoris," *Journal of Orthomolecular Medicine* 6 (3/4) (1991): 144-146.

"X-Ray Crystallography and the Nature of The Chemical Bond," in *The Chemical Bond: Structure and Dynamics*, Ahmed Zewail, ed., New York: Academic Press, 1992, pp. 3-16.

"How I Became Interested in the Chemical Bond: A Reminiscence," in *The Chemical Bond: Structure and Dynamics*, Ahmed Zewail, ed., New York: Academic Press, 1992, pp. 99-109.

"How My Interest in Proteins Developed," *Protein Science* 2 (6), 1060-1063 (1993).

"Analysis of the Ground-State Band and a Closely Related Intercalated Band of $^{235/92}$Ul$_{143}$ by the Two-Revolving-Cluster Model with Consideration of Symmetric and Antisymmetric Resonance of the Two Dissimilar Clusters," *Proceedings of the National Academy of Science* 90 (1993): 5901-5903. [Linus Pauling and Barclay Kamb].

"Hardin-Jones Biostatistical Analysis of Mortality Data for a Second Set of Cohorts of Cancer Patients with a Large Fraction Surviving at the Termination of the Study and a Comparison of Survival Times of Cancer Patients Receiving Large Regular Oral Doses of Vitamin C and Other Nutrients with Similar Patients Not Receiving These Doses," *Journal of Orthomolecular Medicine* 8 (3) (1993): 157-167. [A. Hoffer and Linus Pauling].

"Analysis of A Hyperdeformed Band of $^{152}_{66}Dy_{86}$ on The Basis of a Structure with Two Revolving Clusters, Each with a Previously Unrecognized Two-Tiered Structure," *Proceedings of the National Academy of Science* 91 (1994): 897-899.

SELECTED BOOKS BY LINUS PAULING

The Structure of Line Spectra (New York: McGraw-Hill, 1930)

Introduction to Quantum Mechanics (New York: McGraw-Hill, 1935)

The Nature of the Chemical Bond (Ithaca, New York: Cornell University Press, 1939)

General Chemistry (San Francisco, W.H. Freeman and Company, 1947)

College Chemistry (San Francisco: W.H. Freeman and Company, 1950)

No More War! (London: Victor Gollancz Ltd., 1958)

The Architecture of Molecules (San Francisco: W.H. Freeman and Company, 1964)

The Chemical Bond (Ithaca, New York: Cornell University Press, 1967)

Vitamin C and the Common Cold (San Francisco: W.H. Freeman and Company, 1970)

Orthomolecular Psychiatry (San Francisco: W.H. Freeman and Company, 1973)

Chemistry (San Francisco: W.H. Freeman and Company, 1974)

Vitamin C, the Common Cold, and the Flu (San Francisco: W.H. Freeman and Company, 1976)

How to Live Longer and Feel Better (New York: W.H. Freeman and Company, 1985)

SELECTED BOOKS AND ARTICLES ABOUT LINUS PAULING

Brian, Denis. "Linus Pauling" in *Genius Talk: Conversations with Nobel Scientists and Other Luminaries*. New York: Plenum Press, 1995: pp. 1-34.

Crick, Francis. "The a Helix," in *What Mad Pursuit: A Personal View of Scientific Discovery*. New York: Basic Books, Inc., 1988: pp. 53-61.

Crick, Francis. "The Impact of Linus Pauling on Molecular Biology: A Reminiscence" in *The Chemical Bond: Structure and Dynamics*, Ahmed Zewail, ed., New York: Academic Press, 1992, pp. 87-98.

Goertzel, Ted, Mildred Goertzel, and Victor Goertzel. "Linus Pauling: The Scientist as Crusader," in *The Antioch Review* 38 (3) (Summer 1980): pp. 371-382.

Goertzel, Ted and Ben Goertzel. *Linus Pauling: A Life in Science and Politics*. New York: Basic Books, 1995.

Goodstein, Judith. "Atoms, Molecules, and Linus Pauling," in *Social Research* 51 (3) (Autumn 1984): pp. 691-708.

Hager, Thomas. *Force of Nature: The Life of Linus Pauling.* New York: Simon and Schuster, 1995.

Hager, Thomas. *Linus Pauling and the Chemistry of Life.* New York: Oxford University Press, 1998.

Huemer, Richard P., ed. *The Roots of Molecular Medicine.* New York: W.H. Freeman and Company, 1986.

Linus Pauling: a Man of Intellect and Action. [Tokyo]: Cosmos Japan International, c1991.

Maksic, Zvonimir B., and Mirjana Eckert-Maksic, eds. *Molecules in Natural Science and Medicine: An encomium for Linus Pauling.* New York: Ellis Horwood Limited, 1991.

Maksic, Z.B., and W.J. Orville-Thomas, eds. *Pauling's Legacy: Modern Modelling of the Chemical Bond.* Amsterdam: Elsevier, 1999.

Marinacci, Barabara, ed. *Linus Pauling: In His Own Words.* New York: Simon and Schuster, 1995.

Marinacci, Barbara, and Ramesh Krishnamurthy. *Linus Pauling on Peace.* Los Altos, California: Rising Star Press, 1998.

Newton, David E. *Linus Pauling: Scientist and Advocate.* New York: Facts on File, 1994.

Nye, Mary Jo. *From Chemical Philosophy to Theoretical Chemistry.* Berkeley: University of California Press, 1993.

Rich, Alexander, and Norman Davidson, eds. *Structural Chemistry and Molecular Biology.* San Francisco: W.H. Freeman, 1968.

Richards, Evelleen. *Vitamin C and Cancer: Medicine or Politics?* London: MacMillan Professional and Academic Ltd., 1991.

Servos, John W. *Physical Chemistry from Ostwald to Pauling.* Princeton, New Jersey: Princeton Umiversity Press, 1990.

White, Florence Meiman. *Linus Pauling: Scientist and Crusader.* New York: Walker and Company, 1980.

INDEX